83|84

graphis annual

The International Annual of Advertising and
Editorial Graphics

Das internationale Jahrbuch der Werbe-
graphik und der redaktionellen Graphik

Le répertoire international de l'art graphique
publicitaire et rédactionnel

Edited by / Herausgegeben von / Réalisé par:

Walter Herdeg

Graphis Press Corp., Zurich (Switzerland)

GRAPHIS PUBLICATIONS

GRAPHIS, International bi-monthly journal of graphic art and applied art
PHOTOGRAPHIS, The international annual of advertising and editorial photography
GRAPHIS POSTERS, The international annual of poster art
GRAPHIS PACKAGING VOL. 4, An international survey of package design
CHILDREN'S BOOK ILLUSTRATION VOL. 3, VOL. 4, An international survey of children's book illustration
GRAPHIS DIAGRAMS, The graphic visualization of abstract data
FILM + TV GRAPHICS 2, An international survey of the art of film animation
ARCHIGRAPHIA, Architectural and environmental graphics
GRAPHIS EPHEMERA, Artists' Self-Promotion

GRAPHIS-PUBLIKATIONEN

GRAPHIS, Die internationale Zweimonatsschrift für Graphik und angewandte Kunst
PHOTOGRAPHIS, Das internationale Jahrbuch der Werbephotographie und der redaktionellen Photographie
GRAPHIS POSTERS, Das internationale Jahrbuch der Plakatkunst
GRAPHIS PACKUNGEN BAND 4, Internationales Handbuch der Packungsgestaltung
KINDERBUCH-ILLUSTRATION BAND 3, BAND 4, Eine internationale Übersicht über die Kinderbuch-Illustration
GRAPHIS DIAGRAMS, Die graphische Visualisierung abstrakter Gegebenheiten
FILM + TV GRAPHICS 2, Ein internationaler Überblick über die Kunst des Animationsfilms
ARCHIGRAPHIA, Architektur- und Umweltgraphik
GRAPHIS EPHEMERA, Künstler-Eigenwerbung

PUBLICATIONS GRAPHIS

GRAPHIS, La revue bimestrielle internationale d'arts graphiques et d'arts appliqués
PHOTOGRAPHIS, Le répertoire international de la photographie publicitaire et rédactionnelle
GRAPHIS POSTERS, Le répertoire international de l'art de l'affiche
GRAPHIS EMBALLAGES VOL. 4, Répertoire international des formes de l'emballage
ILLUSTRATIONS DE LIVRES D'ENFANTS VOL. 3, VOL. 4, Un aperçu international des illustrations de livres d'enfants
GRAPHIS DIAGRAMS, La visualisation graphique de données abstraites
FILM + TV GRAPHICS 2, Un panorama international de l'art du film d'animation
ARCHIGRAPHIA, La création graphique appliquée à l'architecture et à l'environnement
GRAPHIS EPHEMERA, Autopromotion des artistes

Distributors / Auslieferung / Distribution:

USA: WATSON-GUPTILL PUBLICATIONS, INC., 1515 Broadway, New York, N.Y. 10036 – **(ISBN: 0-8230-2153-X)**
CANADA: HURTIG PUBLISHERS, 10560-105 Street, Edmonton, Alberta T5H 2W7, tel. (403) 426-2469
FRANCE: GRAPHIS DISTRIBUTION, Milon-la-Chapelle, F-78470 St-Rémy-lès-Chevreuse, tél. 052-13-26
ITALIA: INTER-ORBIS, Via Lorenteggio, 31/1, I-20146 Milano, tel. 422 57 46
SPAIN: COMERCIAL ATHENEUM, S.A., Consejo de Ciento, 130-136, Barcelona 15, tel. 223 14 51-3
AMERICA LATINA, AUSTRALIA, JAPAN AND OTHER ASIAN COUNTRIES, AFRICA:
FLEETBOOKS S.A., c/o Feffer & Simons, Inc., 100 Park Avenue, New York, N.Y. 10017, tel. (212) 686-0888

All other countries / Alle anderen Länder / Tout autres pays:

GRAPHIS PRESS CORP., 107 Dufourstrasse, CH-8008 Zurich (Switzerland)

PUBLICATION No. 172 (ISBN 3-85709-183-5)

Contents   Inhalt   Sommaire

Abbreviations   Abkürzungen   Abréviations

Argentina	ARG	Argentinien	ARG	Afrique du Sud	SAF
Australia	AUS	Australien	AUS	Allemagne occidentale	GER
Austria	AUT	Belgien	BEL	Argentine	ARG
Belgium	BEL	Brasilien	BRA	Australie	AUS
Brazil	BRA	Bulgarien	BUL	Autriche	AUT
Bulgaria	BUL	Dänemark	DEN	Belgique	BEL
Canada	CAN	Deutschland (BRD)	GER	Brésil	BRA
Columbia	COL	Finnland	FIN	Bulgarie	BUL
Cuba	CUB	Frankreich	FRA	Canada	CAN
Czechoslovakia	CSR	Grossbritannien	GBR	Colombie	COL
Denmark	DEN	Hongkong	HKG	Cuba	CUB
Finland	FIN	Indien	IND	Danemark	DEN
France	FRA	Iran	IRN	Espagne	SPA
Germany (West)	GER	Irland	IRL	Etats-Unis	USA
Great Britain	GBR	Israel	ISR	Féd. Émirats arabes unis	UAE
Hong Kong	HKG	Italien	ITA	Finlande	FIN
India	IND	Japan	JPN	France	FRA
Iran	IRN	Kanada	CAN	Grande-Bretagne	GBR
Ireland	IRL	Kolumbien	COL	Hongkong	HKG
Israel	ISR	Korea	KOR	Inde	IND
Italy	ITA	Kuba	CUB	Iran	IRN
Japan	JPN	Kuweit	KUW	Irlande	IRL
Korea	KOR	Mexiko	MEX	Israël	ISR
Kuwait	KUW	Niederlande	NLD	Italie	ITA
Mexico	MEX	Norwegen	NOR	Japon	JPN
Netherlands	NLD	Österreich	AUT	Korea	KOR
Norway	NOR	Polen	POL	Koweit	KUW
Poland	POL	Portugal	POR	Mexique	MEX
Portugal	POR	Schweden	SWE	Norvège	NOR
South Africa	SAF	Schweiz	SWI	Pays-Bas	NLD
Spain	SPA	Spanien	SPA	Pologne	POL
Sweden	SWE	Südafrika	SAF	Portugal	POR
Switzerland	SWI	Tschechoslowakei	CSR	Suède	SWE
United Arab Emirates	UAE	USA	USA	Suisse	SWI
USA	USA	Ver. Arabische Emirate	UAE	Tchécoslovaquie	CSR

Cover Design / Umschlag / Couverture: Jean Michel Folon

Our cordial thanks goes to all those whose cooperation has enabled us to compile this far-ranging international survey of a year of graphic design and illustration.

Unser herzlicher Dank gilt allen, deren Mitarbeit es uns ermöglicht hat, diese vielfältige, internationale Übersicht auf dem Gebiet des Graphik-Design und der Illustration zusammenzustellen.

C'est grâce à la collaboration de tous nos correspondants que nous avons pu composer ce panorama diversifié de l'art graphique et de l'illustration et nous aimerions les remercier ici très chaleureusement.

JEAN MICHEL FOLON, who designed our cover (see also articles in GRAPHIS 130 and 156), was born in Brussels in 1934. He gave up the study of architecture to devote himself to graphic design and illustration and has since been successful in many areas: his drawings have appeared in the world's leading magazines, he has done giant murals for a subway station in Brussels and for Waterloo Station in London, he has made animated films and in recent years has given much of his time to watercolours, etchings, book illustrations (for Kafka, Lewis Carroll, Jacques Prévert, Apollinaire, etc.) and to stage sets. His work has been exhibited all over the world, and he has won numerous international awards. A retrospective of his oeuvre is taking place at the Picasso Museum in Antibes in 1983.

JEAN MICHEL FOLON, der Gestalter des Umschlags (s. auch Graphis No. 130 und 156), wurde 1934 in Brüssel geboren. Zugunsten der graphischen Kunst gab er sein Architekturstudium auf, und er hat sich seither auf vielen Gebieten bewährt: Seine Zeichnungen erschienen in führenden Zeitschriften; für eine Brüsseler Métro-Station und den Londoner Bahnhof Waterloo schuf er riesige Wandbilder; es entstanden Trickfilme, in den letzten Jahren vor allem aber Aquarelle, Radierungen, Buchillustrationen (u.a. Kafka, Lewis Carroll, Jacques Prévert, Apollinaire etc.), eigene Bücher (z.B. *Conversation,* in Zusammenarbeit mit Milton Glaser) und Bühnenbilder. Seine Werke wurden in aller Welt ausgestellt, und er erhielt zahlreiche internationale Auszeichnungen. Im Picasso-Museum in Antibes findet 1983 eine Retrospektive seiner Werke statt.

JEAN MICHEL FOLON, le créateur de notre couverture (voir aussi Graphis no 130 et no 156), fut né en 1934 à Bruxelles. Il abandonna ses études d'architecture en faveur de l'art graphique et réussit par la suite à s'imposer dans des domaines nombreux: ses dessins parurent dans les magazines les plus importants et ses tableaux gigantesques décorent une station de métro à Bruxelles ainsi que la gare londonienne Waterloo. Sous sa main naquirent des séquences de dessins animés insolites. Au cours de ces dernières années, il se voua avant tout aux aquarelles, gravures à l'eau-forte, décorations scéniques, illustrations de livres (entre autres Kafka, Lewis Carroll, Jacques Prévert, Apollinaire) ainsi qu'à des publications propres (p.ex. *Conversation,* en collaboration avec Milton Glaser). Ses créations firent le tour du monde et furent distinguées à plusieurs reprises par des prix internationaux. Une rétrospective de son œuvre a été organisée en 1983 au Musée Picasso à Antibes.

Massimo Vignelli

Preface

Born in Milan in 1931, Massimo Vignelli studied architecture in Milan and Venice, and since then has worked with his wife Lella, an architect, on the design of corporate identity and graphic programmes; transportation and architectural graphics; books, magazines, and newspapers; exhibitions and interiors and, through Vignelli Designs, furniture and a variety of industrial products.
Originally based in Milan, the firm has long been working for major American and European companies and institutions. Based in the USA since 1965, the Vignellis have had their work exhibited throughout the world and are represented in the permanent collections of several museums. Massimo Vignelli has taught and lectured on design in the major cities and universities of the USA and elsewhere. Among his many awards: the 1973 Industrial Arts Medal of the American Institute of Architects, an Honorary Doctorate from the Parsons School of Design, New York, entry to the Art Directors Club Hall of Fame New York (1982), and the 1983 Gold Medal of the American Institute of Graphic Arts.

The extremely exciting, seductive and dangerously probing attitude of the eighties has brought us a devouring desire to reassess the philosophy of our profession, its origins and its meaning as it stands today.

We feel a tremendous need for historical investigation into the roots of our profession, not only of the modern movement, but even before the industrial revolution. We need to rediscover the friendliness of design prior to the industrial revolution. We need to understand the motivations of the creative minds that preceded the modern movement. We are all offspring of the modern movement and we want to know more about our intellectual forebears. We need our roots. We need to know who the protagonists were, what prompted them to operate as they did, who their clients were and how their rapport generated a climate of creativity which affected others.

Historical information, introspection and interpretation are almost totally missing in our profession, and I think we feel a tremendous need to fill that gap.

The development of graphic design theory in this century is a corollary of the development of the major arts. This condition has culturally humiliated our profession. The consequences are a total vacuum of theory and a surplus of transitory superficial fads. It is time that theoretical issues be expressed and debated to provide a forum of intellectual tension out of which meanings spring to life. Pretty pictures can no longer lead the way in which our visual environment should be shaped. It is time to debate, to probe the values, to examine the theories which are part of our heritage and to verify their validity to express our times. It is time for the word to be heard. It is time for Words and Vision.

The emergence of semiotics could and will have a deep impact on our profession. It will establish a discipline of awareness and expression unreached before. The theoretical implications of new technologies for the way we conceive and express the printed word and the graphic image are a tremendous field of exploration which is still to be tapped. Again the lack of appropriate professional publications deprives all of us of the stimulation that could emerge from dialogue.

It should be no surprise that, along with the lack of history and theory, criticism is totally missing. The main function of criticism is not that of providing flattering or denigrating reviews but that of providing creative interpretations of the work, period or theory being analysed. Out of those creative interpretations a new light is cast on the objects, and new nuances and reflections are brought to our notice.

With criticism, designers will be offered the possibility of multi-layered reading of the work of other designers, or the opportunity of focusing on the meaning of particular expressive movements. Criticism will prevent, to a great extent, the superficial spreading of fads, or in any case will provide ground for their evaluation in the proper context. Graphic design will not be a profession until we have criticism.

The need for reassessment calls for documentation. We are thirsty for documentation that could provide us with sources of information for the re-evaluation of periods, people or events. Graphic design publications around the world provide a good source of documentation, although most of the time in a very disengaged way.

We need to arouse the awareness that every gesture of the present is a document for the future, and that our present will be measured only by these gestures.

In the early eighties I was amazed by the development of issues in the last twenty years, particularly by the way some issues reversed themselves completely from the sixties to the eighties. To visualize the phenomenon, I prepared the following chart which, like all charts, is quite schematic. However it still intrigues me as food for thought for the inquisitive mind.

SCHEMATIC CHART OF IDEOLOGICAL AND DESIGN CHANGES FROM THE 60s TO THE 80s

'60	'70	'80
discipline	appropriateness	ambiguity
idealism	pluralism	semiotics
objectivity	specificity	subjectivity
simplicity	complex simplicity	complexity
structure	programme	meaning
absolute	consistent	relative
geometry	articulate geometry	contradicting geometries
one stylistic code	contrasting stylistic codes	double stylistic coding
form follows function	form + function	semiotic form
no symbolism	controlled symbolism	expressive symbolism
no humour	surprise as humour	contradiction as humour
anti-metaphor	towards metaphor	metaphor
anti-ornament	structure as ornament	ornament
orthodox grid	loose grid	complex grid
one typeface (Helvetica)	few typefaces	variety of types
one type size	few type sizes	hierarchy concept
primary colours + black + red	rainbow	muted colours
high gloss	soft	contrasting textures
asymmetry	dynamic symmetry	symmetry plus asymmetry
sameness	identity	diversity
rigid systems	modular systems	accidental systems
less is more	less is a bore	the more the better

Massimo Vignelli

Vorwort

Massimo Vignelli, 1931 in Mailand geboren, studierte Architektur in Mailand und Venedig. Zusammen mit seiner Frau Lella, einer Architektin, spezialisierte er sich auf Firmenidentitäts- und graphische Programme; Signalisierungs- und Architekturgraphik; Bücher, Magazine und Zeitungen; Ausstellungs- und Innenausstattungen und, durch Vignelli Designs, auf Möbel und eine Anzahl weiterer Produkte.
Ursprünglich in Mailand zu Hause, hat das Unternehmen für grosse amerikanische und europäische Firmen und Institutionen gearbeitet. Seit 1965 leben und arbeiten die Vignellis in den USA. Ihre Arbeiten wurden in der ganzen Welt ausgestellt und in die Sammlungen mehrerer Museen aufgenommen. Massimo Vignelli hat Design gelehrt und in den grossen Städten und Universitäten der USA sowie auch in Übersee Vorlesungen gegeben. Zu seinen vielen Auszeichnungen zählen: Die Industrial Arts Medal (Auszeichnung für Industrie-Design) des American Institute of Architects, Ehrendoktorat der Parsons School of Design, New York, Aufnahme in die Art Directors Club 1982 Hall of Fame (höchste Auszeichnung des Art Directors Club New York) und 1983 die Goldmedaille des American Institute of Graphic Arts.

Der forschende Geist der 80er Jahre, der zugleich begeisternd, verführerisch und gefährlich ist, hat in uns den unbezähmbaren Wunsch nach einer Neueinschätzung der Philosophie unseres Berufes geweckt, seiner Ursprünge und seiner heutigen Bedeutung.

Wir verspüren ein enormes Bedürfnis nach geschichtlicher Untersuchung unseres Standes, wobei nicht nur die Wurzeln der modernen Bewegung sondern auch jene aus der Zeit vor der industriellen Revolution wichtig erscheinen. Wir müssen die Freundlichkeit des Designs aus jener Zeit wiederentdecken. Wir müssen die Beweggründe des kreativen Denkens vor Ausbruch der Moderne begreifen lernen. Wir sind alle Kinder der modernen Bewegung, und wir möchten mehr über unsere intellektuellen Vorfahren wissen. Wir brauchen unsere Wurzeln. Wir müssen wissen, wer die Vorkämpfer waren, was sie veranlasste, so zu handeln wie sie es taten, wer ihre Kunden waren und wie aus der Zusammenarbeit ein kreatives Klima entstand, das andere beeinflusste.

Historische Information, Selbstwahrnehmung und Interpretation fehlen in unserem Beruf beinahe ganz, und wir verspüren, glaube ich, ein grosses Bedürfnis, diese Lücke zu schliessen. In diesem Jahrhundert hat sich die Theorie des Graphik-Designs in völliger Abhängigkeit von jenem der freien Künste entwickelt. Dieser Umstand ist eine kulturelle Demütigung für unseren Stand. Die Konsequenzen sind ein völliges Theorie-Vakuum und ein Überfluss an vorübergehenden, belanglosen Modetorheiten. Es wird Zeit, dass theoretische Fragen formuliert und diskutiert werden, damit ein Forum intellektueller Spannung entstehen kann, aus dem Sinngehalte geboren werden. Schöne Bilder können nicht mehr aufzeigen, wie unsere visuelle Umwelt gestaltet werden sollte. Es ist Zeit zu debattieren, die Werte zu ergründen, die in unserem Erbe enthaltenen Theorien zu prüfen und ihre Gültigkeit für unsere Zeit festzustellen. Es ist an der Zeit, dass das Wort Gehör findet. Es ist Zeit für das Wort und das Bild.

Das Auftauchen der Semiotik kann und wird einen tiefgreifenden Einfluss auf unseren Beruf haben. Es wird eine bisher unerreichte Strenge der Wahrnehmung und des Ausdrucks ermöglichen. Die theoretische Bedeutung neuer Technologien für die Art, wie wir das gedruckte Wort und das graphische Bild begreifen und ausdrücken, ist ein enormes Gebiet, das es noch zu erforschen und zu nutzen gilt. Auch hier lässt uns der Mangel an geeigneten professionellen Publikationen die Stimulation missen, die aus dem Dialog entstehen könnte.

Es überrascht nicht, dass mit dem Mangel an Geschichte und Theorie auch die Kritik völlig fehlt. Die Hauptfunktion der Kritik ist nicht, schmeichelnde oder verunglimpfende Besprechungen zu liefern, sondern kreative Deutungen der untersuchten Arbeiten, Zeitläufte oder Theorien. Kreative Interpretation wirft ein neues Licht auf den Gegenstand der Besprechung, und neue Nuancen und Überlegungen kommen zum Vorschein.

Kritik gibt dem Designer die Möglichkeit einer vielschichtigen Betrachtung der Arbeit anderer Designer, oder die Gelegenheit, sich auf die Bedeutung bestimmter Ausdrucksrichtungen zu konzentrieren. Kritik wird die oberflächliche Verbreitung von Marotten weitgehend verhindern, oder auf jeden Fall eine Basis für ihre Auswertung im richtigen Zusammenhang bieten. Graphik-Design wird kein vollwertiger Beruf sein, bis es diese Form der Kritik gibt.

Die Neueinschätzung bedarf einer Dokumentation. Wir sehnen uns nach einer Dokumentation, die uns als Informationsquelle für die Neubewertung von Perioden, Leuten oder Ereignissen dienen könnte. Graphik-Design-Publikationen auf der ganzen Welt bieten eine gute Quelle der Dokumentation, obwohl in den meisten Fällen auf eine sehr unverbindliche Art.

Wir müssen das Bewusstsein wecken, dass jede Geste der Gegenwart ein Dokument für die Zukunft ist und dass unsere Zeit nur an diesen Gesten gemessen werden wird.

Die frühen 80er Jahre versetzen mich in Erstaunen über die Entwicklung der Kernfragen der letzten zwanzig Jahre, ganz besonders was die völlige Umkehrung einiger Werte zwischen den 60er und den 80er Jahren betrifft. Um dieses Phänomen sichtbar zu machen, habe ich die folgende Tabelle aufgestellt, die, wie alle Tabellen, ziemlich schematisch ist. Trotzdem glaube ich, dass sie einem wissbegierigen Geist Anregung bietet.

SCHEMATISCHE TABELLE DER IDEOLOGISCHEN UND DESIGN-WECHSEL VON DEN 60er BIS ZU DEN 80er JAHREN.

'60	'70	'80
Disziplin	Zweckmässigkeit	Mehrdeutigkeit
Idealismus	Pluralismus	Semiotik
Objektivität	Sachbezogenheit	Subjektivität
Einfachheit	vielschichtige Einfachheit	Vielschichtigkeit
Struktur	Programm	Bedeutung
absolut	beständig	relativ
Geometrie	klar erkennbare Geometrie	entgegengesetzte geometrische Darstellungen
eine stilistische Regel	kontrastierende stilistische Regeln	zweigleisige stilistische Regeln
Form folgt Funktion	Form und Funktion	semiotische Form
kein Symbolismus	kontrollierter Symbolismus	expressiver Symbolismus
kein Humor	Überraschung als Humor	Widerspruch als Humor
Anti-Metapher	in Richtung Metapher	Metapher
Anti-Ornament	Struktur als Ornament	Ornament
genormter Raster	gelöster Raster	komplexer Raster
eine Schrift (Helvetica)	wenige Schriften	verschiedene Schriften
eine Schriftgrösse	wenige Schriftgrössen	hierarchisches Konzept
Grundfarben + Schwarz + Rot	Regenbogen	gedämpfte Farben
Hochglanz	matt	kontrastierende Strukturen
Asymmetrie	dynamische Symmetrie	Symmetrie plus Asymmetrie
Gleichheit	Identität	Diversität
starre Systeme	Modularsysteme	Zufallssysteme
weniger ist mehr	weniger ist langweilig	je mehr desto besser

Massimo Vignelli

Préface

Né à Milan en 1931, Massimo Vignelli fait des études d'architecture à Milan et à Venise, puis se voue avec sa femme Lella, qui est architecte, à l'élaboration de programmes d'identité globale de marque, de programmes graphiques; de réalisations graphiques appliquées aux transports et à l'architecture; de livres, magazines et journaux; d'expositions et de décorations intérieures; ainsi que, à travers Vignelli Designs, d'ameublements et d'une grande variété de produits divers.
D'abord installée à Milan, l'entreprise a travaillé pour des grandes sociétés et institutions américaines et européennes. Aux Etats-Unis depuis 1965, les Vignelli ont vu leurs œuvres exposées dans le monde entier et incorporées dans les collections permanentes de plusieurs musées. Massimo Vignelli est un professeur et conférencier de design apprécié du public des principales villes et universités américaines et étrangères. Le couple Vignelli a remporté de nombreux prix, dont l'Industrial Arts Medal de l'American Institute of Architects en 1973, un doctorat honoris causa de la Parsons School of Design, New York, l'inclusion dans le Hall of Fame de l'Art Directors Club New York en 1982 et la médaille d'or de l'American Institute of Graphic Arts en 1983.

La tendance au repositionnement qui s'est fait jour depuis le début des années 1980 comporte énormément de séductions et pas mal de dangers. Elle nous a valu un désir ardent de remettre en question la philosophie de notre profession, de remonter à ses origines et d'en redéfinir le sens hic et nunc.

Nous éprouvons un besoin dévorant de rechercher les racines de notre profession en remontant le cours du temps non seulement jusqu'à l'aube des temps modernes, mais par-delà même la révolution industrielle. Nous avons besoin de redécouvrir l'aménité du design des temps jadis, avant la révolution industrielle. Nous avons besoin d'élucider les motivations des créateurs qui précédèrent les temps modernes. Nous sommes tous les descendants de ces pionniers et aimerions mieux connaître nos ancêtres intellectuels. Nous avons besoin de retrouver nos racines. Nous avons besoin de savoir qui étaient les maîtres du jeu, ce qui les poussait à agir de la manière qu'ils le firent, quels étaient leurs clients et comment les relations qu'ils entretinrent avec eux donnèrent corps à un climat de créativité qui en vint influencer d'autres.

L'information au plan historique, l'introspection et l'interprétation sont presque totalement absents de notre profession; à mon avis, c'est là une lacune que nous avons bien besoin de combler.

Le développement de la théorie de la création graphique en ce siècle est un corollaire de celui des arts majeurs. C'est là une condition historique qui constitue une source d'humiliation culturelle pour notre profession. La conséquence en est un vide quasi total sur le plan théorique et un excès de modes et d'engouements passagers fort superficiels. Il est grand temps que les questions de théorie soient exprimées et débattues afin de constituer un forum animé d'une tension intellectuelle qui permette aux significations de prendre vie. Des jolies images ne peuvent plus servir de panneaux indicateurs sur la voie menant à l'aménagement visuel de notre environnement. Il est temps de discuter, de soumettre à examen les valeurs absolues, de se pencher de près sur les théories qui font partie de notre héritage et de vérifier si elles se prêtent à l'expression de notre époque. Il est temps que le verbe soit entendu. Le temps du Verbe et de la Vision est venu.

L'émergence de la sémiotique pourrait avoir et aura très certainement une influence déterminante sur notre profession. Elle contribuera à imposer une discipline de prise de conscience et d'expression inconnue jusqu'ici. Les implications théoriques des nouvelles technologies pour la manière dont nous concevons et exprimons le mot imprimé et l'image graphique constituent un extraordinaire champ d'exploration qui reste encore à défricher. Une fois de plus, la pénurie de publications professionnelles adéquates nous prive tous de la stimulation que provoque le dialogue.

Il n'est guère étonnant que le manque d'histoire et de théorie s'accompagne d'une absence totale de critique. La fonction majeure de toute critique n'est pas celle de la flatterie ou de la dénigration, mais celle de l'interprétation créatrice de l'œuvre, de la période ou de la théorie considérée. C'est de cette interprétation créatrice que jaillit une lumière neuve sur les objets et que des teintes et réflexions nouvelles enrichissent l'expérience.

La critique autorise la lecture multiple de l'œuvre des autres designers, la concentration sur la signification de mouvements expressifs déterminés. La critique prévient dans une large mesure la diffusion de modes et engouements passagers et superficiels ou en permet pour tout le moins une appréciation raisonnée qui les replace dans leur contexte. Le design graphique ne sera une profession que dans la mesure où se développera la critique.

Le besoin de repositionnement présuppose un effort documentaire. Nous sommes assoiffés de documentation, d'une source de renseignements permettant d'aborder les périodes, les individus ou les événements en toute connaissance de cause. Les publications d'art graphique au plan international constituent une bonne source documentaire, quoique trop souvent de manière peu engagée. Nous avons besoin de prendre conscience de ce que chaque geste du temps présent est un document pour l'avenir et de ce que notre présent ne sera mesuré qu'en fonction de ces gestes.

Au début des années 1980, j'ai été fortement impressionné par l'évolution qu'ont connue les grandes questions de notre profession depuis vingt ans, et en particulier par certaines positions complètement inversées lorsque l'on passe des années 60 aux années 80. Afin de visualiser le phénomène, j'ai préparé le tableau qui suit, un tableau évidemment schématisé comme tout tableau, et qui pourtant continue de m'intriguer en tant qu'aliment utile pour tout esprit curieux.

TABLEAU SCHÉMATIQUE DES TRANSFORMATIONS INTERVENUES ENTRE LES ANNÉES 60 ET LES ANNÉES 80 AU DOUBLE PLAN DE L'IDÉOLOGIE ET DU DESIGN

Années 60	70	80
discipline	à-propos	ambiguïté
idéalisme	pluralisme	sémiotique
objectivité	spécificité	subjectivité
simplicité	simplicité complexe	complexité
structure	programme	signification
absolu	consistant	relatif
géométrie	géométrie articulée	géométries contradictoires
code stylistique unique	codes stylistiques contrastés	double codage stylistique
la forme suit la fonction	forme et fonction	forme sémiotique
pas de symbolisme	symbolisme contrôlé	symbolisme expressif
pas d'humour	la surprise fait fonction d'humour	la contradiction fait fonction d'humour
anti-métaphore	en route vers la métaphore	métaphore
anti-ornement	la structure fait fonction d'ornement	ornement
grille orthodoxe	grille lâche	grille complexe
un type de caractères (Helvetica)	petit nombre de caractères	variété de caractères
un corps de lettre	petit nombre de corps	conception hiérarchisée
couleurs primaires plus noir et rouge	arc-en-ciel	couleurs atténuées
brillant	adouci	textures contrastées
asymétrie	symétrie dynamique	symétrie plus asymétrie
ressemblance	identité	diversité
systèmes rigides	systèmes modulaires	systèmes accidentels
le moins est le plus	le moins, c'est ennuyeux	plus il y a, mieux c'est

Index to Artists
Verzeichnis der Künstler
Index des Artistes

Index to Designers
Verzeichnis der Gestalter
Index des Maquettistes

Index to Art Directors
Verzeichnis der künstlerischen Leiter
Index des Directeurs Artistiques

Index to Publishers
Verzeichnis der Verleger
Index des Editeurs

Index to Agencies and Studios
Verzeichnis der Agenturen und Studios
Index des Agences et Studios

Index to Advertisers
Verzeichnis der Auftraggeber
Index des Clients

■ Entry instructions may be requested by anyone interested in submitting samples of exceptional graphics or photography for possible inclusion in our annuals. No fees involved. Closing dates for entries:
GRAPHIS ANNUAL (advertising and editorial art and design): 31 January
PHOTOGRAPHIS (advertising and editorial photography): 30 June
GRAPHIS POSTERS (an annual of poster art): 30 June
Write to: Graphis Press Corp., Dufourstrasse 107, 8008 Zurich, Switzerland

■ Einsendebedingungen können von jedermann angefordert werden, der uns Beispiele hervorragender Photographie oder Graphik zur Auswahl für unsere Jahrbücher unterbreiten möchte. Es werden keine Gebühren erhoben.
Einsendetermine:
GRAPHIS ANNUAL (Werbe- und redaktionelle Graphik): 31. Januar
PHOTOGRAPHIS (Werbe- und redaktionelle Photographie): 30. Juni
GRAPHIS POSTERS (ein Jahrbuch der Plakatkunst): 30. Juni
Adresse: Graphis Verlag AG, Dufourstrasse 107, 8008 Zürich, Schweiz

■ Tout intéressé à la soumission de travaux photographiques et graphiques recevra les informations nécessaires sur demande. Sans charge de participation.
Dates limites:
GRAPHIS ANNUAL (art graphique publicitaire et rédactionnel): 31 janvier
PHOTOGRAPHIS (photographie publicitaire et rédactionnelle): 30 juin
GRAPHIS POSTERS (annuaire sur l'art de l'affiche): 30 juin
S'adresser à: Editions Graphis SA, Dufourstrasse 107, 8008 Zurich, Suisse

Editor and Art Director: Walter Herdeg
Assistant Editor: Stanley Mason
Project Managers: Heinke Jenssen, Maja Zwahlen
Designers: Marino Bianchera, Martin Byland,
Art Assistant: Walter Zuber

1

What better way to build your business than with another entrepreneur?

Building toward your business goals becomes a lot easier with the help of someone who shares many of the same dreams.

Like you, Penn Mutual representatives are entrepreneurs. That's why they understand your needs so well.

They realize the necessity of strengthening cash flow and building cash reserves. And they can provide valuable services to help you achieve those goals.

They know the importance of mini-

mizing tax liability. So they'll help you shelter income, defer taxes, and maximize your retirement benefits.

They understand your need for protection. And they'll work with you to safeguard your business, your key employees, and your estate.

No matter what business goals you're building toward, your Penn Mutual agent can help you bridge the gap between your dreams and reality.

If you want to talk to someone about

building your business, call 1-800-331-1750—Operator 932 (In Oklahoma, call 1-800-622-3600—Operator 932). Ask about Penn Mutual's business building programs. We'll put you in touch with the Penn Mutual representative nearest you.

Penn Mutual
Where independence begins

The Penn Mutual Life Insurance Company, Independence Square, Philadelphia, PA 19172

1

Why do some people manage to make more money from the money they manage?

Don't look for green thumbs. Or secret formulas. To find out why some asset managers achieve higher yields, look at the way they use their resources.

One such resource is Penn Mutual's new *Diversifier*sm multiple-option investment contract.

By offering three different investment options in a single contract, *The Diversifier* helps asset managers choose the right alternative for each need.

For rapid asset growth and maxi-

mum liquidity, there's a short-term investment option that features high money market yields.

For long-term growth, there's a common stock option that has outperformed both the Dow-Jones Industrials and the S&P 500 in recent years.

And, for maximum protection of capital, there's a guaranteed investment account option for as little as $5,000.

The Diversifier gives you all this—plus monthly statements, 5-day written

confirmations and more—for a remarkably low annual charge. Without the expense of front-end loading.

To find out how *The Diversifier* can help you make more money from the money you manage, call collect: (215) 629-0600 and ask for Sam Taylor, Vice President, Pension Marketing.

Penn Mutual
Where independence begins

The Penn Mutual Life Insurance Company, Independence Square, Philadelphia, PA 19172

2

SECURITY
a world of certainty

Safety and security are basic needs. And we should expect to have them met, particularly in our homes. This is why Four-Leaf Towers is engineered and built the way it is.

A high-rise condominium community in the heart of Houston, Four-Leaf Towers brings this international city a classic style of living that is safe and secure. Its well-lighted grounds are protected by on-premise security patrol. A TV system monitors the interiors and the underground garage which is connected to the main lobbies by shuttle elevators that open in full view of each concierge.

Door keys to the residences cannot be duplicated, and each residence features an emergency call system. The twin, 40-story towers have smoke detectors, extensive sprinkler systems, and emergency power generators. Residences are separated from each other by 15" walls and from public spaces by 12" concrete walls.

Designed by Cesar Pelli, developed by Interfin Corporation, Four-Leaf Towers will be available for occupancy early in 1982.

Come, discover the certainty of our world.

FOUR-LEAF TOWERS

3

LOCATION
a world of choices

The world's great international cities have their special places: Zona Rosa, Fifth Avenue, Via Condotti, Mayfair, Rive Droit. Each personifies some element of city life: entertainment, living, shopping, dining, lodging.

In Houston these elements come together in one place: the Post Oak area. All the choices Houston has to offer are either here or they are coming here: world class hotels, the Galleria, international cuisine, couture shops, exclusive clubs, entertainment, corporate offices, fine residential neighborhoods.

Now, into this thoroughly urban setting, in the world's newest international city, comes the first truly international residence: Four-Leaf Towers.

A high-rise condominium community set in a quiet, private nine-acre park, Four-Leaf Towers promises to bring a classic style of living to Houston's expressive heart.

Designed by Cesar Pelli and developed by Interfin Corporation, Four-Leaf Towers will be available for occupancy early in 1982. Come discover its world of choices.

FOUR-LEAF TOWERS

4

Advertisements / Anzeigen / Annonces

1, 2 Two full-page advertisements in black and white for the *Penn Mutual* insurance company, offering special investments for companies and individuals. (USA)
3–6 Double-spread advertisements and an illustration in original size taken from an image advertising campaign for high-rise luxury condominiums in Four-Leaf Towers. These advertisements offer purchasers many of the requirements they desire nowadays. Fig. 3: Water-colour; Fig. 4: Oil-pastel; Figs. 5, 6: Mixed techniques. All in full colour. (USA)

1, 2 Zwei ganzseitige Anzeigen in Schwarzweiss für die Versicherungsgesellschaft *Penn Mutual*, die Unternehmern Investitionsverträge anbietet. (USA)
3–6 Doppelseitige Anzeigen und eine Illustration in Originalgrösse aus einer Werbekampagne für luxuriöse Eigentumswohnungen in den «Four-Leaf Towers». Sicherheit, die schöne Lage im Herzen der Stadt und Sorgfalt in der Ausführung sind die Themen dieser Inserate für die 40stöckigen Wohnungstürme. Abb. 3: Aquarell. Abb. 4: Ölpastell. Abb. 5/6: Mischtechnik. Alle in Farbe. (USA)

ARTIST / KÜNSTLER / ARTISTE:

1, 2 Geoffrey Moss
3   James McMullen
4   John Hylton
5, 6 Milton Glaser

DESIGNER / GESTALTER:

1, 2 Jack Bythrow
3–6 Steven Sessions

ART DIRECTOR:

1, 2 Jack Bythrow
3–6 Steven Sessions

AGENCY / AGENTUR / AGENCE:

1, 2 Spiro Assoc., Inc.
3–6 Baxter & Korge Inc.

5

6

1, 2 Deux annonces pleine page, en noir et blanc, pour la compagnie d'assurances *Penn Mutual*, qui offre aux chefs d'entreprise des contrats d'investissements. (USA)
3–6 Annonces double page, ainsi qu'une illustration au format original; éléments d'une campagne en faveur d'appartements luxueux en copropriété dans des gratte-ciel de quarante étages. Thèmes: la sécurité, la situation centrale au cœur de la ville et les soins apportés à l'aménagement. Fig. 3: aquarelle. Fig. 4: pastel à l'huile. Fig. 5/6: technique mixte. Le tout en couleur. (USA)

Advertisements
Anzeigen
Annonces

7, 8 Full-page illustration and complete double-page advertisement used to advertise *Quest* magazine, recommending its "Urban Renewal for the City Mind". (CAN)
9–11 Illustration and complete examples from a series of double-page advertisements for the radio and television magazine *Télérama*, which publishes information about radio, TV, cinema and music. (FRA)

7, 8 Ganzseitige Illustration und vollständiges, doppelseitiges Inserat für das Magazin *Quest*, das sich als «Belebung für den städtischen Geist» empfiehlt. (CAN)
9–11 Illustration und vollständige Beispiele aus einer Serie von doppelseitigen Anzeigen für die Radio- und TV-Zeitschrift *Télérama*, die Informationen zu Radio- und Fernsehprogrammen, Kino und Musik bietet. (FRA)

7, 8 Illustration pleine page et annonce double page complète pour le magazine *Quest*, qui se recommande pour la tonalité vivifiante qu'il apporte à l'atmosphère de la ville. (CAN)
9–11 Illustration et examples complets d'une série d'annonces double page pour le journal de TV-radio *Télérama*, où l'on trouve toutes les informations utiles sur les programmes, mais aussi sur la musique et le cinéma. (FRA)

8

ARTIST:

7, 8 John Martin
9–11 André François

ART DIRECTOR:

7, 8 Paul Cade
9–11 Yves Delacroix

AGENCY/AGENTUR:

7, 8 Doyle Dane Bernbach
9–11 Mirabelle

7

9

10

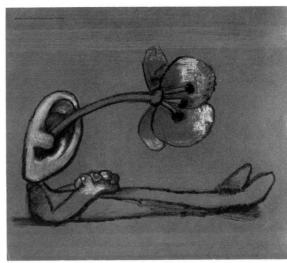

11

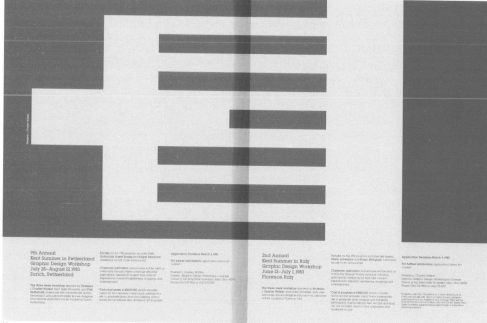

ARTIST / KÜNSTLER / ARTISTE:

12 Michael Terry
13 J. Charles Walker
14 Braldt Bralds
15 Terry Widener
16 Elwood H. Smith
17 Don Weller
18 Gary Templin/Nancy Hoefig

12 Advertisement for *Voetbal International*, a magazine devoted to soccer, presenting a rare male representative of the population who pays no attention to this periodical. It serves the ends of space promotion and refers to the magazine's high circulation. (NLD)
13 Double-spread advertisement for three-week design courses. (USA)
14 Pull-out advertisement for IBM computer programmes, with sketchboards that transpose drafts into data and with screens on which every design can be graphically altered. These computers memorize everything from the first draft to the last technical drawing. (GER)
15 Full-colour advertisement attracting firms to Riverside. (USA)
16 Full-colour ad for the School of Visual Arts in New York. (USA)
17 Advertisement for a series of lectures on advertising and design. Opportunities for skiing are simultaneously offered. (USA)
18 Advertisement for the opening of a new shopping centre. (USA)

12 Anzeige für *Voetbal International*, eine Fussballzeitschrift für Männer. Hier wird ein seltener Vertreter der männlichen Bevölkerung vorgestellt, der nichts von der Zeitschrift hält. Mit Hinweis auf die hohe Auflage wird um Inserenten geworben. (NLD)
13 Doppelseitige Anzeige für dreiwöchige Graphik-Design-Kurse in Zürich und Florenz, organisiert von der Kent State Universität. (USA)
14 Auslege-Anzeige für IBM-Computer-Programme, mit Zeichentischen, die Entwürfe in Daten übersetzen; und mit Bildschirmen, auf denen jedes Design graphisch geändert werden kann. Die Computer speichern alles, vom ersten Entwurf bis zur letzten technischen Zeichnung. (GER)
15 Farbige Anzeige für Riverside, ein Ort in der Nähe von Dallas, in welcher die einzigartige Lage für Firmen hervorgehoben wird. (USA)
16 Anzeige für eine Kunstschule in New York. Mehrfarbig. (USA)
17 Anzeige für einen Kursus über Werbung und Design. Gleichzeitig wird die Möglichkeit zum Skilaufen geboten. (USA)
18 Anzeige anlässlich der Eröffnung eines neuen Einkaufszentrums mit mehr als 125 Läden in New Jersey. (USA)

12 Annonce pour *Voetbal International*, un magazine du football pas pour les hommes du type représenté. Campagne mettant en évidence l'intérêt du fort tirage pour les annonceurs. (NLD)
13 Annonce double page pour des cours d'art graphique à Zurich et Florence organisés par la Kent State University. (USA)
14 Annonce pour des programmes d'ordinateurs IBM permettant de transposer en données tout dessin technique et de le modifier. (GER)
15 Annonce couleurs pour Riverside près de Dallas. (USA)
16 Annonce pour une école d'art newyorkaise. En polychromie. (USA)
17 Annonce pour un cours de publicité et de design offrant l'occasion de faire du ski. (USA)
18 Annonce à l'occasion de l'inauguration d'un nouveau centre commercial dans le New Jersey regroupant plus de 125 commerces. (USA)

How the executives of Dallas and Fort Worth view the executives of Riverside.

Riverside is a corporate community midway between Dallas and Fort Worth. Five minutes from the Dallas/Fort Worth Airport, Riverside is also close to the major cities of the world. □ And Riverside has advantages the executives of any city will view with envy. Like hotels and restaurants, shops and condominiums, a country club and a masters level golf course. All on 450 acres, which makes Riverside quite a site for your company. □ For information about your future at Riverside, contact Bradley Bayoud, President, Bedrock Development Corporation, 630 Texas American Bank Tower, Dallas, Texas 75235. Or call (214) 352-3388. And look closely at Riverside.

RIVERSIDE

15

The Design Conference That Just Happens To Be in Park City '83

A Mind-Bending Experience

Take in the beauty of Park City skiing while you take in the latest in advertising and design. The fifth annual TDCTJHTBIPC is featuring some of the foremost minds in the business. It's an informal experience. Mornings and evenings there will be lectures, films and question and answer sessions. Catch up on state-of-the-art thinking. Afternoons and all day Wednesday you can work out on the slopes, take ski lessons or explore the historic mining town of Park City, Utah. The Conference will be held February 7-11, 1983 at the Holiday Inn in Park City. Ski your way to success at the TDCTJHTBIPC '83.

Scheduled Speakers include:
Sheila Levrant de Brettveille, *Designer/Educator;* The Otis Art Institute of Parsons

School of Design, Los Angeles. **Heather Cooper**, *Illustrator;* Burns, Cooper, Hynes, Ltd., Toronto. **Gene Federico**, *Art Director;* Lord, Geller, Federico, Einstein, Inc., New York. **Errol Gerson**, *Investment, Management and Motivational Advisor*, Los Angeles. **Richard Hess**, *Designer/Illustrator*, Richard Hess, Inc., New York. **Larry Rood**, *Creative Director/V.P.;* Cunningham & Walsh, Los Angeles.
Register now. Only the first 200 reservations can be accepted. The cost of attending the Conference is $200 for five days. Students with current I.D. $75.00. Send form to:

TDCTJHTBIPC '83
c/o Travel International
8907 Wilshire Blvd., Suite 203
Beverly Hills, CA 90211
Tele: 213-655-4430

□ Yes, I want to bend my mind and body.

I am enclosing $_____ (Please make checks payable to: TDCTJHTBIPC '83) for _____ reservation(s).

□ Send me the TDCTJHTBIPC '83 Travel Accommodation Special Rate information.

NAME

ADDRESS

CITY, STATE AND ZIP

PHONE

TITLE OR POSITION

COMPANY

267

17

SCHOOL OF VISUAL ARTS

209 EAST 23RD STREET, NEW YORK, N.Y. 10010 (212) 679-7350

16

← BURLINGTON CENTER IS YOURS FOR THE CHOOSING ON THURSDAY, AUGUST 5. DON'T MISS IT!

18

31

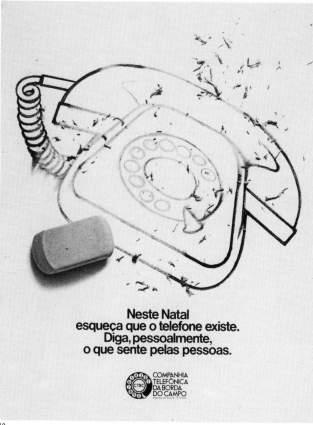

Neste Natal
esqueça que o telefone existe.
Diga, pessoalmente,
o que sente pelas pessoas.

COMPANHIA
TELEFÔNICA
DA BORDA
DO CAMPO

19

SKI FRONTIER'S WEST. Just name where you want to go skiing. And odds are that we can take you there. Frontier flies to more ski resorts than any other airline. 139 ski resorts in all. Throughout our destination cities all up and down the Rockies.

This is the time to dig out your skis and parka from last season and get ready to carve your mark in Montrose. Ride the bumps in Boise. And jump for joy in Jackson. Not to mention our other great skiing destinations like Vancouver, Spokane, Grand Junction, Denver, Durango, Salt Lake City and Reno/Lake Tahoe. The list just goes on and on.

So just call your travel agent or Frontier Airlines. And tell them you'd rather be on the slopes than just reading about them.

FRONTIER AIRLINES
First class comfort at coach prices.

20

ARTIST / KÜNSTLER / ARTISTE:

19 Marcio Scavone
20 Nicholas Gaetano
21 Yutaka Hasegawa
22 Joe Scorsone
23 Józef Sumichrast
24 Fred Otnes

DESIGNER / GESTALTER:

21 Yutaka Hasegawa
22 Joe Scorsone
24 John DeCesare

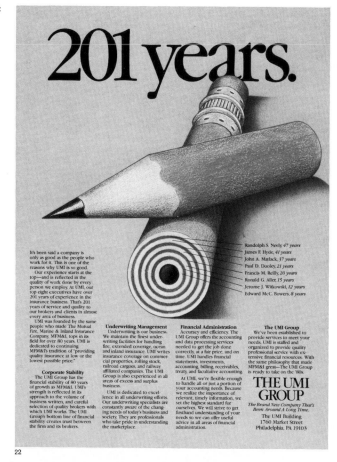

201 years.

It's been said a company is only as good as the people who work for it. This is one of the reasons why UMI is so good.

Our experience starts at the top—and is reflected in the quality of work done by every person we employ. At UMI, our top eight executives have over 201 years of experience in the insurance business. That's 201 years of service and quality to our brokers and clients in almost every area of business.

UMI was founded by the same people who made The Mutual Fire, Marine & Inland Insurance Company, MFM&I, tops in its field for over 80 years. UMI is dedicated to continuing MFM&I's tradition of "providing quality insurance at low or the lowest possible price."

Corporate Stability
The UMI Group has the financial stability and years of growth as MFM&I. UMI's strength is reflected in its approach to the volume of business written, and careful selection of quality brokers with which UMI works. The UMI Group's bottom line of financial stability creates trust between the firm and its brokers.

Underwriting Management
Underwriting is our business. We maintain the finest underwriting facilities for handling fire, extended coverage, ocean and inland insurance. UMI writes insurance coverage on commercial properties, rolling stock, railroad cargoes, and railway affiliated companies. The UMI Group is also experienced in all areas of excess and surplus business.

UMI is dedicated to excellence in all underwriting efforts. Our underwriting specialists are constantly aware of the changing needs of today's business and society. They are professionals who take pride in understanding the marketplace.

Financial Administration
Accuracy and efficiency. The UMI Group offers the accounting and data processing services needed to get the job done correctly, at a fair price, and on time. UMI handles financial statements, investments, accounting, billing, receivables, treaty, and facultative accounting.

At UMI, we're flexible enough to handle all or just a portion of your accounting needs. Because we realize the importance of relevant, timely information, we set the highest standard for ourselves. We will strive to get firsthand understanding of your needs so we can offer useful advice in all areas of financial administration.

The UMI Group
We've been established to provide services to meet your needs. UMI is staffed and organized to provide quality professional service with extensive financial resources. With the same philosophy that made MFM&I great—The UMI Group is ready to take on the '80s.

Randolph S. Neely, 47 years
James F. Hyde, 41 years
John A. Matlack, 37 years
Paul D. Dooley, 21 years
Francis M. Reilly, 20 years
Ronald G. Aller, 15 years
Jerome J. Witkowski, 12 years
Edward McC. Bowers, 8 years

THE UMI GROUP

The Brand New Company That's Been Around A Long Time.

The UMI Building
1760 Market Street
Philadelphia, PA 19103

22

NOW YOU CAN BUY A HOME WITH MONTHLY PAYMENTS YOUR POCKETBOOK CAN LIVE WITH.

SOLD
The Real Estate Members of
Better Homes

Our H.E.L.P™ program can help you buy a home now.

H.E.L.P

H.E.L.P. (Home Equity Leverage Plan) is a unique financing program designed by Better Homes and Gardens® Real Estate Service to reduce monthly payments and make a home purchase easier.

The H.E.L.P. contract, drawn between you and the seller, allows you to negotiate a lower-than-market interest rate.

This lower rate can help you qualify for a home now...or maybe qualify for a higher priced home than you could afford with conventional financing.

For full information and a brochure on our H.E.L.P. program, see the Better Homes and Gardens member in your area.* Or, if you're locating out of town, call toll free for

assistance. 1-800-247-5050
In Iowa, call 1-800-532-1430

*Services and products available only at participating members. Each office independently owned and operated.

The Real Estate Members of
Better Homes

IT'S LIKE MOVING WITH SOMEONE YOU KNOW.

23

ナイス ショット!!————————読者を魅了する『主婦と生活社』の出版物。

主婦と生活
JUNON
週刊女性
angle
健康家族
美しい部屋
じゃるむ
ヘア&メーク
sens
21世紀ブックス
家庭実用書
番町書房の本

主婦と生活社

21

ART DIRECTOR / DIRECTEUR ARTISTIQUE:

19 Carlos Bergamini
20 Clarice Bonzer
21 Yutaka Hasegawa
22 JRA Associates
23 Liz Kell
24 John DeCesare

AGENCY / AGENTUR / AGENCE – STUDIO:

19 Alcantara Machado,
   Periscinoto Comunicações Ltda.
20 Tracy-Locke
22 Friebel Studios
23 Campbell-Mithun Inc.
24 DeCesare Design

19 Annonce de journal de la compagnie brésilienne des téléphones, avec ce slogan: «En cette fête de Noël, oubliez l'existence du téléphone. Dites vos sentiments de vive voix.» (BRA)
20 Petite annonce couleurs pour les *Frontier Airlines* de Denver (Colorado), compagnie aérienne qui dessert la plupart des stations de ski d'Amérique du Nord. (USA)
21 Annonce d'un éditeur japonais, dans un magazine du golf. (JPN)
22 Annonce pour le groupe UMI, une compagnie d'assurances riche de 201 années d'expérience (le total de l'expérience de ses cadres symbolisé par les cernes rouges des crayons jaunes). (USA)
23 Annonce de magazine pour une société immobilière: «Vous pouvez maintenant acheter une maison facile à payer en mensualités intéressantes.» (USA)
24 Pour l'annonce d'une conférence sur la formation médicale. (USA)

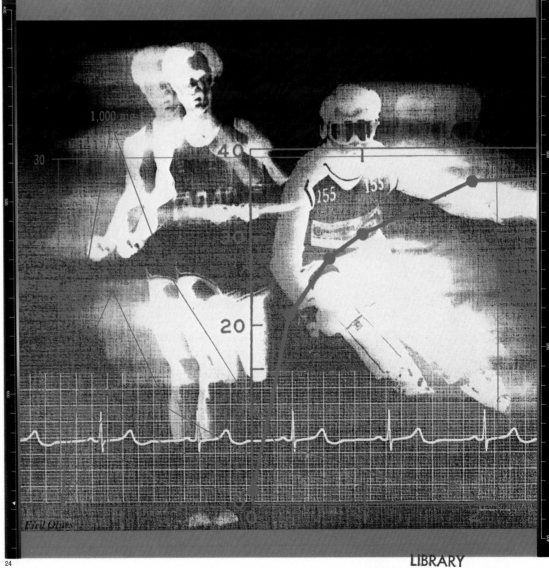

24

33

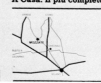

25

26

27

25–27 Examples from an advertising campaign for the *A Casa* furniture company, pointing to the large selection it has on exhibition and to its complete furnishing service. (ITA)
28 Example from a series of work by various artists for the IVECO company, showing here a composite work (five-colour silkscreen and four-colour etching) by Enrico Baj. (ITA)
29, 30 Illustration and complete advertisement showing "Sound Waves", one of a series by contemporary artists commissioned by TDK, manufacturers of music cassettes. (USA)

25–27 Beispiele aus einer Werbekampagne der Möbelfirma *A Casa*, die auf die grosse Auswahl in ihren Ausstellungsräumen und auf einen kompletten Einrichtungsservice hinweist. (ITA)
28 Beispiel aus einer Reihe von Arbeiten verschiedener Künstler für das Unternehmen IVECO, hier eine Collage (Fünffarben-Siebdruck und Vierfarben-Radierung) von Enrico Baj. (ITA)
29, 30 Illustration und vollständige Anzeige aus einer Serie von zeitgenössischen Künstlern für TDK, Hersteller von Musikkassetten, hier zum Thema «Klangwellen». (USA)

25–27 Trois exemples d'une campagne de publicité de la maison d'ameublements *A Casa*, où l'accent est mis sur la diversité de l'offre et sur l'existence d'un service d'aménagements et de décoration complet. (ITA)
28 Exemple des travaux réalisés par divers artistes pour l'entreprise IVECO: collage d'Enrico Baj. Sérigraphie cinq couleurs, eau-forte quatre couleurs. (ITA)
29, 30 Illustration et annonce complète. Série d'artistes contemporains pour TDK, fabricant de musicassettes. (USA)

28

29

30

ARTIST / KÜNSTLER / ARTISTE:

25–27 Anna Pennati
28 Enrico Baj
29, 30 James Marsh

DESIGNER / GESTALTER / MAQUETTISTE:

25–27 Claudio Platania
29, 30 James Marsh

ART DIRECTOR / DIRECTEUR ARTISTIQUE:

25–27 Claudio Platania
29, 30 Chris Baker

AGENCY / AGENTUR / AGENCE – STUDIO:

25–27 Copyright Srl
28 Iveco Image
29, 30 Newton & Godin

Advertisements / Anzeigen / Annonces

31

We bring out the beauty in the beast.

Schroder Real Estate Corporation.

32

31, 32 Illustration in original size and complete advertisement of a real estate company. (USA)
33 From a series of newspaper ads announcing a TV programme about childhood. Linocut in black and white. (USA)
34 Double-spread advertisement of an insurance company. In shades of yellow and orange. (USA)
35 Double-spread *Ingersoll-Rand* advertisement, urging American industry to invest more money in machines and to become aware of this necessity. (USA)
36, 37 Complete advertisement and illustration for *Pioneer* automobile stereo kits. (FRA)

31, 32 Illustration in Originalgrösse und ganzseitige Anzeige einer Immobilienfirma. (USA)
33 Aus einer Serie von Zeitungsanzeigen, mit dem Hinweis auf eine Fernsehsendung zum Thema «Kindheit». Linolschnitt in Schwarzweiss. (USA)
34 Doppelseitiges Inserat einer Versicherungsgesellschaft. In Gelb- und Orangetönen. (USA)
35 Doppelseitige Anzeige der *Ingersoll-Rand*, welche die amerikanische Industrie von der Notwendigkeit vermehrter Investitionen in Maschinen überzeugen will. (USA)
36, 37 Vollständiges Inserat und Illustration für *Pioneer*-Autostereoanlagen. (FRA)

31, 32 Illustration au format original et annonce pleine page d'une société immobilière. (USA)
33 Exemple d'une série d'annonces de journaux. Référence à une émission de TV, «Mais où sont donc passé tous ces enfants?»... trop vite adultes. Linogravure en noir et blanc. (USA)
34 Annonce double page d'une compagnie d'assurances. Jaune et divers oranges. (USA)
35 Annonce double page d'*Ingersoll-Rand* proclamant la nécessité d'investissements accrus dans les équipements industriels mécaniques. (USA)
36, 37 Annonce complète et illustration pour les autoradio stéréo *Pioneer*. (FRA)

33

34

In certain parts of the world, if the powers that be don't like the way you do business, they do more than send you nasty letters.

AFIA
WORLDWIDE INSURANCE

The older we get
the younger we think.

Closed for revitalization?

INGERSOLL-RAND

35

ARTIST / KÜNSTLER / ARTISTE:

31, 32 Dick Mitchell
33 Jerry Jeanmard
34 Eugene Mihaesco
35 Michael Presley
36, 37 Adrian Chisterman

DESIGNER / GESTALTER / MAQUETTISTE:

31, 32 Dick Mitchell
33 Charles Hively
35 John Dolby

ART DIRECTOR / DIRECTEUR ARTISTIQUE:

31, 32 Dick Mitchell/Nancy Hoefig
33 Charles Hively
34 Jerry O'Hara
35 John Dolby

AGENCY / AGENTUR / AGENCE – STUDIO:

31, 32 Richards, Sullivan, Brock & Assoc.
33 Metzdorf Advertising
34 E.R.A.
35 BBDM Advertising

ROULEZ EN PIONEER.

Autostéréo Pioneer. Pour vraiment changer de voiture.

36

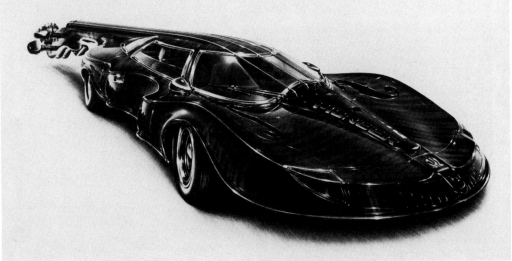

37

Advertisements
Anzeigen
Annonces

Advertisements / Anzeigen
Annonces

38, 39 Full-page magazine advertisements for the Takeo Paper Company. In full colour. (JPN)
40, 41 Examples from an advertising campaign for *Siegwerk* printing inks. (GER)
42 Full-page advertisement for a manufacturer of paints and varnishes. The paint running out from the tin depicts Switzerland while simultaneously marking the locations of this company's branches. (SWI)
43 Full-page advertisement of the *Container Corporation of America*, a leading manufacturer of packaging materials. Yellow lettering on white. (USA)

38, 39 Zwei ganzseitige Zeitschrifteninserate für eine Papierfabrik. Mehrfarbig. (JPN)
40, 41 Beispiele aus einer Inseratenkampagne des Druckfarbenherstellers *Siegwerk*. (GER)
42 Ganzseitige Anzeige eines Herstellers von Farben und Lacken. Die vom Kanister auslaufende Farbe stellt die Schweiz dar und weist gleichzeitig auf die Niederlassungen des Herstellers hin. (SWI)
43 Ganzseitiges Inserat der *Container Corporation of America*, eines führenden Herstellers von Kartonage-Verpackungsmaterialien. Gelbe Schrift auf Weiss. (USA)

38, 39 Annonces de magazines pleine page pour un papetier. Polychrome. (JPN)
40, 41 Deux exemples d'une campagne d'annonces du fabricant d'encres d'imprimerie *Siegwerk*. (GER)
42 Annonce pleine page d'un fabricant de couleurs et vernis. La couleur qui s'écoule du bidon compose la carte des succursales en Suisse. (SWI)
43 Annonce pleine page de la *Container Corporation of America*, l'un des leaders dans le domaine des emballages en carton. Texte jaune sur fond blanc. (USA)

Regenbogen macht Freude

SIEGWERK
DRUCKFARBEN

DER POLYGRAPH 5-82   269

40

Die «Siegfried Keller-Schweiz» in Öl gemalt von Giuseppe Reichmuth

In der Farbe sind wir mitten drin

Und zwar, wie immer man dies auslegt. Mit einer der breitesten Produktepaletten überhaupt. Mit einer technischen Fachberatung, die in heiklen Fällen Rat weiss, mit internationaler Erfahrung, die Ihnen zugute kommt. Und mit einem sprichwörtlich raschen Lieferservice, der selbst Profis immer wieder überrascht.

Von diesem Inseraten-Sujet gibt es auch einen attraktiven Kalender-Poster. Verlangen Sie ihn mit diesem Coupon.

Firmenstempel: 3.1

Siegfried Keller AG
Farben und Lacke · Bautenschutz
Kunststoffputze
8304 Wallisellen · Telefon 01 · 830 32 32

42

Regenbogen macht Freude

SIEGWERK
DRUCKFARBEN

41

43

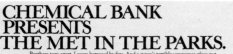

CHEMICAL BANK PRESENTS THE MET IN THE PARKS.

Brothers torn apart. Lovers betrayed by fate. And a gypsy's terrible vengeance plays out. All, set to Verdi's gorgeous music. And all yours, free for the hearing. When Chemical Bank helps bring the Metropolitan Opera to the Great Lawn of Central Park at 81st Street, in Il Trovatore. Tuesday, June 15, at 8:30 p.m.

The cast includes Grace Bumbry, Bianca Berini, Juan Lloveras, Louis Quilico and Dimitri Kavrakos. Conducted by Anton Guadagno, with the Met Orchestra and Chorus.

Chemical supports The Met in The Parks Series of free concert performances of Il Trovatore, and Beethoven's Fidelio. They will play in Brooklyn, the Bronx, Queens, Staten Island and Nassau County in addition to Manhattan. You can get a schedule at any Chemical Branch. Or call 362-6000 for information.

Bringing you great opera brings us great pleasure. It's part of Chemical's tradition of involvement in the life of the community.

The Met in The Parks series of performances is made possible by major grants from Chemical Bank, New York City Department of Cultural Affairs in Cooperation with the Department of Parks and Recreation, The Louis Calder Foundation and The Robert Wood Johnson, Jr. Charitable Trust's Met Parks Concert Fund. Funding has also been received from The National Endowment for the Arts, The Nassau County Office of Cultural Development Affairs, The Barker Welfare Foundation, The Nena B. and Frances Spinghill Foundation and The Edna McConnell Clark Foundation.

Member FDIC

ChemicalBank

44

SONY

にまかせられない音楽に出逢った。

METALLIC·DUAD

45

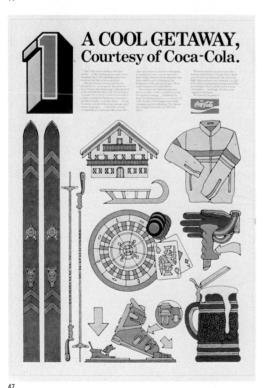

A COOL GETAWAY, Courtesy of Coca-Cola.

47

48

Advertisements / Anzeigen / Annonces

44 Magazine advertisement from an image campaign of the *Chemical Bank*, which financially supports performances by the Metropolitan Opera in New York's Central Park. (USA)
45 Double-spread magazine advertisement in bright colours for *Sony* tapes. (JPN)
46 Full-page advertisement for a new typeface, "Caxton", designed by Les Usherwood for Typographic Systems International Ltd., a division of *Letraset*. In black and white. (GBR)
47 Full-colour *Coca-Cola* advertisements. The best salesmen are rewarded with a ski outfit and a ski holiday in Kitzbühel. (SAF)
48 Large-format magazine ad for *Roth-Händle* cigarettes. (USA)
49 Magazine advertisement for *Chivas Regal* whisky. (USA)
50, 51 Complete advertisement and illustration that appeared in *Vogue* magazine for *Miss Dior* perfume. (FRA)

44 Zeitschrifteninserat aus einer Image-Kampagne der *Chemical Bank*, welche Gratisvorführungen der Metropolitan Opera im Central Park, New York, finanziell unterstützt. (USA)
45 Doppelseitiges Zeitschrifteninserat in leuchtenden Farben für *Sony*-Tonbandkassetten. (JPN)
46 Ganzseitiges Inserat für die neue Schrift «Caxton», entworfen von einem internationalen Schriftgestaltungs-Team, ein Zweig der *Letraset*. Schwarzweiss. (GBR)
47 Anzeige von *Coca Cola*: Die besten Verkäufer erhalten als Belohnung eine Skiausrüstung und Skiferien in Kitzbühel. (SAF)
48 Grossformatiges Zeitschrifteninserat für *Roth-Händle*. (USA)
49 Zeitschriftenanzeige für *Chivas-Regal*-Whisky. (USA)
50, 51 Vollständiges Inserat und Illustration für das Parfum *Miss Dior*, erschienen in der Modezeitschrift *Vogue*. (FRA)

44 Annonce de magazine d'une campagne de prestige de la *Chemical Bank* qui finance partiellement des représentations gratuites du Metropolitan Opera au Central Park de New York. (USA)
45 Annonce de magazine double page aux couleurs éclatantes en faveur des cassettes de magnétophone *Sony*. (JPN)
46 Annonce pleine page pour les nouveaux caractères «Caxton» conçus par une équipe internationale de créateurs d'alphabets au service de *Letraset*. Noir et blanc. (GBR)
47 Annonce polychrome de *Coca Cola*: ses meilleurs vendeurs sont récompensés d'équipements et de vacances de ski. (SAF)
48 Annonce de magazine pour les cigarettes *Roth-Händle*. (USA)
49 Annonce de magazine. Whisky *Chivas Regal* de 12 ans. (USA)
50, 51 Annonce complète et illustration pour le parfum *Miss Dior*. Publicité parue dans le magazine de mode *Vogue*. (FRA)

46

49

50

51

41

ARTIST / KÜNSTLER:

52 Seymour Chwast
53, 54 Nobuyoshi Matsui
55 Jean Soutif
56 Harry Willock

DESIGNER / GESTALTER:

52 John Garr
53, 54 Kenji Takumi
55 Jean Soutif
56 M. D. Wolfe

ART DIRECTOR:

52 John Garr
53, 54 Iwao Matsuura
55 Jean Pétré
56 M. D. Wolfe

AGENCY / AGENTUR:

52 Pushpin Lubalin Peckolick
53, 54 Iwao Matsuura
55 Atelier Pétré
56 Merck Sharp & Dohme

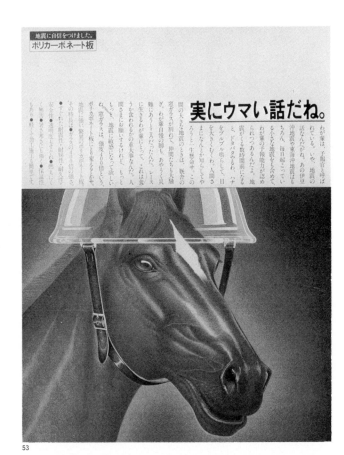

53

54

55

56

52 Illustration from an advertisement that appeared in *Forbes* magazine. (USA)
53, 54 From a series of full-page magazine advertisements for a manufacturer of special glass. The glass helmets demonstrate the strength of this glass. Both are in shades of orange and warm red. Red and black lettering on white. (JPN)
55 Full-colour ad for *Eburex*, an agent for wood protection and care. (FRA)
56 Trade-magazine advertising supplement for *Clinoril*, a new antiinflammatory drug. Golden tablet in a light brown nut, yellow lettering. (SWE)

52 Illustration einer Anzeige für das Wirtschaftsmagazin *Forbes*. (USA)
53, 54 Aus einer Serie von ganzseitigen Zeitschriftenanzeigen für einen Hersteller von Spezialglas. Die Glashelme demonstrieren die Glasstärke. Beide in Orange- und warmen Rottönen. Schrift rot und schwarz auf Weiss. (JPN)

55 Mehrfarbige Anzeige für das Holzschutz- und Pflegemittel *Eburex*, das in acht verschiedenen Farbnuancen erhältlich ist. Rote Titelschrift. (FRA)
56 Fachzeitschriften-Werbebeilage für das entzündungshemmende Arzneimittel *Clinoril*. Goldene Tablette in hellbrauner Nuss, gelbe Schrift. (SWE)

52 Illustration d'une annonce pour le magazine des affaires *Forbes*. (USA)
53, 54 Exemples d'une série d'annonces de magazines pleine page pour un fabricant de verres spéciaux. Les casques de verre symbolisent la résistance du matériau. Divers oranges et rouges chauds. Texte rouge, noir sur blanc. (JPN)
55 Annonce couleurs pour *Eburex*, pour la protection et décoration du bois. (FRA)
56 Encart publicitaire pour l'anti-inflammatoire *Clinoril*, dans des revues spécialisées. Comprimé or dans noix brun clair, texte jaune. (SWE)

43

ARTIST / KÜNSTLER / ARTISTE:

57, 58 Tomi Ungerer
59 Alex Murawski
60 Christian Lang
61, 62 Seymour Chwast
63 Heinz Edelmann

DESIGNER / GESTALTER / MAQUETTISTE:

59 David Bartels
60 Christian Lang
61, 62 Charles Hively

ART DIRECTOR / DIRECTEUR ARTISTIQUE:

57, 58, 63 Robert Pütz
59 David Bartels
60 Christian Lang
61, 62 Charles Hively

AGENCY / AGENTUR / AGENCE – STUDIO:

57, 58, 63 Robert Pütz GmbH & Co.
59 Bartels & Co.
60 Werbung Ciba-Geigy
61, 62 Metzdorf Advertising

57

58

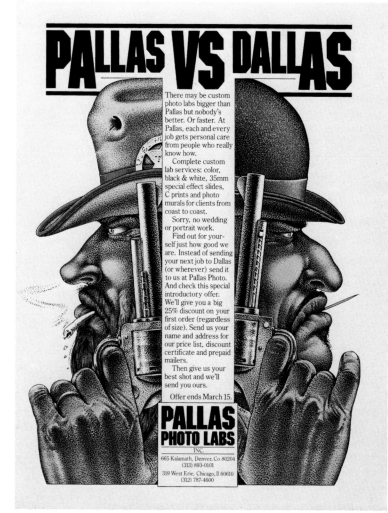

59

60

64, 65 Advertisements for durable synthetic soles. Yellow and blue on white. (ITA)
66 "To understand *Volvic*, look at Auvergne." Double-spread advertisement for *Volvic* mineral waters. The artwork is in oil on canvas. (FRA)
67 Double-spread magazine advertisement announcing the new AZ Encyclopedia supplied in weekly instalments. In full colour. (FRA)
68–70 Examples from an advertising campaign for a manufacturer of a salt substitute, here demonstrated by various kinds of birds. (USA)

64, 65 Inserate für synthetische, widerstandsfähige Schuhsohlen. Gelb und Blau auf Weiss. (ITA)
66 «Um *Volvic* zu verstehen, braucht man nur die Auvergne zu betrachten.» Doppelseitiges Inserat für *Volvic*-Mineralwasser. Die Illustration ist ein Ölgemälde. (FRA)
67 Doppelseitiges Inserat, das im Rahmen der Einführungskampagne für die neue AZ-Enzyklopädie in Zeitschriften erschienen ist. Die Illustration ist ein Ölgemälde. (FRA)
68–70 Beispiele aus einer Werbekampagne für einen Hersteller von einem Salzersatzstoff, dessen Gebrauch von Vögeln demonstriert wird. (USA)

64, 65 Annonces en faveur de syntho-semelles résistantes. Jaune et bleu sur blanc. (ITA)
66 «Pour comprendre *Volvic*, regardez l'Auvergne.» Annonce double page vantant les mérites de l'eau minérale *Volvic*. L'illustration est une peinture à l'huile. (FRA)
67 Annonce de magazine double page pour le lancement de l'Encyclopédie AZ en fascicules hebdomadaires. Ici encore, l'illustration est une peinture à l'huile. (FRA)
68–70 Exemples d'annonces figurant dans une campagne en faveur d'un fabricant de sel de substitution, dont l'usage est démontré par des oiseaux. (USA)

Advertisements
Anzeigen
Annonces

71

Advertisements
Anzeigen
Annonces

71 Double-spread trade magazine advertisement of the *Südzucker* trading company. (GER)
72 Double-spread trade magazine advertisement for *Zerex*, an anti-freeze and summer coolant which gives a three-way protection against freeze-up, boil-over and rust. (USA)
73 Advertisement for *Read*, manufacturer of agricultural buildings and installations. (USA)
74 From a series of full-colour advertisements for a producer of chocolates and sweets. The various illustrations merge into a continuous picture. (NLD)
75, 76 Illustration and complete advertisement for a chocolate spread. (ITA)

71 Doppelseitige Zeitschriftenanzeige der *Südzucker*-Vertriebsgesellschaft. (GER)
72 Doppelseitiges Fachzeitschrifteninserat für einen Auto-Kühlwasserzusatz gegen Rost, Überhitzung und Einfrieren. (USA)
73 Anzeige für *Read*, Hersteller von landwirtschaftlichen Bauten und Installationen. (USA)
74 Aus einer Serie von mehrfarbigen Inseraten für einen Schokoladen- und Süsswarenhersteller. Die verschiedenen Illustrationen ergeben ein fortlaufendes Bild. (NLD)
75, 76 Illustration und ganzseitige Anzeige für einen Schokoladenbrotaufstrich. (ITA)

71 Annonce de magazine double page de la société de commercialisation du sucre *Südzucker*. (GER)
72 Annonce de revue professionnelle, sur double page, pour un additif antirouille, anti-échauffement et antigel dans l'eau de refroidissement des voitures. (USA)
73 Annonce pour *Read*, constructeur de bâtiments et installations agricoles. (USA)
74 D'une série d'annonces polychromes pour un fabricant de chocolat et de confiserie. Les illustrations successives composent un tableau d'ensemble. (NLD)
75, 76 Illustration et annonce pleine page pour une pâte au chocolat à tartiner. (ITA)

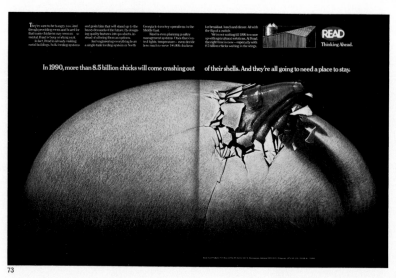

72   73

74

76

75

ECO-Genußscheine der Ersten
Das absetzbare Ja zu A

Der Wiener Arzt Helmut R. glaubte sich unlängst in ein hochkarätiges Steuerparadies versetzt. Was sein Steuerberater über das neue Beteiligungsfondsgesetz und über ECO-Genußscheine zu erzählen wußte war geeignet, den sonst sauren Weg zum Finanzamt erheblich zu versüßen...

77

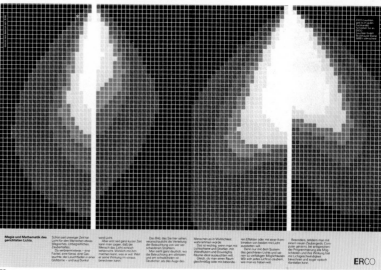

ERCO

78

Advertisements / Anzeigen / Annonces

La straordinaria avventura di una ragazza, un marinaio e un caprone.

80

ARTIST / KÜNSTLER / ARTISTE:

77 Peter Krämer
78 Thomas Rempen
79 Pat Nagel
80 Norberto Civardi
81 Harumi
82–84 Steve Reoutt

DESIGNER / GESTALTER / MAQUETTISTE:

78 Thomas Rempen
79 Woody Pirtle
80 Inocencio Pérez
81 Mariuccia Mandelli
82–84 Richard Cognata

ART DIRECTOR / DIRECTEUR ARTISTIQUE:

77 Hannes Rausch
78 Thomas Rempen
79 Woody Pirtle
80 Inocencio Pérez
82–84 Richard Cognata

AGENCY / AGENTUR / AGENCE – STUDIO:

77 Schretter & Rausch
78 Hildmann, Simon, Rempen & Schmitz
79 Pirtle Design
80 SSC&B Lintas
81 Krizia Industria Confezioni
82–84 Cognata Associates

80a

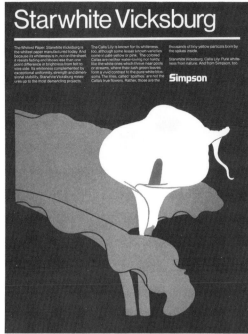

GALLERIA

82

77 Double-spread advertisement for *Eco* participating certificates guaranteeing tax relief. (AUT)
78 Double-spread magazine advertisement from a campaign for *Erco* lamps. (GER)
79 Trade magazine advertisement from the opening campaign for the *Galleria* shopping centre. (USA)
80, 80a Full-page advertisement and illustration in actual size for *Heineken-Bok* beer. (ITA)
81 Illustration from a full-page ad for *Krizia* fashions, showing the sales locations. (FRA)
82–84 Examples of quality paper, used as advertisements for a paper-manufacturer. (USA)

77 Doppelseitiges Inserat für *Eco*-Genussscheine, die dem Erwerber Steuervorteile bringen. (AUT)
78 Doppelseitige Zeitschriftenanzeige aus einer Kampagne für *Erco*-Leuchten. (GER)
79 Fachzeitschriftenanzeige einer Eröffnungskampagne für das neue Einkaufszentrum *Galleria*. (USA)
80, 80a Ganzseitiges Inserat und Illustration in Originalgrösse für *Heineken-Bok*-Bier. (ITA)
81 Illustration eines ganzseitigen Inserates für *Krizia*-Mode, mit Angabe der Verkaufsstellen. (FRA)
82–84 Muster von Qualitätspapieren einer Papierfabrik, welche als Anzeigen verwendet wurden. (USA)

77 Annonce double page pour les bons de jouissance *Eco* aux avantages fiscaux prononcés. (AUT)
78 Annonce de magazine double page. Campagne pour les éclairages *Erco*. (GER)
79 Annonce de revue professionnelle: campagne de lancement du centre commercial *Galleria*. (USA)
80, 80a Annonce pleine page et illustration grandeur originale pour la bière *Heineken-Bok*. (ITA)
81 Illustration d'une annonce pleine page pour les modes *Krizia*; liste des points de vente. (FRA)
82–84 Echantillons de papiers de qualité d'un papetier, utilisés comme annonces. (USA)

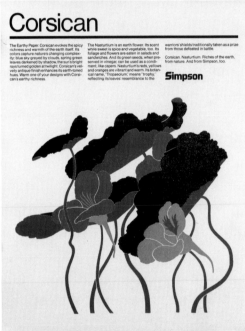

83

81

84

WE WANT A DIRECTOR.

Big fish with top directing skills wanted by outstanding Dallas-based production company. You must be an established director with an impressive reel. You must also be willing to move to Dallas. In return, we will offer you a terrific deal: plenty of work on national accounts. If you can be hooked by opportunity, call Jim Beresford of The James Gang at 214 350-7846.

85

Advertisements / Anzeigen / Annonces

85 Small-format advertisement in black and white. (USA)
86 Large-format cooperative advertisement by ten major New York museums. (USA)
87, 89 Black-and-white advertisements from a campaign in *The Plain Dealer*. (USA)
88 "Many tricks can be used to conceal the truth." Advertisement for Zurich's *Neue Zürcher Zeitung* to attract new subscribers. Black and white. (SWI)
90 Advertisement for *The New York Times*, aimed at job hunters and drawing their attention to vacancies advertised by Labour Exchange offices. (USA)

85 Kleininserat in Schwarzweiss: Gesucht wird ein «grosser Fisch», nämlich ein Direktor! (USA)
86 Grossformatige Gemeinschaftsanzeige für zehn wichtige New Yorker Museen. (USA)
87, 89 Schwarzweisse Anzeigen aus einer Werbekampagne der Zeitung *The Plain Dealer*. Hier wird besonders auf die politische Berichterstattung hingewiesen. (USA)
88 Abonnenten-Werbung für die *Neue Zürcher Zeitung*. Inserat in Schwarzweiss. (SWI)
90 Inserat der *New York Times*, das sich speziell an die Stellensuchenden richtet und hier auf die Vielzahl der Anzeigen von Stellenvermittlungsbüros hinweist. (USA)

85 Petite annonce noir et blanc: on y cherche un «gros poisson», à savoir un directeur... (USA)
86 Annonce collective au grand format pour la promotion de dix grands musées newyorkais. (USA)
87, 89 Annonces noir et blanc d'une campagne du journal *The Plain Dealer*. L'accent est mis ici sur la qualité des reportages politiques. (USA)
88 Recrutement d'abonnés pour la *Neue Zürcher Zeitung*. Annonce en noir et blanc. (SWI)
90 Annonce du *New York Times* destinée au premier chef aux chercheurs d'emplois et soulignant la masse des annonces émanant d'agences de l'emploi publiée dans ce journal. (USA)

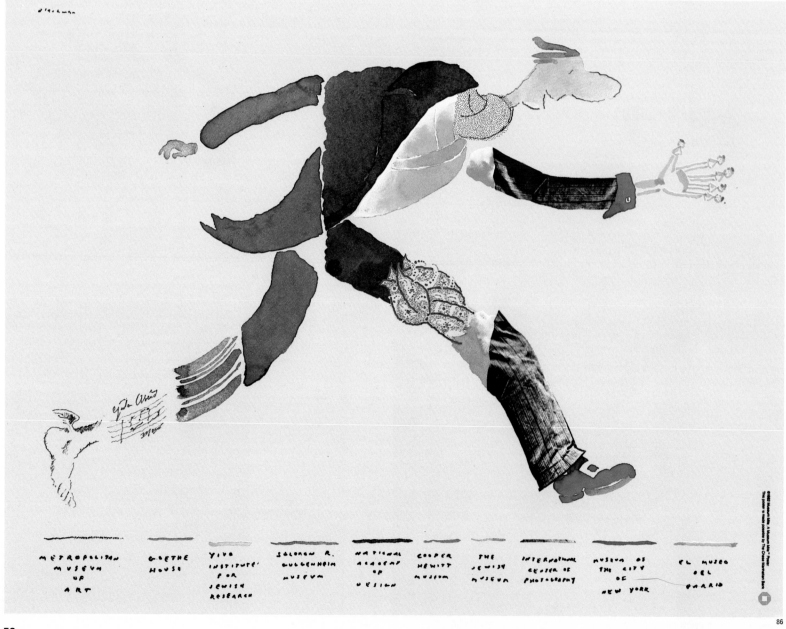

86

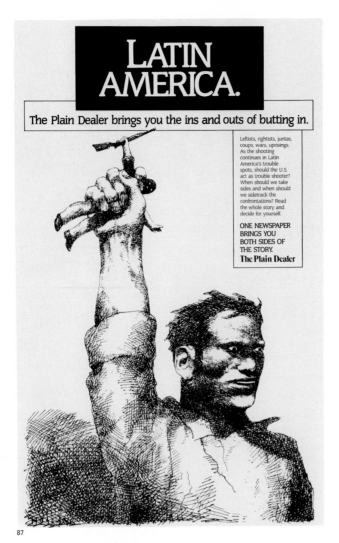

LATIN AMERICA.

The Plain Dealer brings you the ins and outs of butting in.

Leftists, rightists, juntas, coups, wars, uprisings. As the shooting continues in Latin America's trouble spots, should the U.S. act as trouble shooter? When should we take sides and when should we sidetrack the confrontations? Read the whole story and decide for yourself.

ONE NEWSPAPER BRINGS YOU BOTH SIDES OF THE STORY.

The Plain Dealer

87

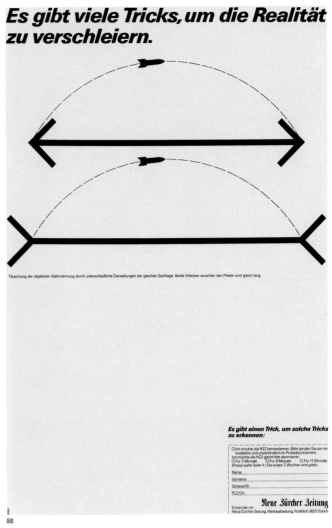

Es gibt viele Tricks, um die Realität zu verschleiern.

Täuschung der objektiven Wahrnehmung durch unterschiedliche Darstellungen der gleichen Sachlage. Beide Strecken zwischen den Pfeilen sind gleich lang.

Es gibt einen Trick, um solche Tricks zu erkennen:

☐ Ich möchte die NZZ kennenlernen. Bitte senden Sie sie mir kostenlos und unverbindlich im Probeabonnement.
Ich möchte die NZZ gleich fest abonnieren.
☐ Für 3 Monate.   ☐ Für 6 Monate.   ☐ Für 12 Monate.
(Preise siehe Seite 4.) Die ersten 2 Wochen sind gratis.

Name

Vorname

Strasse/Nr.

PLZ/Ort

Einsenden an:
Neue Zürcher Zeitung, Werbeabteilung, Postfach, 8021 Zürich

Neue Zürcher Zeitung

88

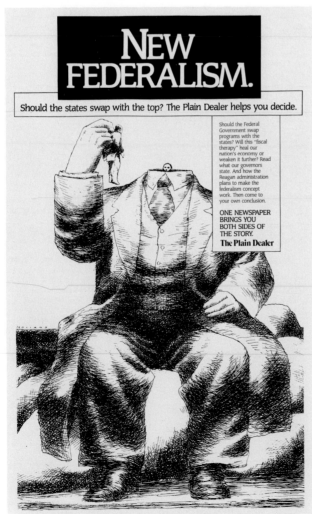

NEW FEDERALISM.

Should the states swap with the top? The Plain Dealer helps you decide.

Should the Federal Government swap programs with the states? Will this "fiscal therapy" heal our nation's economy or weaken it further? Read what our governors state. And how the Reagan administration plans to make the federalism concept work. Then come to your own conclusion.

ONE NEWSPAPER BRINGS YOU BOTH SIDES OF THE STORY.

The Plain Dealer

89

ARTIST / KÜNSTLER:

85 Gary Templin
86 R. O. Blechman
87, 89 Brad Holland
90 David FeBland

DESIGNER / GESTALTER:

85 Gary Templin
88 Willi Bühler
90 Arnold Kushner

ART DIRECTOR:

85 Gary Templin/
    Mark Perkins
86 R. O. Blechman/
    Terry Berkowitz
87, 89 Rick Seich
88 Willi Bühler
90 Andrew Kner

AGENCY / AGENTUR / AGENCE:

85 Richards, Sullivan,
    Brock & Associates
86 R. O. Blechman Inc.
87, 89 Nelson Stern Adv
88 Adolf Wirz AG

Hundreds of professional counselors want to help you find a new job.

Job counselors at Employment Agencies have thousands of job openings right at their finger tips, right now. One... or more... could be exactly right for you.

If they don't find you the job you want, you owe them nothing. If they do find you a terrific job, in most cases your new employer will pay the fee.

Either way, what do you have to lose? Nothing. And you have a whole career to gain.

How do you get in touch with these helpful people? It's so easy.

Pick up a copy of The New York Times any day of the week. Turn to the Help Wanted Classified pages and you'll find Employment Agency ads on every page. On Sundays,

The Times has a whole separate section filled with job ads and Employment Agency listings.

And if you don't want to work full time...or forever...you can still get professional help. Just look for the Temporary Services ads.

Whether you're actively looking, or thinking of looking, the right new job may be ready for you today. Why not let a professional help you find it? Why not choose your professional from the many who advertise regularly in The New York Times?

These times demand The Times.

The New York Times

90

91

92

93

94

91–94 Examples from an advertising campaign for *Mediator* television sets, in particular for the colour style in which these sets are available or can be supplied to order so as to meet the special requirements of customers. (GER)
95 Full-page advertisement in black and white for a festival of the arts in Miami, Florida. Tennessee Williams figures prominently in this ad, for quality productions of his plays and those of his dramatic heirs (known as Off-Broadway productions) are of the standard to which such a festival aspires. An extensive programme of other art forms is also offered. (USA)
96 Full-page advertisement for the *New York Times*, that also appeared as a poster, aimed at potential advertisers making use of an edition with a special overview on education and training possibilities. In grey shades, yellow margin. (USA)
97 *The Washington Post*, one of America's most influential newspapers, issues a full-page black-and-white advertisement. (USA)

91–94 Beispiele aus einer Anzeigen-Kampagne für *Mediator*-Fernsehgeräte. Hier wird besonders auf die verschiedenen vorhandenen Farbausführungen hingewiesen, sowie auf die Möglichkeit, die Geräte in einer Wunschfarbe zu bestellen. (GER)
95 Ganzseitiges Inserat in Schwarzweiss für Festspielwochen in Miami. Thema der Illustration ist die Aufführung eines Stückes von Tennessee Williams und die Vorliebe des Autors für die Mentalität des Südens. «Off-Broadway» ist zu einem Begriff für Aufführungen nicht nur in räumlicher, sondern auch in qualitativer Distanz zum Broadway geworden. (USA)
96 Ganzseitiges, auch als Plakat erschienenes Inserat der *New York Times*, die hier um Inserenten in einer Ausgabe mit einem speziellen Überblick der Ausbildungsmöglichkeiten wirbt. (USA)
97 «Wie man 99% des 97. Kongresses erreicht.» Mit diesem Hinweis auf ihre Leserschaft im Kongress wirbt die *Washington Post* um Inserenten. Ganzseitige Anzeige in Schwarzweiss. (USA)

91–94 Exemples d'annonces publiées dans le cadre d'une campagne en faveur des téléviseurs *Mediator*. On attire ici l'attention sur les coloris des appareils: jaune banane, ambre, «rose éléphant», vert crapaud. (GER)
95 Annonce pleine page, noir et blanc, pour le Festival de Miami. Le thème de l'illustration: la représentation d'une pièce de Tennessee Williams et l'engouement de l'auteur pour la mentalité du sud américain. «Off Broadway» désigne la distance spatiale et qualitative d'une pièce par rapport à celles qui tiennent le haut du pavé à Broadway. (USA)
96 Annonce pleine page, également publiée sous forme d'affiche, où le *New York Times* invite les annonceurs à participer à un numéro contenant un supplément éducatif important. (USA)
97 «Comment toucher le 99% du 97e Congrès.» Annonce pleine page, noir et blanc, du *Washington Post* destinée aux annonceurs potentiels de ce journal lu par tous les députés. (USA)

54

ARTIST / KÜNSTLER / ARTISTE:

91–93 Dominik Burckhardt
94 Sabine Schroer
95 David Levine
96 J. Rafal Olbinski
97 Georg Rauch

DESIGNER / GESTALTER / MAQUETTISTE:

91–94 Dominik Burckhardt
95 David Thall
96 Ellen Kier

ART DIRECTOR / DIRECTEUR ARTISTIQUE:

91–94 Dominik Burckhardt
95 David Thall
96 Ellen Kier
97 Nancy Pentecost-Hanover

AGENCY / AGENTUR / AGENCE – STUDIO:

91–94 Burckhardt, Lüdi
95 BS & Partners
97 Earle Palmer Brown

1983. Your year to attract the strong candidates. Achievers with high expectations. Students with personal ability and initiative who can contribute to academic life both in and out of the classroom. 1983. Your year to use The New York Times. Start your enrollment-building campaign in the Spring Survey of Education. For advertising information call your advertising agency or call Katherine Rees-Jones, Group Manager, Education Advertising Department (212) 556-7221.

96

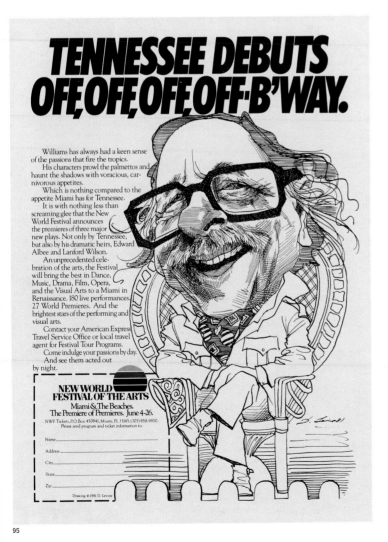

95

97

99

100

98

103

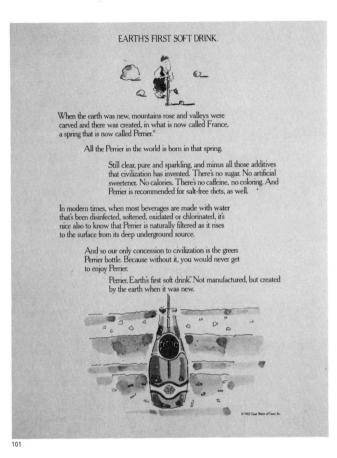

101

102

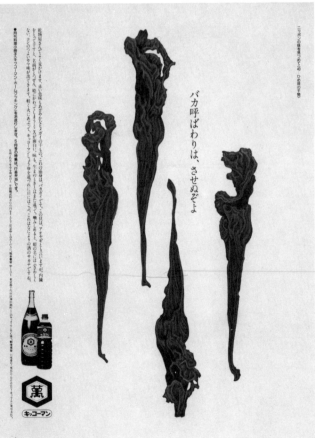

104

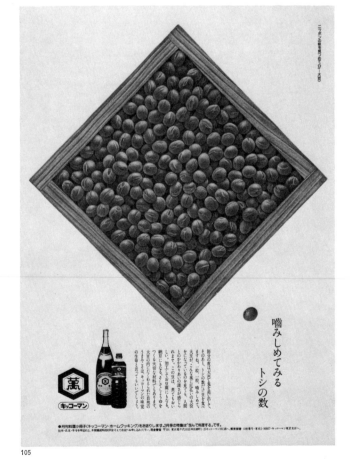

105

98 Inserat für ein Mittel gegen Pilzerkrankungen an Gemüse, hergestellt von dem Chemie-Unternehmen *Kocide*. (USA)
99, 100 Beispiele aus einer Werbekampagne für geräucherte, servierfertige Truthähne von *Sunday House*. Abb. 99 mit einem speziellen Wertgutschein, Mittelbraun auf mattem Blau; Abb. 100: Rotbraun auf Chamois. (USA)
101, 102 «Das erste Tafelgetränk der Erde»; «Eine Million A.C. – ein sehr gutes Jahr.» Beispiele aus einer Inseratenkampagne für *Perrier*-Tafelwasser, deren Thema die unveränderte Reinheit dieses Mineralwassers seit Urzeiten ist – das einzige Zugeständnis an die Zivilisation sei die grüne Flasche. (USA)
103–105 Ganzseitige Anzeigen des Gewürz- und Saucenherstellers *Kikkoman*. Abb. 103 gehört zu einer Serie unter dem Titel «Die Sprichwörter Japans»; das gemeinsame Thema von Abb. 104 und 105 lautet: «Die Geschmäcke Japans». (JPN)

98 Annonce pour un fongicide actif dans la protection des légumes, fabriqué par le groupe pharmaceutique *Kocide*. (USA)
99, 100 Exemples d'annonces figurant dans une campagne en faveur des dindons fumés prêts à la dégustation commercialisés par *Sunday House*. Fig. 99 avec un bon en espèces, brun moyen sur bleu mat; fig. 100 roux sur chamois. (USA)
101, 102 «La première boisson de table sur Terre»; «Un million d'années av. J.-C. – un très bon millésime.» Exemple d'une série d'annonces pour l'eau *Perrier*, axée sur le thème de la pureté inchangée de cette eau minérale depuis les origines, la seule concession à la civilisation étant la bouteille. (USA)
103–105 Annonces pleine page du grossiste en épices et fabricant de sauces *Kikkoman*. La fig. 103 fait partie d'une série de «Proverbes japonais»; les fig. 104 et 105 ont pour sujet commun «Les goûts du Japon». (JPN)

we ❤ the theater

And we love the world's great fragrances. But most of all we love to see you out on the town enjoying them. To celebrate the way we feel, some very special arrangements have been made. We're offering thousands of Bonus Certificates entitling you to purchase two tickets for the price of one at dozens of theaters, concert halls and cabarets in Los Angeles, San Francisco, Portland, Seattle, Chicago and Washington, D.C. You'll receive a Certificate with any 15.00 or more fragrance purchase from us through Sunday, May 9. Others participating in We ❤ The Theater: Century City Playhouse, L.A. Public Theater, Los Angeles Stage Company and more! Tickets for all performances are subject to availability.

You may decide to use your We ❤ The Theater Certificate at the Los Angeles Actors Theater when you purchase Ombre Rose Perfume.

Parfum in hand-blown black lead crystal vial 1 oz. 150.00, Eau de Toilette in clear crystal 6 oz. 55.00. Keep the Certificate or have us include it when we gift-wrap your Ombre Rose selection for Mother's Day. Cosmetics. Minimum delivery charge 2.00. Your American Express Card may be used at I. Magnin.

I. magnin

Open Monday until 6:00 in Los Angeles (387-4111), Beverly Hills (271-2134), Del Amo (370-8561), Santa Ana (547-5911), Palm Springs (325-1531); until 5:30 in Pasadena (793-7101), Santa Barbara (962-0061), La Jolla (459-4081); until 9:00 in Sherman Oaks (788-9600); until 9:30 in South Coast Plaza (957-1511)

106

ARTIST / KÜNSTLER / ARTISTE:

106, 107 Lance G. Klemm
108–110 Antonio Lopez
111 Jill Karla Schwarz

DESIGNER / GESTALTER / MAQUETTISTE:

106, 107 Joe Allen Hong
108, 110 John C. Jay
109 Charles Banuchi

ART DIRECTOR / DIRECTEUR ARTISTIQUE:

106, 107 Zoe Architect
108–110 John C. Jay
111 Keith Gold

AGENCY / AGENTUR / AGENCE – STUDIO:

106, 107 I. Magnin Advertising Dept.
108–110 Bloomingdale's
111 Price/McNabb

Advertisements
Anzeigen
Annonces

106, 107 Newspaper advertisements for the *I. Magnin* department store on the occasion of Mother's Day. Fig. 106: When purchasing a certain perfume, the buyer is entitled to bonus certificates for special theatre ticket offers. Fig. 107: Advertising for *Oscar de la Renta* body cream, also available in gift wrapping. Both in black and white. (USA)
108–110 Newspaper advertisements for *Bloomingdale's*, one of New York's most famous department stores. Figs. 108, 110: Advertising for sports outfits and for the coat collection created by *Calvin Klein*. Fig. 109: Women's fashions in Russian style. (USA)
111 Small-format advertisement in black and white for luxury homes. (USA)

106, 107 Zeitungsanzeigen des Kaufhauses *I. Magnin* zum Muttertag. Abb. 106: Hier werden beim Kauf eines Parfums zwei Theaterbillette zum Preis von einem angeboten, die für mehrere Theater gültig sind. Abb. 107: Werbung für eine Körpercrème von *Oscar de la Renta*, die auch in einer besonderen Geschenkverpackung erhältlich ist. In Schwarzweiss. (USA)
108–110 Zeitungsinserate des Kaufhauses *Bloomingdale's*. Abb. 108, 110: Werbung für Sportbekleidung und die Mantelkollektion von *Calvin Klein*, beide unter dem Motto «Wir glauben an Schwarz». Abb. 109: Damenmode im russischen Stil. (USA)
111 Kleinanzeige in Schwarzweiss für schön gelegene, luxuriöse Eigentumswohnungen. (USA)

106, 107 Annonces de journaux des grands magasins *I. Magnin* à l'occasion de la Fête des Mères. Fig. 106: à l'achat d'un parfum, un billet de théâtre sur deux est gratuit; billets valables pour plusieurs théâtres. Fig. 107: pour une crème d'*Oscar de la Renta* pour les soins du corps, livrée aussi en emballage-cadeau. En noir et blanc. (USA)
108–110 Annonces de journaux des grands magasins *Bloomingdale's*. Fig. 108, 110: pour des vêtements sport et les manteaux *Calvin Klein*, tous deux sous la devise «Nous croyons au noir». Fig. 109: mode féminine de style russe. (USA)
111 Petite annonce noir-blanc pour des appartements luxueux en copropriété. (USA)

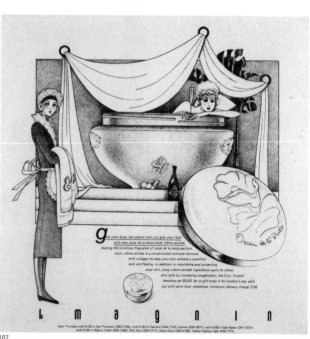

I. magnin

107

ARTIST / KÜNSTLER / ARTISTE:

112 Greg MacNair
113 Christine Middleton
114 Calvin Woo
115 Brian Boyd
116, 117 Brad Holland
118 R. O. Blechman

DESIGNER / GESTALTER / MAQUETTISTE:

112 David Bartels
113 Michael McLaughlin
114 Calvin Woo
115 Brian Boyd/Ron Sullivan
116, 117 Blaine Gutermuth

Bartels Company
Marketing Communications, Planning, Design

AM BI
TI ON

The Objective Is Not To Tame The Concept, But To Capture It.

3284 Ivanhoe, Saint Louis, Missouri 63139 314 781 4350

112

113

We have...
Bamboo Shoots
Waterchestnuts
Kumquats
Seedless Loquats
Pala Manus
Atjar Tjampoer
Mango Chutney
Laos Roots
Straw Mushroom
Sweet White Cucumber
Sweet Red Ginger
Carambola
Coconut Juice
Mixed Ginger
Lotus Roots
Mangoes
Pineapple Chunks
Rambutan
Sugar Cane Juice
Boiled Abalone
Boiled Baby Clams
Stewed Cuttle Fish
Roasted Eel
Fried Fish Paste
Fried Dace
Shark Fin Soup
Bean Curd in water
Grass Jelly
Snow Cabbage & Bean
Lo Han Chai
Sweet Sesame Drink
Electric Rice Cooker
Sweet Almond Drink
Vegetarian Mock Abalone
Vegetarian Mock Duck
Black Fungus
Five Flavor Spice Powder
Achara Pickles
Nata De Coco
Seaweed
Bird's Nests
Szechuan Cabbage Tips
Mustard Hearts
Ko Dong Auh
Dried Shrimp
Black Soy Sauce
Thin Soy Sauce
Soy Sauce
Chili in Oil
Rice Flour
Tapioca Starch
Taro Powder
Wheat Starch
Rice Sticks
Wonton Wrapper
Fresh Hawaiian Poi
Fennel Seed
Sha Ginger
Star Anise
Lichee Black Tea
Loong Tsing Tea
Gum Wo Herb Tea
Boiled Mackerel
Renkon Mizuni
Takuwan
Otsumami Tara
Oyster Flavored Sauces
Instant Demae Itcho Ramen
Longevity Noodle
Rice Cake
Bean Thread

Black Mushroom
Lily Flowers
Sea Moss
Sweet Macapuno
Misua
Sambal Oelek
Chan Pci Apricots
Lychee Nuts
Snow Flower Plum
Almond Cake
Fortune Cookies
Ming Kung Cake
Bagoong
Bak Choy
Salted Plums
Salted Duck Eggs
Quail Eggs in Water
Sweet Banana Chips
Candied Coconut Slices
Indonesian Rose Syrup
Achyete
Waterchestnut Flour
Boemboe Goulash
Boemboe Sambal Goreng
Boemboe Tjap Tjay
Bitter Melon
Gingko Nuts
Button Mushrooms
Pickled Garlic
Onion Powder
Coconut Juice Milk
Sesame Seeds
Hunkweemeel
Nest Egg Noodles
Yeast Balls
Soy Bean Sprouts
Sago Seed
Tapioca Pearls
Kamaboko
Mitsumame
Hot Yellow Chili Sauce
Plum Sauce
Red Bell Pepper Paste
Soy Bean Sauce
Szechuan Pickles
Mung Bean Sprouts
Ajitsuke Nori
Tempura No Moto
Cal Rose Rice
Kanemasa Shiro Miso
Ajinomoto
Noritama Furikake
Japan Shinshu Aka Miso
Kikkoman Soy Sauce
Ginseng Tea
Noh Korean BBQ Base
Yaki Soba
Fresh Fish
Chowmein Noodle
Milk Candy
Udon
Salted Salmon
Koya Tofu
Akadama Wine
Hakushika Sake
Smoked Baby Clams
Sesame Candy
Tempura Batter
Arare
Umeboshi Shiozuke
Kimchee
Japanese Sake

Oh-Jing Auh (Dried Fish)
Mee Yuk (Dried Seaweed)
Instant Noodle Soups
Patis
Iso Peanuts
Sushi—su nomoto
Sweet Rice
Panocha
Mirin
Kong Na Mul
Seok Choo Na Mul
Cucumber Kimchee
Pickled Scallions
Ko Chi Jang
Doen Jang
Cha Jang Doen Jang
Bul Do Ki Yang Nyum
Ko chu Ka Ru
Korean Soy Sauce
Instant Curry Sauce
Kan Jang
Ko Chu Jang
Fish Eggs of Alaska
Nak Gee (Small Octopus)
Dried Pomelo Peel in Soy
Szechuan Pickled Mustard
Sukiyaki Pan
Sea Lettuce (Pa Rai)
Dried Kelp (Da Si Ma)
Insam Powder
Barley Tea
Korean Acorn Powder
Thai Ground Coffee
Ground Pepper Mackerel
Crab Oil with Chili
Salted Black Beans
Dried Salted Mussel
Dried Squid
Kang Som Canned Curry
Shrimp Oil
Dried Mint
Tamarind
Japanese Mortar & Pestle
Jujube
Nunya Fish Soup
Salal (Red) Thai Syrup
Dried Sok Fish
Lumpia Wrappers
Pickled Sweet/Sour Mango
Canned Crab Meat
Red & Black Vinegar
Japanese Rice Vinegar
Chinaware
Cookbooks
Woks
... and more.

WOO
CHEE
CHONG
ORIENTAL
FOODS

633 16th Street, San Diego, (714) 233-6311
1415 Third Avenue, Chula Vista, (714) 425-0181

114

The Grand Avenue is grand news for downtown.

The Grand Avenue will soon be open — a very good sign for downtown Milwaukee. Because soon downtown will be grander than ever, with four city blocks of continuous shopping from Gimbels to Boston Store at more than 120 shops, stores, and restaurants in between. All joined together with skywalks that pass over city streets. And full of fountains, trees, and temptations — like Speisegarten, a skylit "dining garden" in the grand Milwaukee tradition of food and drink. • You will find three levels of shopping at The Grand Avenue. Where you can explore the fabulous New Arcade's new shops and stores. And enjoy the fabled Plankinton Arcade, restored to grandeur. Plus you will find special downtown parking in two garages. • On Thursday, August 26, join us at The Grand Avenue at 11 a.m. for a parade. Then stay for the grandest of openings at 12 noon, with singers, dancers, jugglers, and more. And stroll The Grand Avenue, where the grand news for you is grand times in downtown Milwaukee. *The Grand Avenue*

115

116

117

ART DIRECTOR / DIRECTEUR ARTISTIQUE:

112 David Bartels
113 Michael McLaughlin
114 Calvin Woo
115 Brian Boyd
116, 117 Blaine Gutermuth
118 R. O. Blechman

AGENCY / AGENTUR / AGENCE – STUDIO:

112 Bartels & Company
113 Vickers & Benson
114 HumanGraphic
115 Richards, Sullivan, Brock & Assoc.
116, 117 Howard Swink
118 R. O. Blechman Inc.

Catch our Summer line.
JERRY REGENBOGEN
Dresses, Related Separates
Sizes 2 to 14
Deborah Hodge for Regenbogen
Dresses, Sizes 12 to 20
575 Seventh Avenue, New York, N.Y. 10018
(212) 921-7650

118

112 Trade newspaper advertisement for Bartels & Company, a firm operating in marketing communications, planning and design. The illustration of the ant-bear is in black and white. (USA)
113 Newspaper ad for *Cavendish Farms* fruit and vegetables. Full-colour illustration. (CAN)
114 Full-page advertisement with black-and-white illustrations for a brand of oriental foods. (USA)
115 Full-colour advertisement on the occasion of the opening of a new shopping centre. (USA)
116, 117 Illustration and complete advertisement in the *Wall Street Journal* for the *Owens-Illinois* company, emphasizing its cash flow and liquidity strategies for the 80s.(USA)
118 "Catch our Summer Line". Trade newspaper ad for *Jerry Regenbogen's* ready-made clothes. (USA)

112 «Ehrgeiz. – Es geht nicht darum, das Konzept zu zähmen, sondern es zu ergreifen.» Fachzeitungs-Anzeige für ein Werbestudio. Illustration des Ameisenbärs in Schwarzweiss. (USA)
113 Zeitungsinserat für Gemüse und Obst von *Cavendish Farms*. Farbillustration in der Mitte. (CAN)
114 Ganzseitige Anzeige mit Schwarzweiss-Illustrationen für fernöstliche Nahrungsmittel. (USA)
115 Inserat anlässlich der Eröffnung eines Einkaufszentrums in Milwaukee. In Farbe. (USA)
116, 117 Illustration und vollständiges Inserat im *Wall Street Journal* für *Owens-Illinois*, ein Unternehmen, das auf seine Liquidität in den stürmischen 80er Jahren hinweist. (USA)
118 «Fang unsere Sommerkollektion ein.» Fachzeitungsinserat für eine Konfektionsfirma. (USA)

112 «Ambition. – L'objectif ne consiste pas à dompter le concept, mais à le capturer.» Annonce de revue professionnelle pour un studio publicitaire. Illustration du tamanoir en noir et blanc. (USA)
113 Annonce de journal pour les fruits et légumes *Cavendish Farms*. En couleurs. (CAN)
114 Annonce pleine page (illustrations noir-blanc) pour des aliments extrême-orientaux. (USA)
115 Annonce pour l'inauguration d'un centre commercial à Milwaukee. En couleurs. (USA)
116, 117 Illustration et annonce complète, dans le *Wall Street Journal*, pour *Owens-Illinois*, une entreprise disposant du cash flow nécessaire pour aborder les orages des années 80.(USA)
118 «Attrapez nos collections d'été.» Annonce de revue pour un confectionneur. (USA)

119

120

121

119–121 From a series of advertisements for a programming language that quickly and effortlessly reaches desired goals as opposed to more complicated means. Black and white, green arrows. (GER)
122 Double-spread trade magazine advertisement with a full-colour illustration, for *Nixdorf* computers. (GER)
123–125 Advertisements and illustration in original size from an image campaign for *Volkswagen*. Fig. 123 refers to "Father's Day", and Figs. 124, 125 to "Mother's Day". (BRA)

119–121 Beispiele aus einer Serie von Anzeigen für eine Programmiersprache, die schnell und mühelos zum gewünschten Ziel führen soll. Schwarzweiss mit grünen Pfeilen. (GER)
122 Doppelseitiges Fachzeitschrifteninserat mit mehrfarbiger Illustration für *Nixdorf*-Computer. (GER)
123–125 Inserate und Illustration in Originalgrösse aus einer Image-Kampagne für *Volkswagen*. Abb. 123 bezieht sich auf den «Vatertag», Abb. 124, 125 auf den «Muttertag». (BRA)

119–121 Exemples d'annonces vantant les mérites d'un langage de programmation qui s'apprend aisément et simplifie l'emploi de l'ordinateur. Noir et blanc, flèches vertes. (GER)
122 Annonce de revue spécialisée sur double page (illustration polychrome) pour les ordinateurs *Nixdorf*. (GER)
123–125 Annonces et illustration grandeur nature tirées d'une campagne de prestige pour *Volkswagen*. La fig. 123 a trait à la Fête des Pères, les fig. 124, 125 à celle des Mères. (BRA)

ARTIST / KÜNSTLER / ARTISTE:

119–122 Heinz Edelmann
123–125 Bjarne Norking

ART DIRECTOR / DIRECTEUR ARTISTIQUE:

119–122 Robert Pütz
123–125 Bjarne Norking

AGENCY / AGENTUR / AGENCE – STUDIO:

119–122 Robert Pütz GmbH & Co.
123–125 Alcantara Machado,
Periscinoto Comunicações Ltda.

122

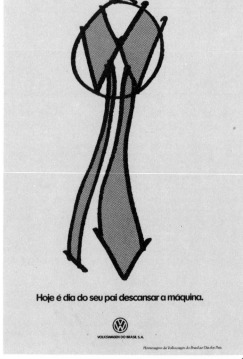

123

124

Encha seu tanque de amor.

125

63

Fein in Schale

– schippern sie über die sieben Meere der Welt. Die Pepperoni und Pommeranzen. Die Kiwis und Dividivis. Die Mangos und Melonen. Die Papayas und Pampelmusen. Avocados und Kiwis. Exoten aller Herren Länder vereinigen sich in Europa. Schiffe von Hapag-Lloyd sind schon

Über die Meere gesegelt und gedampft, als von Lebensqualität überhaupt noch niemand sprach. Und schon gar nicht von der Haute Cuisine oder Haute Couture. 1848 nach Nordamerika, 1871 in die Karibik, 1872 nach Südamerika, 1886 nach Ostasien und Australien. Und sie

holten heran, was uns Europäern das Leben versüßte und ihm die rechte Würze gab. Zum Beispiel Kaffee und Kakao, Wolle und Seidenstoffe, exotische Früchte und oder Tabak. Hapag-Lloyd Schiffe sind in alle Welt gefahren; auch dahin, wo der Pfeffer wächst.
Heute gäbe es ohne die Fracht über See kaum einen Markt-Platz auf dieser Welt. Keinen Morgenkaffee. Keinen Fünf-Uhr-Tee. Kein Papier für die Zeitung. Kein Wachstum und keine Industrialisierung in dem Maße, wie wir sie heute kennen. Nichts, was uns Spaß macht und wir

zum Leben miteinander brauchen.
Mit 24 Containerschiffen ist Hapag-Lloyd an dem weltumspannenden Handel beteiligt. Und mit 85.000 Containern, in denen Frachtgüter sicher und "fein in Schale" reisen.

◀◀ HAPAG-LLOYD

126

Richtungweisend

– war einst Christoph Columbus für die Schiffahrt unserer Welt. Aber wie auch immer: Alle Seefahrer jener Zeit hatten viel Wasser aufgewirbelt und den Europäern die Richtung gewiesen.
Die Wiederentdeckung Amerikas (und damit der Beginn enger wirtschaftlicher Beziehungen) fand erst

Jahrhunderte später statt. 1848 setzte die Hamburg-Amerika Linie ihre Schnellsegler "Deutschland" unter Wind; er brauchte für die Rundreise 98 Tage. Zehn Jahre danach fuhr die "Bremen", das erste Überseeschiff des Norddeutschen Lloyd, unter Dampf nach New York. Dann kamen die Verschnellsteiner; die

schnellen Atlantiker nannte. Die Flotte wurde immer leistungsstärker, der Dienste regelmäßiger, das Netz der Verbindungen immer dichter. Heute ist kaum noch Neuland zu entdecken; zumindest nicht für Hapag-Lloyd. Die Dienste umspannen die Welt. Containerschiffe und konventionelle Frachter sind überall zu Hause, wo es wichtige Märkte gibt oder neue wirtschaftliche Bande geknüpft werden sollen. In Nord-, Mittel- und Südamerika. In Australien und Neu-

seeland. In Ostasien, Südostasien und Saudi-Arabien. An den Küsten des indischen Ozeans. Mit 257 Anlaufhäfen sind die wichtigsten Wirtschaftszentren in diesem dichte Netz "verstrickt".
Frachtschiffahrt mit Hapag-Lloyd: das ist fur den Güteraustausch in der Welt der Kompass, der die Richtung weist.

◀◀ Hapag-Lloyd AG

127

ARTIST / KÜNSTLER / ARTISTE:

126–128 Barbara Geissler
130 Seymour Chwast
131 Michael David Brown

DESIGNER / GESTALTER / MAQUETTISTE:

126–128 Hannes & Barbara Geissler
129 Dave Neville
131 Michael David Brown

ART DIRECTOR / DIRECTEUR ARTISTIQUE:

126–128 Horst Rickmann
129 Brian Morrow
130 Seymour Chwast

AGENCY / AGENTUR / AGENCE – STUDIO:

126–128 Geissler Design
129 TBWA Ltd.
130 Pushpin Lubalin Peckolick
131 Michael David Brown, Inc.

Meeresknoten

– mit Seemannsgarn gesponnen. Das ist die phantasievolle Darstellung jenes Knotens, mit denen Seeleute die Schnelligkeit eines Schiffes messen.
Die Hapag-Lloyd Flotte hatte schon eine Menge Meeresknoten, als die Zeiten für den Handel und Wandel noch windig waren. Und je mehr

Dampf dahinter kam, desto schneller wurden die Schiffe. 1848 zum Beispiel schaffte der Segler "Deutschland" die Reise von Hamburg nach New York in 49 Tagen. 1858 stach das Dampfsegelschiff "Bremen I" zum erstenmal in See; mit 150 Tons Frachtgüter an Bord. Bis es schließlich die spektakulären atlantischen

Rekorde gab. 1929 fuhr die berühmte "Bremen" in 4 Tagen, 14 Stunden und 30 Minuten von Bremerhaven nach New York und holte sich die be-

gehrte Trophäe, das "Blaue Band". Heute hat der Knoten für Hapag-Lloyd eine andere Bedeutung. Denn Schnelligkeit ist zwar gut, Pünktlichkeit und Regelmäßigkeit aber sind viel besser. Die handeltreibende Wirtschaft muß wissen, wann ein Schiff welchen Hafen anläuft und ihn wieder verläßt. Deshalb betreibt Hapag-Lloyd den Güteraustausch im Liniendienst; mit regelmäßigen Abfahrtszeiten zum Beispiel einmal wöchentlich über den Nordatlantik. Deshalb ist Hapag-Lloyd an allen

wirtschaftlichen Knotenpunkten präsent. Mit 450 Vertretungen überall in der Welt. Mit 22 eigenen Frachtkontoren in Europa. Und mit einem

zentral gesteuerten und weltweit funktionierenden Datenverarbeitungs- und Kommunikationsnetz.
Frachtliniendienste von Hapag-Lloyd sorgen für den reibungslosen Service in allen Phasen des Transports. Knotenpunkt für Knotenpunkt.

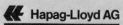 ◀◀ Hapag-Lloyd AG

128

126–128 Examples from an advertising campaign in daily newspapers for *Hapag-Lloyd* container traffic and transport. Fig. 126 refers to international trade—today in containers, earlier in frigates and steamships. Fig. 127: "Freight shipping with *Hapag-Lloyd*: this is the compass that points in the right direction for goods exchange." Fig. 128: an imaginative creation of the knot, the unit by which the speed of ships is measured. (GER)
129 Full-page newspaper advertisement with the addresses of *Land Rover* dealerships in Great Britain. (GBR)
130 Full-page advertisement in black and white for Haber Typographers, Inc., New York. The text and illustration are based on a play upon words. (USA)
131 Small-format advertisement for a cinema, announcing a film directed by Alfred Hitchcock. (USA)

126–128 Beispiele aus einer Inseratenkampagne in Tageszeitungen für den *Hapag-Lloyd*-Container-Verkehr. Abb. 126 bezieht sich auf den weltumspannenden Handel – heute in Containern, früher in Segel- und Dampfschiffen; Abb. 127: «Frachtschiffahrt mit *Hapag-Lloyd*: das ist für den Güteraustausch der Kompass, der die Richtung weist»; Abb. 128: Phantasie-Darstellung des Knotens, jener Einheit, mit der die Seeleute die Schnelligkeit eines Schiffes messen. In Schwarzweiss. (GER)
129 Ganzseitiges Zeitungsinserat mit den Adressen der *Land-Rover*-Vertretungen in Grossbritannien. (GBR)
130 Ganzseitiges Inserat in Schwarzweiss für den New Yorker Schriften-Hersteller *Haber*, der in seinen Anzeigen häufig selbst dargestellt ist. Text und Illustration basieren auf einem Wortspiel. (USA)
131 Kleinformatige Anzeige eines Kinos für die Ankündigung des Hitchcock-Films *Die 39 Stufen*. (USA)

126–128 Exemples d'annonces figurant dans une campagne de quotidiens en faveur des transports de conteneurs *Hapag-Lloyd*. La fig. 126 se rapporte au commerce international effectué aujourd'hui par conteneurisation, autrefois par voile ou vapeur; fig. 127: «le fret maritime, c'est *Hapag-Lloyd*, la boussole qui marque la direction que doivent prendre les cargaisons»; fig. 128: représentation imagée du nœud, l'unité de mesure de vitesse utilisée en navigation maritime. Noir et blanc. (GER)
129 Annonce de journal pleine page: liste des agences *Land Rover* en Grande-Bretagne. (GBR)
130 Annonce pleine page, en noir et blanc, pour la fonderie de caractères *Haber*, dont le propriétaire figure souvent dans la publicité. Le texte et l'illustration s'inspirent d'un jeu de mots. (USA)
131 Petite annonce de cinéma pour la projection des *39 Marches* de Hitchcock. (USA)

130

129

131

2

Booklets

Folders

Catalogues

Programmes

Broschüren

Faltprospekte

Kataloge

Programme

Brochures

Dépliants

Catalogues

Programmes

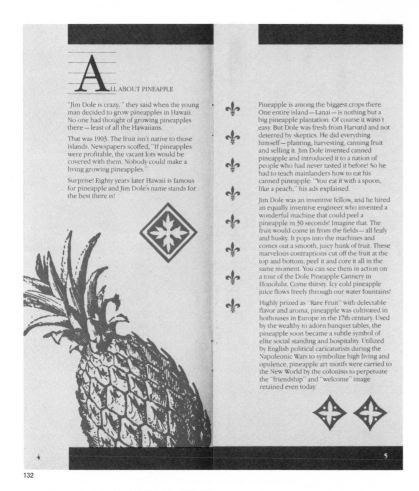

All About Pineapple

"Jim Dole is crazy," they said when the young man decided to grow pineapples in Hawaii. No one had thought of growing pineapples there — least of all the Hawaiians.

That was 1903. The fruit isn't native to those islands. Newspapers scoffed, "If pineapples were profitable, the vacant lots would be covered with them. Nobody could make a living growing pineapples."

Surprise! Eighty years later Hawaii is famous for pineapple and Jim Dole's name stands for the best there is!

Pineapple is among the biggest crops there. One entire island — Lanai — is nothing but a big pineapple plantation. Of course it wasn't easy. But Dole was fresh from Harvard and not deterred by skeptics. He did everything himself — planting, harvesting, canning fruit and selling it. Jim Dole invented canned pineapple and introduced it to a nation of people who had never tasted it before! So he had to teach mainlanders how to eat his canned pineapple: "You eat it with a spoon, like a peach," his ads explained.

Jim Dole was an inventive fellow, and he hired an equally inventive engineer who invented a wonderful machine that could peel a pineapple in 30 seconds! Imagine that. The fruit would come in from the fields — all leafy and husky. It pops into the machines and comes out a smooth, juicy hunk of fruit. These marvelous contraptions cut off the fruit at the top and bottom; peel it and core it all in the same moment. You can see them in action on a tour of the Dole Pineapple Cannery in Honolulu. Come thirsty. Icy cold pineapple juice flows freely through our water fountains!

Highly prized as "Rare Fruit" with delectable flavor and aroma, pineapple was cultivated in hothouses in Europe in the 17th century. Used by the wealthy to adorn banquet tables, the pineapple soon became a subtle symbol of elite social standing and hospitality. Utilized by English political caricaturists during the Napoleonic Wars to symbolize high living and opulence, pineapple art motifs were carried to the New World by the colonists to perpetuate the "friendship" and "welcome" image retained even today.

4 / 5

132

Lunch

Add chilled Dole Chunk Pineapple in Syrup (drained) to your favorite chicken salad … water chestnuts for crunch, and voila! It's special.

And when you're making tuna salad (or chicken, or turkey salad) add a small can of Dole Chunk or Crushed Pineapple to the fixings. Here are some combinations to try:
Tuna Salad … tuna, crushed pineapple, raisins, chopped carrot and mayo.
Chicken Salad … diced chicken, crushed pineapple, chopped peanuts, chutney and sour cream.
Ham Salad … diced ham, fresh dill, crushed pineapple and mayo. Peanut Butter & … pineapple! Really good and refreshing. Better than the SOS (Same Old Sandwich).
B-L-P … you guessed it — bacon, lettuce and pineapple.

Turn regular macaroni salad into "Super Salad!" Add a well-drained can of Dole Pineapple Chunks, sliced radishes and chopped green onion to your macaroni. Then … dress with mayonnaise, flavored to taste with mustard and horseradish. Irresistible!

Unexpected guests for lunch? They'll think they've dropped into the best deli in town if you serve this quick and easy salad: Dole canned pineapple chunks (drained), small chunks cream or cheddar cheese and ham or corned beef. Add a little finely chopped green onion and seasoned oil and vinegar dressing. Serve on crisp chunks of lettuce … Is that "to go," or for here?

Jazz up coleslaw with a 20-oz. can of Dole Chunk Pineapple in Syrup (drained) and a handful of peanuts.

Dole Chunk Pineapple in Syrup also dresses up potato salad. Stir drained chunks into your usual potato salad and taste how good it can be!

◆ A satisfying supper sandwich is so easy to make, you'll be hooked once you try this one! Arrange Dole Pineapple slices on generous slices of ham, turkey or chicken. Cover with grated cheese. Broil until melted, then lift onto a buttered English muffin.

◆ Dole Burgers are classic: Place a slice of Dole Pineapple on top of a hamburger during the last few minutes of cooking. Whether you cook 'em in a skillet, or under the broiler, Dole Burgers are good and easy.

◆ Top an open-face grilled cheese sandwich with a drained Dole pineapple slice and taste the juicy difference.

◆ Hotdog! Crushed pineapple with franks on a bun.

12 / 13

133

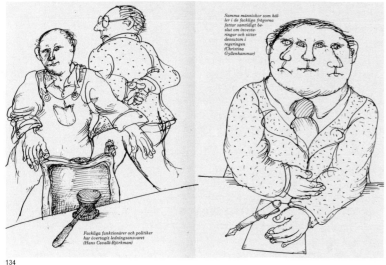

Samma människor som håller i de fackliga frågorna fattar samtidigt beslut om investeringar och sitter dessutom i regeringen (Christina Gyllenhammar)

Fackliga funktionärer och politiker har övertagit ledningsansvaret (Hans Cavalli-Björkman)

134

Der fromme Besuch stand ins britische Haus, die frommen Geschäftsleute rieben sich die Hände: Beim Andenken-Handel waren zusätzliche Einnahmen zu erwarten. Indes, dies war ein frommer Wunsch.

135

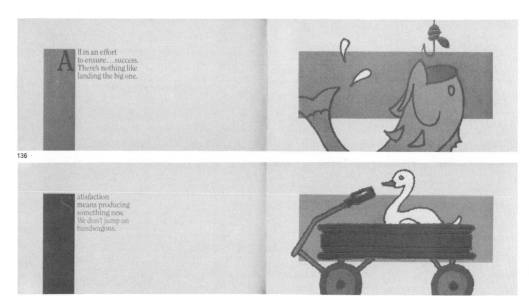

All in an effort to ensure … success. There's nothing like landing the big one.

Satisfaction means producing something new. We don't jump on bandwagons.

136

137

132, 133 Double spreads from an advertising brochure for *Dole* tinned pineapple. In green and yellow. (USA)
134 Inside spreads of a political brochure dealing with economic questions and problems. (SWE)
135 Woodcut illustration from *Donkey Post*, a customer magazine that has been distributed for years as self-promotion by the graphic designer Eduard Prüssen. (GER)
136, 137 Double spreads from a self-promotion brochure of a graphic design team. In complementary colours. (USA)
138–142 Complete recto and illustration taken from the programme of an annual festival held in Perth. (AUS)
143 Invitation brochure of a financial concern for the inauguration of its new company building. (USA)

132, 133 Doppelseiten aus einer Werbebroschüre für *Dôle*-Ananas-Konserven mit dem Titel: «Alles über Ananas.» Rezepte und Geschichte des Anbaus auf Hawaii. In Grün und Gelb. (USA)
134 Innenseiten aus einer politischen Broschüre, die über wirtschaftliche Fragen und Probleme informiert. (SWE)
135 Holzschnitt-Illustration aus der Kundenzeitschrift *Donkey Post*, die der Graphiker Eduard Prüssen seit Jahrzehnten als Eigenwerbung monatlich verschickt. (GER)
136, 137 Doppelseiten aus einer Broschüre, die für ein Graphikerteam wirbt. In Komplementärfarben. (USA)
138–142 Vollständige Vorderseite und Illustrationen aus dem Programm des jährlich stattfindenden Festival of Perth. (AUS)
143 Einladungs-Broschüre einer Finanzgesellschaft zur Einweihung ihres Neubaus, mit Hinweis für die Anfahrt. (USA)

132, 133 Doubles pages d'une brochure publicitaire pour les conserves d'ananas *Dôle* intitulée «Tout sur l'ananas». Recettes et histoire des cultures hawaiiennes. Vert, jaune. (USA)
134 Pages intérieures d'une brochure politique d'information sur les questions et problèmes économiques. (SWE)
135 Gravure sur bois illustrant le *Donkey Post*, une revue mensuelle du graphiste Eduard Prüssen qu'il publie depuis des décennies à l'intention de ses clients. (GER)
136, 137 Doubles pages de la revue autopromotionnelle d'une équipe de graphistes. Couleurs complémentaires. (USA)
138–142 Page de titre complète et illustrations du programme du Festival annuel de Perth. (AUS)
143 Brochure d'une société financière invitant à l'inauguration de son nouvel immeuble, avec indication de la route. (USA)

139

140

138

141

142

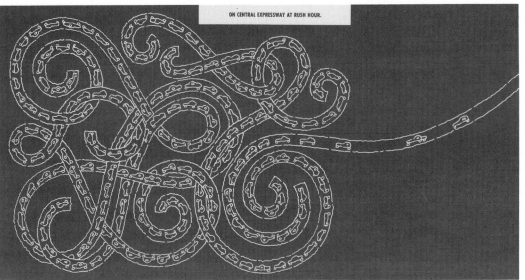
143

144

145

146

ARTIST / KÜNSTLER / ARTISTE:

144 Michael Doret/Todd Schorr
146 Fernando Puig Rosado
147 Lonnie Sue Johnson
148 Ken Cato/Ray Condon

DESIGNER / GESTALTER / MAQUETTISTE:

145 John Marken
147 Dana Kasarsky
148 Ken Cato

ART DIRECTOR / DIRECTEUR ARTISTIQUE:

144 Murray Smith
145 John Marken
147 Lonnie Sue Johnson
148 Ken Cato

AGENCY / AGENTUR / AGENCE – STUDIO:

148 Ken Cato Design Company Pty Ltd

144 Title for the film *Alien*, presented by *20th Century Fox*. (USA)
145 Recto of a folder issued by the *Brooklyn Union Gas* company. Black reel, red background. (USA)
146 Postcard for Amnesty International entitled "Brainwashing". (FRA)
147 Illustrated card used as self-promotion for the artist Lonni Sue Johnson. Manhattan's skyscrapers in violet on a white background. (USA)
148 Double spread from a brochure for a printing firm, presenting its various types of print and typesetting as well as a programme of cultural activities. (AUS)

144 Titel des Films *Alien* der Filmgesellschaft *20th Century Fox*. (USA)
145 Vorderseite eines Faltprospekts der Firma *Brooklyn Union Gas*, die ihren Kunden Filme anbietet, hier mit Kochrezepten aus aller Welt. Schwarze Filmspule auf rotem Hintergrund. (USA)
146 Postkarte für Amnesty International mit dem Titel «Gehirnwäsche». (FRA)
147 Illustrierte Karte als Eigenwerbung einer Künstlerin. Manhattans Wolkenkratzer in Veilchenblau auf weissem Hintergrund. (USA)
148 Doppelseite aus einer Broschüre für eine Druckerei, die ihre verschiedenen Druckarten und gleichzeitig einen Veranstaltungskalender kultureller Aktivitäten präsentiert. (AUS)

144 Titre du film *Alien* de la *20th Century Fox*. (USA)
145 Recto d'un dépliant de la *Brooklyn Union Gas* offrant des films culinaires à sa clientèle, ici un film présentant des recettes du monde entier. Bobine noire sur fond rouge. (USA)
146 Carte postale pour Amnesty International intitulée «Lavage de cerveau». (FRA)
147 Carte illustrée autopromotionnelle de l'artiste Lonni Sue Johnson. Les gratte-ciel de Manhattan violacés sur fond blanc. (USA)
148 Double page d'une brochure pour une imprimerie présentant ses divers imprimés en même temps qu'un calendrier de manifestations culturelles. (AUS)

147

Booklets / Prospekte / Brochures

148

Week Thirty
Battle Of Flowers
As part of the British celebrations on the coronation of Edward VII and Queen Alexandra in 1902, the Channel Island of Jersey staged a Battle of Flowers. This magnificent floral spectacle was such an outstanding success that it is now held regularly on the Thursday before the first Monday in August. It is Europe's greatest floral carnival. Millions of blooms are grown voluntarily and preparations begin soon after Christmas. About 50,000 people flock to Jersey and line the mile-long route for the floral procession in St Helier. Afterwards, the Battle of Flowers starts at a pre-arranged signal. The strictest precautions are taken by the organisers to guard against any irresponsible stripping of the exhibits and to ensure that all flowers used in the battle are free of stems, thorns and wires.

Week Thirty One
Doggett's Coat and Badge Race
As near as possible to August 1, the Worshipful Company of Fishmongers stage the oldest rowing event in the world, for Doggett's Coat and Badge. The race takes place on the Thames in London and is always against an adverse tide, requiring great strength, skill and stamina on the part of the oarsmen.
Thomas Doggett was an 18th Century actor who initiated the race in 1716 with a poster announcing 'This being the day of His Majesty George I's happy Accession to the Throne, there will be given by Mr Doggett an Orange Livery with a Badge representing Liberty to be rowed for by six Watermen that are out of their time within the year past. They are to row from London Bridge to Chelsea. It will be continued annually on the same day forever'.
It was open only to watermen who had just completed their apprenticeships, and so no man has more than one chance to win the coveted Coat and Badge.
The winner still gets his pleated, quilted coat with its silver buttons and the silver badge bearing the prancing White Horse of the House of Hanover and the word Liberty emblazoned on it.
In the wake of the contestants follows a barge carrying past winners, wearing their coats and badges complete with the headgear, breeches, silk stockings and buckled shoes which go with the prize.

Week Thirty Two
The Watermelon Festival
This early August celebration is held annually at Rush Springs, Oklahoma, and includes a rodeo, fiddlers contest and prizes for the best watermelons. In between events, lucky folks attending the festivities get to slurp their way through more than 20,000 kilograms of free watermelons.

149 Greetings card for a publisher's self-promotion, posted in a grass-green envelope. (USA)
150 Unfolded invitation card for an exhibition of office furniture. The *Hauserman* company offers open or closed-in spaces, according to one's wishes. (USA)
151–153 Segmented inside spreads from a brochure containing the programme for a univesity's summer festival. (USA)
154, 155 Card in folding and cut-out technique designed to announce a competition inviting designers and architects to utilize *Colorcore*, a new type of plastic surface material. (USA)

149 Grusskarte als Eigenwerbung eines Verlagshauses. In einem grasgrünen Umschlag. (USA)
150 Aufklappbare Einladungskarte für eine Büromöbel-Ausstellung. Die Firma *Hauserman* bietet offenen Raum an, wo man ihn will, aber auch Abgeschlossenheit, wenn gewünscht. (USA)
151–153 Kapitelseiten aus der Broschüre der Penn State University für das Sommer-Festwochenprogramm. (USA)
154, 155 Karte in Falt- und Stanztechnik im Umschlag versandt: Wettbewerb unter Designern und Architekten für die Anwendung des neuen Plastik-Oberflächenmaterials *Colorcore*. (USA)

149 Carte de vœux utilisé pour la promotion d'un éditeur. Expédiée sous enveloppe vert prairie. (USA)
150 Carte d'invitation dépliante pour une exposition de meubles de bureau. La société *Hauserman* offre des aménagements créant des espaces clos ou ouverts au gré du preneur. (USA)
151–153 Pages intérieures en tête des sections d'une brochure de la Penn State University sur son Festival d'été. (USA)
154, 155 Carte dépliante obtenue par pliage et découpage: concours de graphistes et d'architectes pour l'application du nouveau matériau plastique surfaçant *Colorcore*. (USA)

Universal Spring.

149

150

LIST OF SIDEWALK ARTISTS WITH LOCATION

51

151

EXHIBITIONS

152

ARTISTS-IN-ACTION

15

153

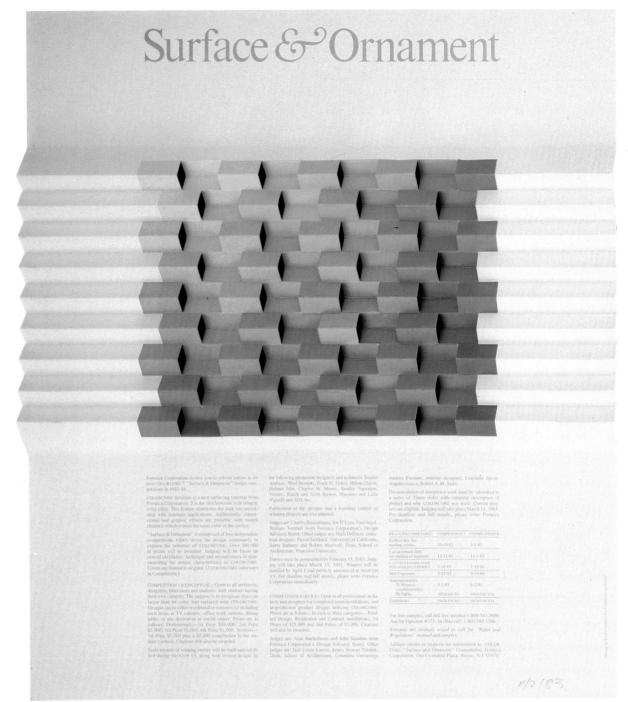

154

155

156

158

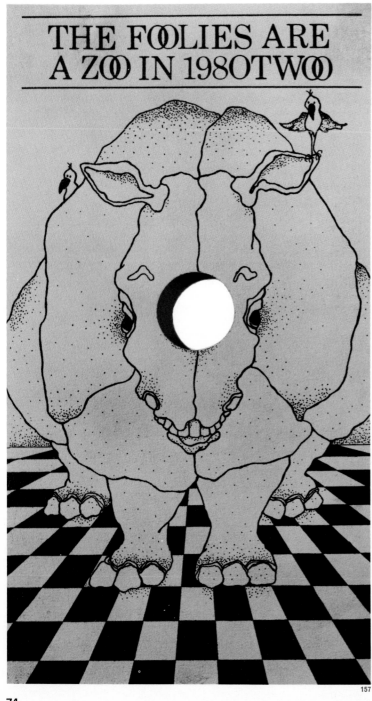

157

159

160

DON'T GIVE US THAT OLD, "I CAN'T COME BECAUSE I DON'T HAVE A COSTUME," ROUTINE.
THE FIFTH ANNUAL HALLOWEEN BLOCK PARTY STARTS SCREAMING AGAIN SATURDAY, OCTOBER 30 AT 6. BETWEEN 1177 AND 1189 VIRGINIA AVENUE, N.E.
EVEN PEOPLE WHO LOOK SCARY ALL-YEAR AROUND ARE DIGGING A LITTLE TO CREATE A COSTUME. BECAUSE ONCE AGAIN THERE WILL BE PRIZES FOR BEST. NEXT BEST. AND NEXT TO NEXT BEST.
PLUS, THERE WILL BE BEER, WINE, FOOD AND LIVE ENTERTAINMENT. BEYOND THE SHOW YOU'LL PUT ON.
BUT EVEN IF YOU CAN'T COME UP WITH A COSTUME OF YOUR OWN, YOU CAN STILL COME TO THE PARTY. JUST PUT A BAG OVER YOUR HEAD. BROUGHT TO YOU BY RICHARD HOFLICH, PHOTOGRAPHY. BRYON REED, DENTIST. REIDER FILM & TELEVISION, INC. PETER HAND, AIA, BEN DOOLEY, AIA, ROGER MACUCH, PHOTOGRAPHY. MARY CARUSO, CHIROPRACTOR. BROOKS BOWMAN, PHOTOGRAPHY. SULLIVAN AND/OR HAAS, CREATIVE ADVERTISING SERVICE. TOM HICKS, REALTOR.

ILLUSTRATION BY BILL MAYER. TYPE BY TYPE DIRECTION. MECHANICAL BY PENNY REDFERN. CONCEIVED, DESIGNED, WRITTEN AND PRODUCED BY SULLIVAN AND/OR HAAS.

161

162

156, 157 Rectos of unfolded cards containing the programme for slide and film shows of the Penn State Graphic Design School. In Fig.156 the inserted finger becomes an elephant's trunk, in Fig.157 a rhinoceros's horn. (USA)
158 Cover of a folder used as self-promotion by Florian, a photo- and graphic-design studio. (FRA)
159 Self-promotion in the form of a prospectus with drawings of "very distinguished people". (POR)
160, 161 Complete art work and illustration of a paper bag which served as an invitation to a Halloween party, urging people to come with just a bag over their head if they did not possess any kind of fancy costume. (USA)
162 Invitation to a Halloween party, also serving as self-promotion for an artist. (USA)

156, 157 Vorderseiten aufklappbarer Karten, für Dia- und Filmvorführungen der Penn-State-Graphic-Design-Schule. In Abb.156 wird der Finger zum Elephantenrüssel, in Abb.157 zum Horn des Nashorns. (USA)
158 Umschlag einer Mappe als Eigenwerbung für das Photo- und Graphikstudio Florian. (FRA)
159 Eigenwerbung in Form eines Prospektes mit Zeichnungen von «sehr feinen Leuten». (POR)
160, 161 Vollständige Abbildung und Illustration eines Papiersackes, der als Einladung zu einer Halloween-Party dient, mit dem Hinweis: «Auch wenn Sie kein eigenes Kostüm besitzen, können Sie mit einem Sack über dem Kopf erscheinen». (USA)
162 Einladungskarte für eine Halloween-Kostüm-Party, die als Eigenwerbung eines Künstlers dient. (USA)

156, 157 Rectos de cartes dépliantes pour les projections de diapos et de films à l'Ecole d'art graphique de la Penn State University. Le doigt introduit dans l'illustration devient trompe d'éléphant (156) ou corne de rhino (157). (USA)
158 Couverture d'un album autopromotionnel du studio d'art graphique et photographique Florian. (FRA)
159 Autopromotion sous forme d'un prospectus illustré de dessins de «gens très comme il faut». (POR)
160, 161 Image complète et illustration d'un sac en papier servant d'invitation à une fête de Halloween: «Même si vous n'avez pas de costume à mettre, vous pourrez toujours venir avec un sac sur la tête». (USA)
162 Carte d'invitation à une fête costumée de Halloween, en même temps qu'un rappel autopromotionnel de l'artiste. (USA)

163

164

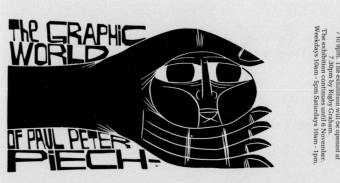

THE GRAPHIC WORLD

OF PAUL PETER PIECH·

You are cordially invited to attend a preview of an exhibition of the Graphic Work of Paul Peter Piech at the Kimberlin Exhibition Hall, Mill Lane, Leicester Polytechnic on Friday 22 October from 7 to 9pm. The exhibition will be opened at 7.30pm by Rigby Graham. The exhibition continues until 6 November. Weekdays 10am - 5pm Saturdays 10am - 1pm.

165

ARTIST / KÜNSTLER / ARTISTE:

163 Thomas Kern
165 Paul Peter Piech
166 Fernando Puig Rosado

DESIGNER / GESTALTER / MAQUETTISTE:

163 Thomas Kern
164 Gerry Rosentswieg

ART DIRECTOR / DIRECTEUR ARTISTIQUE:

163 Thomas Kern
164 Gerry Rosentswieg

AGENCY / AGENTUR / AGENCE – STUDIO:

163 Thomas Kern Design
164 The Graphics Studio

166

163 Self-promotion by the illustrator David Kern. (USA)
164 Enclosure of a circular letter issued by the Art Directors Club of Los Angeles. Golden lettering on a red pencil. (USA)
165 Invitation to the preview of an artist's exhibition. Linocut in blue on white. (GBR)
166 Invitation card of the Spanish artist Fernando Puig Rosado for an exhibition held at the Bartsch & Chariau gallery in Munich. (GER)

163 Eigenwerbung des Illustrators David Kern mit dem Titel: «Weisse Augen einer Eiche». (USA)
164 Beilage eines Rundschreibens des Art Director Clubs, Los Angeles. Goldene Schrift auf rotem Bleistift. (USA)
165 Einladungskarte für eine Voranzeige der Ausstellung eines Plakatkünstlers in Leicester. Linolschnitt. (GBR)
166 Einladungs-Karte zu einer Ausstellung in der Galerie Bartsch & Chariau in München. (GER)

163 Autopromotion de l'illustrateur David Kern. Titre: «Les yeux blancs d'un chêne.» (USA)
164 Annexe à une circulaire de l'Art Directors Club de Los Angeles. Texte or sur crayon rouge. (USA)
165 Carte d'invitation au vernissage d'une exposition individuelle. Linogravure, bleu sur blanc. (GBR)
166 Carte d'invitation de l'artiste espagnol Fernando Puig Rosado à une exposition organisée à la galerie Bartsch & Chariau de Munich. (GER)

Booklets / Prospekte / Brochures

167

168

169

ARTIST / KÜNSTLER / ARTISTE:

171 Mark Hess

DESIGNER / GESTALTER / MAQUETTISTE:

167, 168 Susan Skoorka
169, 170 Walter Lefmann
171 Mark Hess

ART DIRECTOR / DIRECTEUR ARTISTIQUE:

167–170 Walter Lefmann
171 Mark Hess

AGENCY / AGENTUR / AGENCE – STUDIO:

167–170 Time Promotion Art Dept.

170

167–170 Once a year, an original artifact is conceived, designed and mailed to a small group of *Time* magazine's clients. These pieces are made in the tradition of the art and produced in limited quantity, with great attention paid to quality and artistic integrity. The theme is always patriotic and symbolic of an intriguing or fanciful aspect of America's history as a nation. All this is incorporated in *Time* magazine's "July 4th promotion". In full colour. (USA)
171 An artist's self-promotion. Illustration in actual size. (USA)

167–170 Verschiedene patriotische und symbolische Gegenstände, entworfen von Künstlern im Auftrag der Zeitschrift *Time*, die jährlich am amerikanischen Nationalfeiertag (4. Juli) an einen kleinen Teil ihrer Kundschaft versandt werden. Bei den Arbeiten wird speziell auf die künstlerische Qualität geachtet, die Auflage ist jeweils limitiert. Hier George Washington, Yankee Doodle (in bemaltem Holz), ein Briefbeschwerer mit dem ersten Zusatzartikel der amerikanischen Verfassung, sowie Papierteller in den amerikanischen Farben. (USA)
171 Eigenwerbung für einen Künstler. In Originalgrösse. (USA)

167–170 Divers objets patriotiques et symboliques conçus par des artistes pour *Time* et envoyés à un petit nombre de lecteurs du magazine à l'occasion de la Journée de l'Indépendance, le 4 juillet. L'accent est mis sur l'originalité et la qualité artistique de ces productions dont le tirage est limité. On voit ici George Washington, un Yankee chantant le yankee doodle (bois peint), un presse-papier avec le premier amendement à la Constitution, et des assiettes en papier. (USA)
171 Autopromotion d'un artiste. Illustration grandeur nature. (USA)

172

ARTIST / KÜNSTLER / ARTISTE:

172 Wendell Minor
173 Ed Acuna
174 Na, Jae-Oh
175, 176 Paul Peter Piech

DESIGNER / GESTALTER / MAQUETTISTE:

172 Wendell Minor
173 Hal Florian
175, 176 Paul Peter Piech

ART DIRECTOR / DIRECTEUR ARTISTIQUE:

172 Louise Noble
173 Hal Florian
175, 176 Paul Peter Piech

AGENCY / AGENTUR / AGENCE – STUDIO:

172 W. Minor Designs
173 Ketchum Advertising

172 An artist's illustration, used for self-promotional purposes by his agency. (USA)
173 Direct mail from the *Schering Corporation* referring to allergies caused by detergents. (USA)
174 Title of an exhibition promoting Korea. Recto of a brochure. (KOR)
175, 176 Postcards protesting the stationing of Cruise missiles in Great Britain. Black linocuts on a light yellow background. (GBR)

172 Illustration eines Künstlers, als Eigenwerbung von seiner Agentur verwendet. (USA)
173 Direktwerbung der *Schering Corporation*: Hinweis auf mögliche Allergien, die von Reinigungsmitteln verursacht werden können. (USA)
174 «Das Gesicht Koreas» ist der Titel dieser Ausstellung. Vorderseite einer Broschüre. (KOR)
175, 176 Postkarten gegen die Stationierung von Nuklearraketen in England. Schwarze Linolschnitte auf hellgelbem Hintergrund. (GBR)

172 Illustration d'un artiste, employée comme autopromotion par son agence. (USA)
173 Publicité directe de la *Schering Corporation*: on met ici en garde contre les allergies que peuvent provoquer les détergents. (USA)
174 «Visage de la Corée»: page de titre d'une brochure d'exposition. (KOR)
175, 176 Cartes postales contre le stationnement de missiles nucléaires en Angleterre. Linogravures noires sur fond jaune clair. (GBR)

173

174

175

176

177 Self-promotion for a Chinese design consultancy in the form of a leporello. Green lettering on a light brown brush, sand-coloured background. (USA)
178, 180 From a series of large sheets entitled: "My beautiful garden is a paradise for your advertising." They were sent to potential advertisers on behalf of the magazine *Mein schöner Garten*, issued and published by the *Burda* company. Fig. 178 in a mixed technique. (GER)
179 Direct advertising of the Whole Hog Studios, with a plea and an illustration for a Save-a-Pig campaign based on humorous allusions to these studios' symbol. Black on cream-coloured paper. (USA)

177 Eigenwerbung für eine chinesische Design-Beraterfirma in Form eines Leporellos. Grüne Schrift auf hellbraunem Pinsel, sandfarbener Hintergrund. (USA)
178, 180 Aus einer Serie von Kunstblättern mit dem Titel: «*Mein schöner Garten* ist das Paradies für Ihre Werbung». Sie wurden für die Zeitschrift *Mein schöner Garten*, aus dem Verlagshaus *Burda*, an potentielle Anzeigenkunden verschickt. Abb. 178: Mischtechnik. (GER)
179 Direktwerbung des Whole Hog Studios, ein Graphiker-Studio, welches das Schwein in seinem Namen hat und mit der Illustration für die Erhaltung dieses Tiers – und des Studios durch Aufträge – plädiert. Wie hier angedeutet, wird Schweineleder für die Herstellung von amerikanischen Fussbällen verwendet. Schwarz auf crèmefarbenem Papier. (USA)

177 Autopromotion pour une société chinoise de conseils en design. Dépliant en accordéon. Texte vert sur le pinceau brun clair, arrière-plan sable. (USA)
178, 180 Exemples de gravures composant une série intitulée «Mon beau jardin, c'est le paradis pour votre publicité» distribuée aux annonceurs potentiels du magazine *Mein schöner Garten* (Mon beau jardin) des Editions *Burda*. Fig. 178: technique mixte. (GER)
179 Publicité directe du Whole Hog Studio d'art graphique. «Hog» veut dire «cochon», et cette illustration plaide pour la préservation de cet animal, ainsi que du studio (sous forme de commandes). Comme on l'indique ici, le cuir du porc sert à la confection de ballons du football américain. Noir sur papier crème. (USA)

177

178

ARTIST / KÜNSTLER / ARTISTE:

178 Edward Sorel
179 John Breakey
180 Milton Glaser

DESIGNER / GESTALTER:

177 Hoi Ling Chu/Benjamin Perez
179 Ron Mabey

ART DIRECTOR:

177 Hoi Ling Chu
178, 180 Robert Pütz
179 Ron Mabey

AGENCY / AGENTUR / AGENCE:

177 H. L. Chu & Co., Ltd.
178, 180 Robert Pütz GmbH & Co.
179 Whole Hog Studios

Yes fans, that football is made of genuine, all-American, grade-A pigskin. What with pee-wee football, high school football, college football and professional football, it's only a matter of time before demand outstrips supply and pigs will be extinct. Just think…no more ham, sausage, pig's knuckles, bacon, hog jowl or sow belly. We'll all be Jewish whether we want to be or not. Worst of all there'll be no more Miss Piggy. This frivolous use of pigskin just to line the pockets of Pete Rozelle must stop! Search your heart and think of the three little pigs. Think of Porky Pig. Think of the pig you dated in high school. Think of how horny Kermit will be and you'll open your wallet as well as your heart. Send your taxable contributions or your next commercial art job to S.A.P. (Save A Pig) c/o Whole Hog Studios, 1205 Spring St., Atlanta, Georgia 30309 or call us at (404) 873-4021.

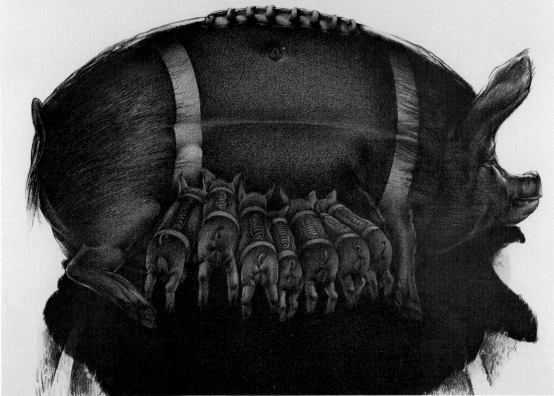

179

180

181

ARTIST / KÜNSTLER / ARTISTE:

181 Bascove
183 Giuseppe Reichmuth

DESIGNER / GESTALTER / MAQUETTISTE:

182 Katherine McCoy/Constance Birdsall

ART DIRECTOR / DIRECTEUR ARTISTIQUE:

181 Bascove
182 Katherine McCoy
183 Albert Ernst

AGENCY / AGENTUR / AGENCE – STUDIO:

182 Cranbrook Academy of Art
183 Fabrik Atelier am Wasser

181 Illustration as self-promotion for Bascove, a woman artist. Oil on canvas. (USA)
182 Recto of a brochure issued by the Cranbrook Academy of Art, Michigan, showing a signet of this institution. The brochure refers to the school's educational possibilities and to its fifty-year history, opportunity being the keyword. Black lettering and signet, pastel background. (USA)
183 A postcard which was also used as a poster, for "Green 80", a gardening exhibition in Basle. The saurian was reproduced in life-size and placed in the exhibition. In full colour. (SWI)

181 Illustration als Eigenwerbung für die Künstlerin Bascove. Öl auf Leinwand. (USA)
182 Vorderseite einer Broschüre der Cranbrook Academy of Art, Michigan, mit dem Signet der Schule. Ausbildungsmöglichkeiten und die fünfzigjährige Geschichte dieser Kunstschule werden darin vorgestellt. Schrift und Signet in Schwarz auf pastellfarbenem Hintergrund. (USA)
183 Postkarte, die auch als Poster verwendet wurde, für eine Gartenbauausstellung in Basel. Der Saurier wurde in Lebensgrösse nachgebildet und in der Ausstellung plaziert. In Farbe. (SWI)

181 Illustration autopromotionnelle de l'artiste Ms Bascove. Huile sur toile. (USA)
182 Recto d'une brochure de la Cranbrook Academy of Art (Michigan) avec l'emblème de l'école. On y présente les cycles de formation et l'histoire des 50 premières années de l'Académie. Texte et emblème sont exécutés en noir sur fond pastel. (USA)
183 Carte postale aussi utilisée comme affiche pour une exposition horticole à Bâle. Le dinosaure, reconstitué en grandeur nature, était le clou de l'exposition. En couleurs. (SWI)

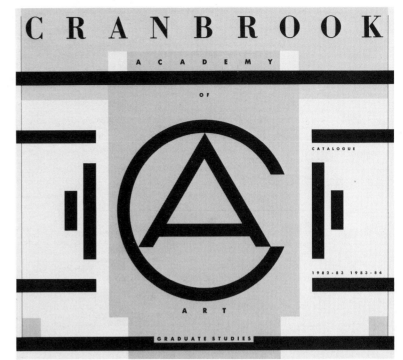

182

183

184

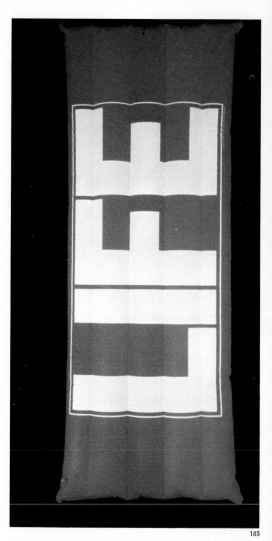

185

186

187

188

189

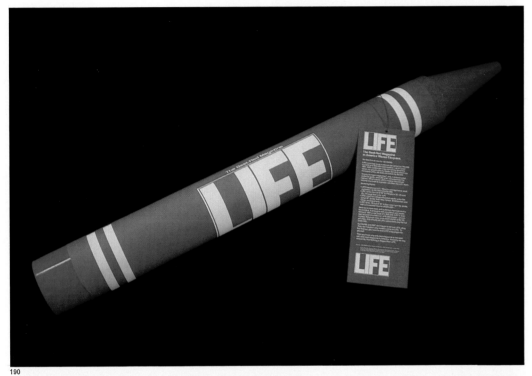

190

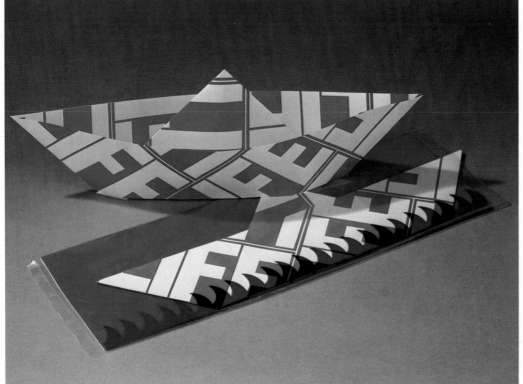

191

DESIGNER / GESTALTER / MAQUETTISTE:

184–191 Gilbert Lesser

ART DIRECTOR / DIRECTEUR ARTISTIQUE:

184–191 Gilbert Lesser

184 Red film reel with concertina-type folder citing some of the merits of *Life*. (USA)
185 Inflatable plastic raft with a card inviting advertisers to "make a big splash with *Life*". (USA)
186 A plastic shopping or bathing bag. (USA)
187 A mug containing matchbooks, plus a reprint folder. (USA)
188, 189 Carton and the "media maze" puzzle contained in it (Fig. 189), in which a small steel ball must be guided into a compartment bearing a *Life* logo. (USA)
190 A giant red pencil with a *Life* logo. (USA)
191 Personal invitation to a launch party of *Life*. (USA)

184 Rote Filmspule mit angeklebtem Leporello, der einige der Vorteile von *Life* erwähnt. (USA)
185 Luftmatratze mit Einladungskarte an die Inserenten, «mit *Life* Wellen zu schlagen». (USA)
186 Einkaufs- oder Badetasche aus Plastik. (USA)
187 Becher mit Streichholzbriefchen gefüllt sowie eine Mappe für Separatdrucke. (USA)
188, 189 Packung und Geschicklichkeitsspiel in Form eines Labyrinthwürfels (Abb. 189). Eine kleine Stahlkugel muss durch die Plastikrinnen der Würfeloberflächen so geführt werden, dass sie in ein mit dem *Life*-Logo markiertes Feld gelangt. (USA)
190 Riesen-Rotstift mit *Life*-Logo. (USA)
191 Einladung zu einer Schiffsparty, um *Life* zu feiern. (USA)

184 Bobine de film rouge au format répété sur un dépliant qui vante les mérites de *Life*. La bobine a été expédiée dans une boîte en aluminium. (USA)
185 Matelas pneumatique assorti d'une carte invitant les annonceurs de *Life* à «faire des vagues à l'aide de *Life*». (USA)
186 Sac de plage ou de commissions en plastique. (USA)
187 Chope contenant des pochettes d'allumettes et un dossier pour les tirés à part du magazine. (USA)
188, 189 Emballage et jeu d'adresse qu'il contient sous forme d'un cube-labyrinthe (fig. 189) à la surface duquel une bille d'acier doit rejoindre un compartiment signalé *Life*. (USA)
190 Crayon rouge géant illustré du logo *Life*. (USA)
191 Invitation à une fête *Life* organisée sur un bateau. (USA)

ARTIST / KÜNSTLER / ARTISTE:

192 André François
195 Christian Lang
198 Maurizio Milani

DESIGNER / GESTALTER / MAQUETTISTE:

193 Nigel Kuzimski
194 Joel Katz
195 Christian Lang
196 Risa Glickman
197 Ivan Chermayeff
198 Maurizio Milani

ART DIRECTOR / DIRECTEUR ARTISTIQUE:

192 Robert Delpire
193 Keith Murgatroyd
194 Richard Saul Wurman
195 Christian Lang
196 Risa Glickman
197 Ivan Chermayeff
198 Armando & Maurizio Milani

AGENCY / AGENTUR / AGENCE – STUDIO:

192 Ideodis
193 Royle Murgatroyd Design Assoc.
195 Werbung Ciba-Geigy
197 Chermayeff & Geismar Assoc.
198 Armando & Maurizio Milani

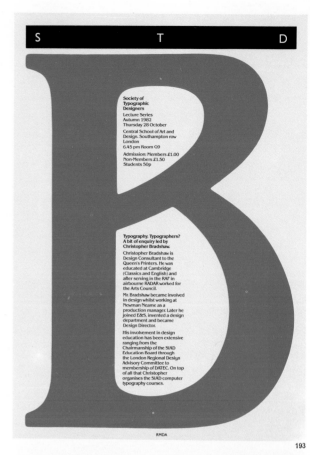

193

192

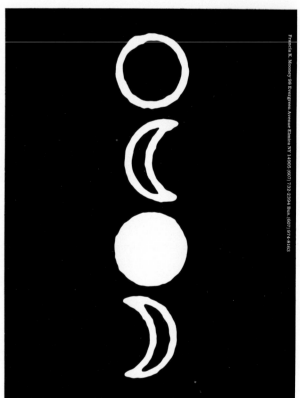

196

192 Invitation to an exhibition in Paris of cats' pictures. (FRA)
193 Invitation to a lecture series in London. (GBR)
194 Recto of a newsletter issued by the Office of Housing and Community Development in Philadelphia. Newspaper format, blue and black print. (USA)
195 From a brochure with illustrated interpretations of the causes and symptoms of depression, issued by *Ciba-Geigy* for the anti-depressive medicament *Ludiomil*. The subject of this page: dizziness. (SWI)
196 Self-promotion of an industrial/interior designer. White on black. (USA)
197 Advertising for Precision Inc., manufacturers of components, parts and tools for the aluminium smelter industry. Here the recto of three hinged aluminium sheets with red print. (USA)
198 Invitation to an exhibition of jewellery, silver and paintings at Dino Ceccuzzi's in Milan. Black and white with two grey shades. (ITA)

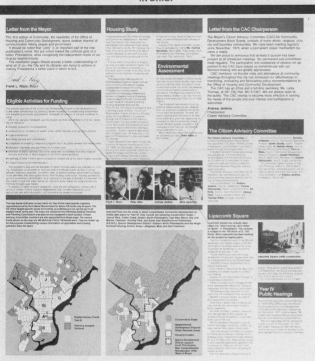

194

195

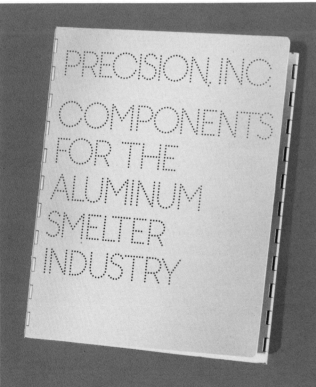

197

198

Booklets / Prospekte / Brochures

192 Einladung zu einer Ausstellung von Katzenbildern in Paris. (FRA)
193 Einladung zu Vorträgen der *Society of Typographic Designers*, London. (GBR)
194 Vorderseite eines Mitteilungsblattes des Amtes zur Förderung des sozialen Wohnungsbaus in Philadelphia. Zeitungsformat, blau und schwarz bedruckt. (USA)
195 Aus einer Broschüre mit zeichnerischen Interpretationen der Ursachen und Symptome der Depression, herausgegeben von *Ciba-Geigy* für das Antidepressivum *Ludiomil*. Das Thema dieser Seite: Schwindel. (SWI)
196 Eigenwerbung einer Industrie-Designerin. Weiss auf Schwarz. (USA)
197 Werbung eines Herstellers von Zulieferteilen und Werkzeugen für Aluminium-Schmelzhütten. Hier die Vorderseite von drei durch Scharniere miteinander verbundenen Aluminium-Blättern, die rot bedruckt sind. (USA)
198 Einladung zu einer Ausstellung von Schmuck, Silber und Bildern in einem Juwelier- und Uhrengeschäft. Schwarzweiss mit zwei Grautönen. (ITA)

192 Invitation à une exposition de portraits de chats à Paris. (FRA)
193 Invitation aux conférences de la *Society of Typographic Designers* de Londres. (GBR)
194 Page de titre d'un bulletin de l'Office du développement de logements sociaux de Philadelphie. Format journal, impression en noir et bleu. (USA)
195 Page consacrée à l'illustration du vertige, dans une brochure *Ciba-Geigy* expliquant les vertus de l'antidépresseur *Ludiomil* et remplie de dessins interprétant les causes et les symptômes de la dépression. (SWI)
196 Autopromotion d'une esthéticienne industrielle. Blanc sur noir. (USA)
197 Publicité pour Precision Inc., un fabricant d'accessoires et d'outillage pour fonderies d'aluminium. Dessus de trois feuillets d'aluminium reliés par charnières. Le texte est imprimé en rouge à même l'aluminium. (USA)
198 Invitation à une exposition de bijoux, d'argenterie et de tableaux dans une horlogerie-bijouterie. Noir et blanc, deux gris. (ITA)

89

199

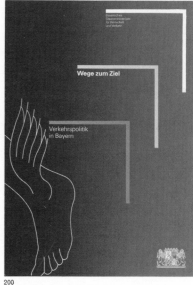

200

ARTIST / KÜNSTLER / ARTISTE:

199 Massimo Dolcini
200–202 Tomasz Ruminski
203, 204 Emanuel Schongut
206 Mario Bartolomeo
207 Ray Condon

DESIGNER / GESTALTER / MAQUETTISTE:

200–202 Barbara Miedaner/Rolf Müller
203, 204 Carol Carson
205 Jeffrey Mueller
206, 207 Ken Cato

ART DIRECTOR / DIRECTEUR ARTISTIQUE:

199 Paolo de Robertis
200–202 Rolf Müller
203, 204 Carol Carson
205 Deborah Sussmann
206, 207 Ken Cato

AGENCY / AGENTUR / AGENCE – STUDIO:

199 Fuorischema
200–202 Büro Rolf Müller
203, 204 Pushpin Lubalin Peckolick
205 Sussman/Prejza & Co. Inc.
206, 207 Cato Hibberd Design

Booklets / Prospekte / Brochures

199 Greetings card as self-promotion for IVECO. Illustration in actual size. Five colours. (ITA)
200–202 "Ways to a destination." Recto and double spreads of a brochure dealing with transport politics in Bavaria, issued by the Bavarian State Ministry for Economics and Transport. (GER)
203, 204 From a series of illustrations of various animal species. Direct mail sent by *Scholastic Magazine* to schools and other institutions of learning. (USA)
205 Recto of a brochure of the real estate company Cadillac Fairview/California Inc., Los Angeles. (USA)
206 Spread from a large-format brochure for the State Bank Centre in Melbourne. Shown here is the disposition of nineteen super-fast lifts that serve the centre's fourtythree storeys. (AUS)
207 Cover of a sleeve containing the loose folded sheets of a *Vega* "violet" calendar. (USA)

199 Grusskarte als Eigenwerbung für IVECO. Illustration in Originalgrösse. Fünffarbendruck. (ITA)
200–202 Vorderseite und Doppelseiten einer Broschüre über Verkehrspolitik in Bayern, herausgegeben vom Bayerischen Staatsministerium für Wirtschaft und Verkehr. (GER)
203, 204 Aus einer Serie von Illustrationen verschiedener Tierarten. An Schulen gerichtete Direktwerbung der pädagogischen Zeitschrift *Scholastic Magazine*. (USA)
205 Vorderseite einer Broschüre der Immobilienfirma *Cadillac Fairview* in Los Angeles. (USA)
206 Seite aus einer grossformatigen Broschüre für das State Bank Centre in Melbourne. Hier wird die Anordnung der 19 superschnellen Aufzüge gezeigt, welche die 43 Stockwerke bedienen. (AUS)
207 Vorderseite einer Hülle für lose, gefaltete Blätter eines *Vega*-Kalenders. (AUS)

199 Carte de vœux autopromotionnelle d'IVECO. Illustration grandeur nature. Cinque couleurs. (ITA)
200–202 Page de titre et doubles pages intérieures d'une brochure sur la politique des transports en Bavière publiée par le Ministère bavarois de l'Economie et des Transports. (GER)
203, 204 Série d'illustrations de différentes espèces animales. Publicité directe de la revue pédagogique *Scholastic Magazine* destinée aux écoles. (USA)
205 Page de titre d'une brochure de la société immobilière *Cadillac Fairview* de Los Angeles. (USA)
206 Page d'une brochure au grand format pour le State Bank Centre de Melbourne. On voit ici le plan des dix-neuf ascenseurs express qui desservent les quarante-trois étages du Centre. (AUS)
207 Couverture d'un étui contenant les feuillets mobiles pliés d'un calendrier *Vega* «violet». (AUS)

205

201

202

203

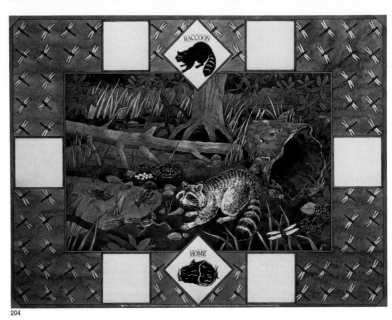

204

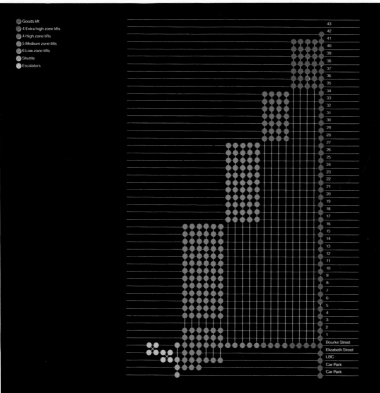

206

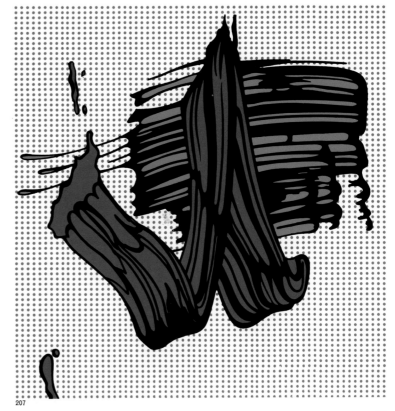

207

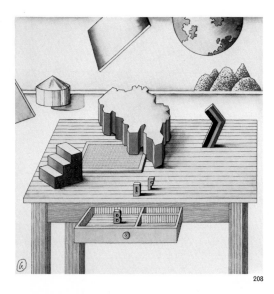

208

210

209

208–210, 215 Full-colour spreads from a brochure of the Belgian branch of *Beiersdorf*, one of which is in actual size. Fig. 208: dynamics within Belgium's framework; Fig. 209: dynamics without borders; Fig. 210: products serving health; Fig. 215: the cosmetics programme with the classic *Nivea* cream. (BEL)
211, 212 Design for the introductory pages of chapters and complete file for IBM instructions for use, inspired by Jasper Johns's numerical pictures. In each case, the number of the corresponding chapter is printed in colour. (USA)
213 Outside of a programme for an office-furniture trade fair whose theme is the humanization of high tech design for work environments. Silver, white and chamois shades with black. (CAN)
214 Double spread from a *Geigy* brochure for *Lopressor*, a medicament prescribed to combat high blood pressure. (USA)

208–210, 215 Farbseiten aus einer Broschüre der belgischen Filiale von *Beiersdorf*, eine davon in Originalgrösse. Abb. 208: Dynamik im Rahmen Belgiens; Abb. 209: Dynamik ohne Grenzen; Abb. 210: Produkte im Dienste der Gesundheit; Abb. 215: das kosmetische Programm mit der klassischen *Nivea*-Creme. (BEL)
211, 212 Von Jasper Johns' Zahlenbildern inspirierte Gestaltung der Kapiteldeckblätter und vollständiger Ordner für IBM-Gebrauchsanweisungen. Die Nummer des entsprechenden Kapitels ist jeweils farbig gedruckt. (USA)
213 Aussenseite eines Programms für eine Büromöbel-Messe, deren Thema die Harmonie zwischen fortschrittlichem Design und menschlichen Bedürfnissen ist. (CAN)
214 Doppelseite aus einer *Geigy*-Broschüre für das Medikament *Lopressor* gegen zu hohen Blutdruck. (USA)

208–210, 215 Pages couleurs d'une brochure de la succursale belge de *Beiersdorf*, dont l'une au format original. Fig. 208: une dynamique dans le cadre de la Belgique; fig. 209: une dynamique sans frontières; fig. 210: produits au service de la santé; fig. 215: programme cosmétique avec la crème *Nivéa* classique. (BEL)
211, 212 Manuels de l'usager IBM: classeur complet et feuillets en tête des chapitres, inspirés des «numbers» de Jasper Johns. Le numéro de chaque chapitre apparaît en couleur. (USA)
213 Côté extérieur d'un programme de foire du meuble de bureau axée sur l'harmonisation d'un design avancé et des besoins humains au sein de l'environnement du travail. Argent, blanc, chamois avec du noir. (CAN)
214 Double page d'une brochure *Geigy* consacré à l'hypotenseur *Lopressor*. (USA)

211

212

213

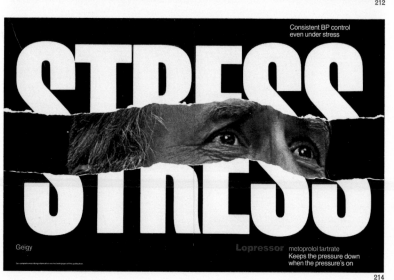

214

ARTIST / KÜNSTLER / ARTISTE:

208–210, 215 Josse Goffin

DESIGNER / GESTALTER / MAQUETTISTE:

208–210, 215 Gill Fiszmann
211, 212 Steff Geissbuhler/Jim Yestadt
213 Les Holloway/Stuart Ash
214 Bob Paganucci

ART DIRECTOR / DIRECTEUR ARTISTIQUE:

208–210, 215 Josse Goffin
211, 212 Steff Geissbuhler
213 Gottschalk & Ash International
214 Bob Paganucci

AGENCY / AGENTUR / AGENCE – STUDIO:

208–210, 215 Dechy Univas
211, 212 Chermayeff & Geismar Associates
213 Gottschalk & Ash International
214 Ciba-Geigy Advertising

215

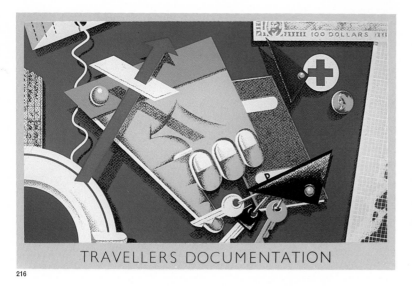

TRAVELLERS DOCUMENTATION

216

CAR FERRIES

217

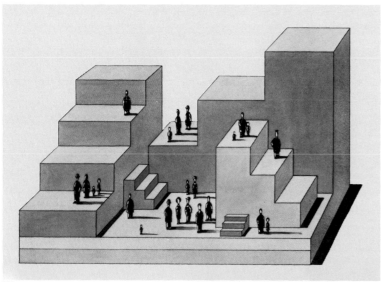

218

219

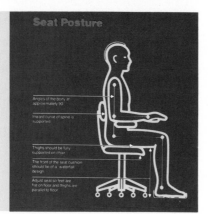

▶ Seating should provide sufficient clearance for the flesh of the thigh in order to prevent reduction of blood circulation. The front of the seat should be of a "waterfall" design.

▶ For tasks requiring frequent lateral movements, seats should swivel.

▶ Holding the same seated position for long periods of time causes fatigue. The diagram opposite illustrates the best posture for sitting for long periods.

▶ In order to achieve this posture it may be necessary to adjust the work station height. This is the reason that typewriters are placed on a lower work surface at secretarial work stations.

Seat Posture

220

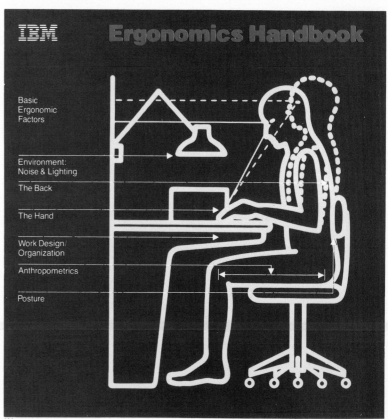

IBM **Ergonomics Handbook**

Basic Ergonomic Factors

Environment: Noise & Lighting

The Back

The Hand

Work Design/ Organization

Anthropometrics

Posture

221

Booklets / Prospekte
Brochures

ART DIRECTOR / DIRECTEUR ARTISTIQUE:

216, 217 David Hillman
218, 219 Gill Fiszmann
220, 221 Bruce Blackburn

AGENCY / AGENTUR / AGENCE – STUDIO:

216, 217 Pentagram
220, 221 Danne & Blackburn, Inc.

216, 217 Rectos of information folders taken from a comprehensive campaign for the Wakefield Fortune Travel company. (GBR)
218, 219 Colour illustrations from the brochure of an insurance company. Dealt with here are personnel insurance and company liability. (BEL)
220, 221 Double spread and cover of a handbook issued by IBM. Small format with uniform colour design in bright yellow and medium blue with red titles; here a yellow drawing on a blue ground. (USA)
222 Illustration in actual size for the recto of a prospectus containing information and advertising rates for the *Zeit* and *Zeitmagazin*. (GER)

216, 217 Vorderseiten von Dokumentationsmappen eines Reisebüros. In Abb. 216 geht es um die notwendigen Papiere und die empfohlene Ausrüstung, in Abb. 217 um Autofähren. Aus einer umfangreichen Kampagne. (GBR)
218, 219 Mehrfarbige Illustrationen aus der Broschüre einer Versicherungsgesellschaft. Hier geht es um Angestelltenversicherung und Unternehmens-Haftpflicht. (BEL)
220, 221 Doppelseite und Umschlag eines von IBM herausgegebenen, kleinformatigen Handbuchs über Ergonomie. Einheitliche Farbgestaltung in leuchtendem Gelb und Mittelblau, mit roten Titeln; hier gelbe Zeichnungen auf blauem Grund. (USA)
222 Illustration für die Vorderseite eines Prospekts mit Informationen und Anzeigentarifen der *Zeit* und des *Zeitmagazins*. (GER)

216, 217 Pages de titre de dossiers documentaires d'une agence de voyages. Fig. 216: les visas et l'équipement; fig. 217: les ferry-boats. Campagne de grande envergure. (GBR)
218, 219 Illustrations polychromes pour une brochure de compagnie d'assurance; on y examine les prestations suivantes: assurance en faveur du personnel; responsabilité civile de l'entreprise. (BEL)
220, 221 Double page et couverture d'un manuel d'ergonomie publié par IBM. Uniformisation des couleurs: jaune vif et bleu moyen, titres rouges; ici dessins jaunes sur fond bleu. (USA)
222 Illustration au format original pour le recto d'un dépliant donnant des reseignements sur les périodiques *Zeit* et *Zeitmagazin* et leurs tarifs d'annonces. (GER)

222

95

ARTIST / KÜNSTLER / ARTISTE:

223 Bob La Cava
224 Haruo Miyauchi
228 Josse Goffin

DESIGNER / GESTALTER / MAQUETTISTE:

223 Jon Craine
224 Haruo Miyauchi
225 Richard Tiney
226 Mervyn Kurlansky/Paul Vickers
227 Fred Troller

ART DIRECTOR / DIRECTEUR ARTISTIQUE:

223 Jon Craine
224 Haruo Miyauchi
225 Richard Tiney
226 Mervyn Kurlansky
227 Fred Troller
228 Josse Goffin

AGENCY / AGENTUR / AGENCE – STUDIO:

223 Compton Advertising
225 Cato Yasumura Behaeghel
226 Pentagram
227 Fred Troller Associates

223 Leporello prospectus announcing an IBM orientation seminar. Violet, red and yellow, and a white ground. (USA)
224 Example from a series of self-promotional cards issued by Haruo Miyauchi. (JPN)
225 Sales kit for company representatives, issued by IBM. (GBR)
226 Self-promotion by *Pentagram Design* in the form of a small brochure containing the rules for "Mora", a finger-game. The illustration is in black and white with a skin-coloured hand on grey, background in cream. (GBR)
227 Invitation issued by AIGA (American Institute of Graphic Arts) for a competition covering typographical design solutions using just type or hand lettering. Black with red on cream-coloured paper. (USA)
228 Cover in actual size for a small catalogue by the illustrator and painter Josse Goffin. (BEL)

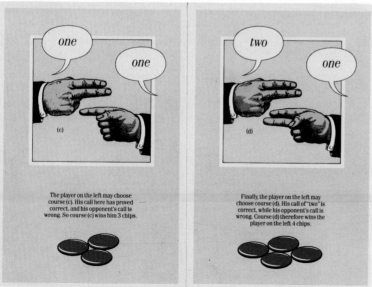

228

Booklets / Prospekte / Brochures

223 Leporello-Prospekt für die Ankündigung eines Computer-Fachseminars, veranstaltet von IBM. Violett, Rot und Gelb auf weissem Grund. (USA)
224 Beispiel aus einer Serie von Eigenwerbungskarten des Japaners Haruo Miyauchi. (JPN)
225 Mappe mit losen Informationsblättern als Verkaufsunterlagen für IBM-Vertreter. (GBR)
226 Eigenwerbung von *Pentagram Design*, in Form einer kleinen Broschüre mit den Spielregeln für «Mora», bei dem es um das Zeigen und gleichzeitige Erraten der vom Gegner gezeigten Anzahl von Fingern geht. Schwarzweiss-Illustration mit hautfarbener Hand auf Grau. (GBR)
227 Auseinandergefaltete Einladung des AIGA (American Institute of Graphic Arts) zur Einsendung von typographisch gelösten Design-Aufgaben für eine jurierte Ausstellung und ein entsprechendes Buch. Schwarz mit Rot auf crèmefarbenem Papier. (USA)
228 Umschlag für einen Werkkatalog des Illustrators und Kunstmalers Josse Goffin. (BEL)

223 Prospectus en accordéon annonçant un séminaire d'informatique spécialisé organisé par IBM. Violet, rouge, jaune sur fond blanc. (USA)
224 Exemple d'une série de cartes autopromotionnelles du Japonais Haruo Miyauchi. (JPN)
225 Dossier à feuillets mobiles pour la force de vente d'IBM. (GBR)
226 Autopromotion de *Pentagram Design* sous forme d'une petite brochure contenant les règles du jeu de «Mora», où il s'agit de montrer un certain nombre de doigts et de deviner le nombre de ceux que montre l'adversaire. Illustration noir-blanc, main chair sur gris, fond crème. (GBR)
227 Invitation dépliée de l'AIGA (American Institute of Graphic Arts) à soumettre des travaux de design réalisés en typo au jury d'une exposition, avec publication ultérieure en volume. Noir, avec du rouge, sur papier crème. (USA)
228 Couverture (format original) d'un petit catalogue du peintre-illustrateur Josse Goffin. (BEL)

229

ARTIST / KÜNSTLER / ARTISTE:

229 Yves Le Fevre
230, 231 Cook & Shanosky Assoc. Inc.
232 Kim Milnazik

DESIGNER / GESTALTER:

229 Pierre Victor Massin
230, 231 Roger Cook/Don Shanosky
232 William Milnazik
233 Tommy Landen/Marten Smith

ART DIRECTOR:

229 Pierre Victor Massin
230, 231 Roger Cook/Don Shanosky
232 William Milnazik
233 Tommy Landen

AGENCY / AGENTUR / AGENCE:

229 UCB
230, 231 Cook & Shanosky Associates, Inc.
232 Mueller & Wister Studio
233 Tommy Landen Reklamestudio AB

230

231

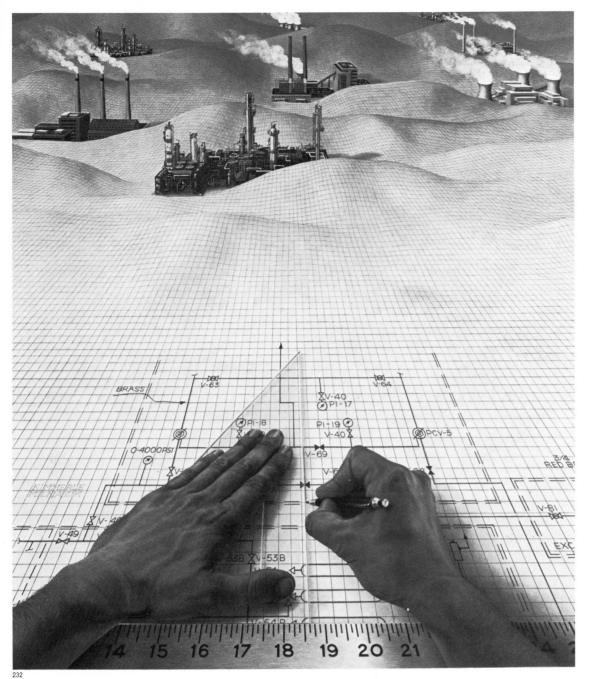

232

229 "Vertigo". Illustration from a brochure of the UCB pharmaceutical company. (BEL)
230, 231 Folder issued by an art college. In three colours. (USA)
232 Cover illustration for a brochure issued by *Air Products & Chemicals*. (USA)
233 Space promotion for an evening newspaper. All supper courses depicted in this illustration, here mortadella on toast and Emmentaler cheese, have been stamped true to life. (SWE)

229 «Schwindelgefühle.» Illustration aus einer Broschüre für den Pharmakonzern UCB. (BEL)
230, 231 Faltprospekt einer Kunstakademie. Die Illustration dient als Dankeschön für finanzielle Unterstützung und, umgedreht, als Bitte um weitere Beiträge. Dreifarbig. (USA)
232 Umschlagillustration für eine Broschüre von *Air Products & Chemicals*, Industrieanlagen für die Herstellung von Gas. (USA)
233 Inserentenwerbung einer Abendzeitung. Alle dargestellten Bestandteile des Abendbrots, hier Mortadella auf Toastbrot und Emmentaler, sind naturgetreu ausgestanzt. (SWE)

229 «Vertiges.» Illustration d'une brochure du groupe pharmaceutique UCB. (BEL)
230, 231 Dépliant d'une académie des beaux-arts. L'illustration sert de remerciement pour l'aide financière accordée; inversée, elle invite à continuer ce soutien. En trichromie. (USA)
232 Illustration de couverture d'une brochure d'*Air Products & Chemicals* (installations servant à équiper l'industrie du gaz). (USA)
233 Publicité-annonceurs d'un journal du soir. Découpe au format original des composants d'un repas du soir suédois type – mortadelle, toast, fromage d'Emmental. (SWE)

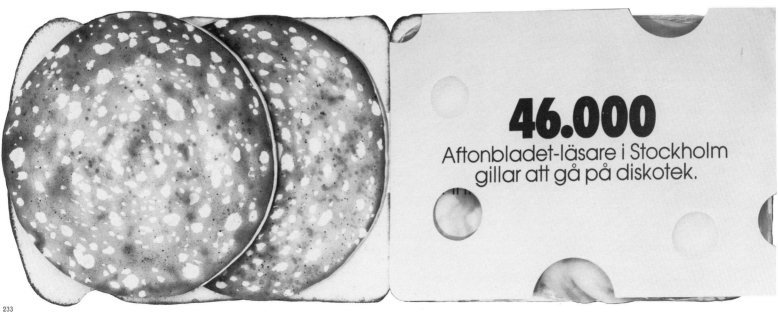

233

46.000
Aftonbladet-läsare i Stockholm gillar att gå på diskotek.

234 Cover of a brochure for the prevention of traffic accidents, issued by the Ministry of Transport in Cuba. In black and white. (CUB)
235, 236 "For this and for other cases, *Gothaer*, the quick service." Full-colour pastel drawings as cover illustrations of prospectuses in a series for the *Gothaer* accident-insurance company. The crocodile is to be found throughout. Fig. 235 with a red and yellow, Fig. 236 with a grass-green crocodile. (GER)
237 Reproduction of a collage on canvas as advertising for a publishing company. (USA)

234 Umschlag einer Broschüre zur Verhütung von Verkehrsunfällen, herausgegeben vom kubanischen Verkehrsministerium. In Schwarzweiss. (CUB)
235, 236 Farbstiftzeichnungen als Umschlagillustrationen von Prospekten aus einer Serie für die *Gothaer*-Unfallversicherung. Das Krokodil taucht in allen Zeichnungen und klein auch im Text auf. Abb. 235 mit rot-gelbem, Abb. 236 mit grasgrünem Krokodil. (GER)
237 Reproduktion einer Collage auf Leinwand als Werbung für einen Verlag. (USA)

234 Couverture d'une brochure de prévention des accidents publiée par le Ministère cubain des Transports. Noir et blanc. (CUB)
235, 236 Design aux crayons couleurs illustrant les couvertures de prospectus publiés en série par la compagnie d'assurances-accidents *Gothaer*. Le crocodile se retrouve dans tous les dessins, jaune rouge dans 235, vert prairie dans 236, et aussi miniaturisé dans le texte. (GER)
237 Reproduction d'un collage sur toile pour la publicité d'un éditeur. (USA)

Booklets / Prospekte / Brochures

ARTIST / KÜNSTLER / ARTISTE:

235, 236 Josse Goffin
237 Fred Otnes

DESIGNER / GESTALTER / MAQUETTISTE:

234 Félix Beltrán

ART DIRECTOR / DIRECTEUR ARTISTIQUE:

234 Félix Beltrán
235, 236 Robert Pütz
237 Margaret Kaeser

AGENCY / AGENTUR / AGENCE – STUDIO:

234 Félix Beltrán
235, 236 Robert Pütz GmbH & Co.
237 Kaeser Wilson Design Ltd.

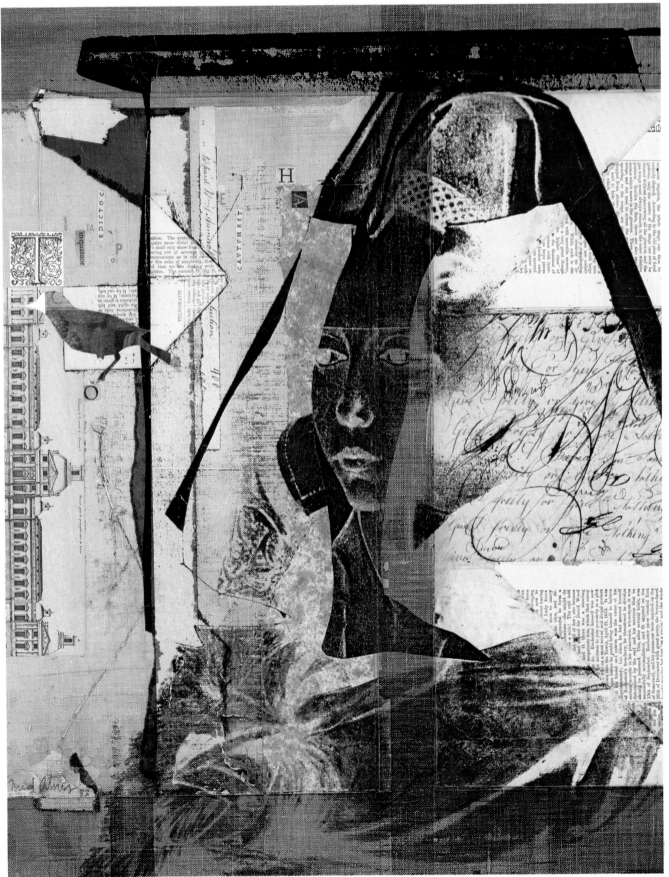

237

Booklets / Prospekte / Brochures

238

ARTIST / KÜNSTLER / ARTISTE:

238, 239 Bob Gadbois
241 Randall Hensley
242 Don Ivan Punchatz

DESIGNER / GESTALTER / MAQUETTISTE:

238, 239 David Bartels
240 G. Knecht
241 Randall Hensley
242 Steve D. Harding

ART DIRECTOR / DIRECTEUR ARTISTIQUE:

238, 239 David Bartels
240 Albert Ernst
241 Randall Hensley
242 Steve D. Harding

AGENCY / AGENTUR / AGENCE – STUDIO:

238, 239 Bartels & Company
240 Fabrikatelier am Wasser
241 Articulation
242 3 D/International

238, 239 Postal wrapper (brown on white) and cover (mainly in red and green) for a brochure of the Illinois Masonry Advisory Council. (USA)
240 From an advertising folder for the Karl Bösch AG engineering company. The folder's loose sheets depict variants of the letter B as well as illustrating the firm's specialised fields. Shown here are the cover (dark blue) with a cut-out B and one of the sheets. (SWI)
241 Double spread from a booklet documenting the growing relationship of the business and arts communities in Kansas City. (USA)
242 Cover of a booklet issued by the *Granada Corporation*, dealing with the quality and disposition of agrarian soil. (USA)

238, 239 Streifband für den Postversand (Braun auf Weiss) und Umschlag (vorwiegend rot und grün) der Broschüre einer Informationsstelle für die Verarbeitung von Ziegeln. (USA)
240 Aus einer Werbemappe für das Ingenieurbüro Karl Bösch AG, mit losen Einlageblättern, die mit Varianten des Buchstabens B illustriert sind und auf die Spezialgebiete der Firma hinweisen. Hier der Umschlag (dunkelblau) mit ausgestanztem B und eines der Blätter. (SWI)
241 Doppelseite aus einer Broschüre über die fruchtbare Beziehung zwischen Geschäftswelt und Kunst in Kansas City. (USA)
242 Die Beschaffenheit des Agrarbodens ist das Thema dieses Umschlags einer Broschüre für die *Granada Corporation*. (USA)

238, 239 Bande d'expédition postale et couverture (tons rouges et verts prédominants) de la brochure d'un centre d'information en briqueterie. (USA)
240 Dossier promotionnel du bureau de constructions Karl Bösch AG, à feuillets mobiles illustrés de variations sur la lettre B et présentant les prestations spécialisées du bureau. On voit ici la couverture (bleu foncé) avec son B découpé et l'un des feuillets. (SWI)
241 Double page d'une brochure qui met en évidence les relations fructueuses qu'entretiennent à Kansas City le milieu des affaires et celui des arts. (USA)
242 La composition du sol favorable à l'agriculture est le thème de la couverture de cette brochure de la *Granada Corporation*. (USA)

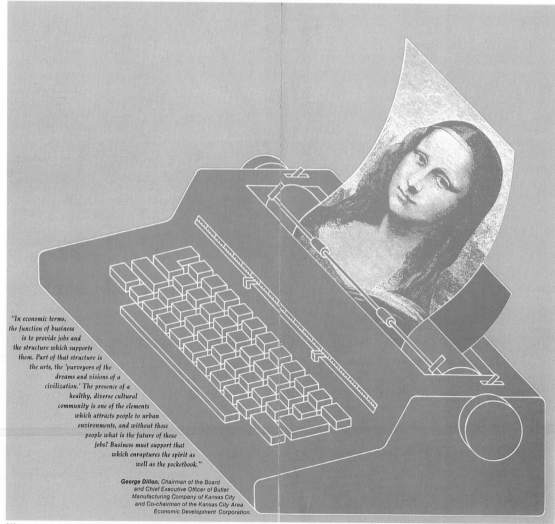

241

239

240

GRANADA CORPORATION

243

Rotgut whiskey declined to a price of $2 per bottle, down from its 1930 high of $3.00. It is hoped the level can return to the peak established when the florist Dion O'Banion was removed from competition. For civic leaders, actresses, brokers, sportswriters, lawyers, and others who demand high class booze no matter how bad the national economy may

be, we will continue to import products from Canada and the Caribbean, with a steady product flow insured by our company-owned-and-operated fleets off Long Island, Florida, and across the Great Lakes.

Various foods, pharmaceuticals, flowers and hardware have

suffered from labor unrest and broken-down distribution. Imported cheese is rotting on the Jersey docks; elaborate floral pieces, for funerals and other important business occasions, are wilting in shuttered greenhouses; explosives and stench bombs are backfiring; and counterfeit kosher hot dogs have been found to contain chitlins. Alcohol-related products we manufacture, such as paint, varnish, and fusel oil, are now being drunk in place of alcohol itself, reducing our total sales volume, as well as the number of customers.

244

Booklets / Prospekte / Brochures

ARTIST / KÜNSTLER / ARTISTE:

243 Jean Claverie
244 Dennis Zaminski/John Mattos/
Ed Jaciow/Norman Orr
246 Miro Malish

DESIGNER / GESTALTER / MAQUETTISTE:

244 Steven Jacobs
245 Yutaka Satoh
246 Louis Fishauf

ART DIRECTOR / DIRECTEUR ARTISTIQUE:

243 Brigitte Sidjanski
244 Steven Jacobs
245 Yutaka Satoh
246 Louis Fishauf

243 Cover of a small prospectus issued by the *Nord-Süd-Verlag* publishing concern, dealing with new publications of children's books in French. Mainly in beige and brown shades. (SWI)
244 Spread taken from a small, humorous booklet of *Simpson* paper company. (USA)
245 Recto of private printed matter for Toshio and Kimie Yasui. (JPN)
246 Full-page illustration from a brochure containing the programme of the Canadian Opera Company, here for the opera *Jenufa* by the Czech composer Leos Janacek. (CAN)

243 Umschlag eines kleinen Prospekts des *Nord-Süd-Verlags* über Kinderbuch-Neuerscheinungen in französischer Sprache. Vorwiegend in Beige- und Brauntönen. (SWI)
244 Seite aus einer kleinen, humorvollen Broschüre des Papierherstellers *Simpson*. (USA)
245 Vorderseite einer privaten Drucksache für Toshio und Kimie Yasui. (JPN)
246 Ganzseitige Illustration aus einer Broschüre mit dem Programm der Canadian Opera Company, hier zur Oper *Jenufa* von dem tschechischen Komponisten Leos Janacek. (CAN)

243 Couverture d'un petit prospectus des Editions *Nord-Süd-Verlag* annonçant des livres pour enfants en langue française. Tons beige et bruns prédominants. (SWI)
244 Page d'une petite brochure humoristique du papetier *Simpson*. (USA)
245 Recto d'un imprimé privé pour Toshio et Kimie Yasui. (JPN)
246 Illustration pleine page d'une brochure-programme de la Canadian Opera Company: opéra *Jenufa* du compositeur tchèque Leos Janacek. (CAN)

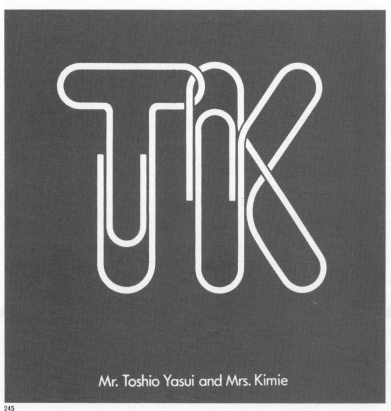

Mr. Toshio Yasui and Mrs. Kimie

245

Great Coats

In Which We Demonstrate How Coated Papers From Champion Capture the Imagination

247

Best Industries
A SPERRY UNIVAC UNIS
Success Story

SPERRY ✦ UNIVAC

248

Booklets / Prospekte / Brochures

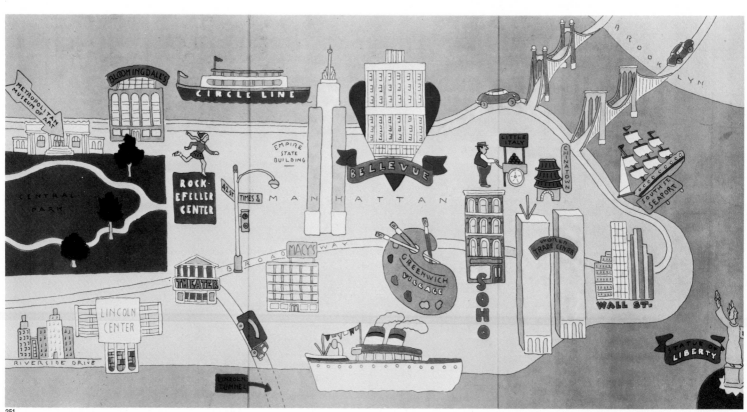

251

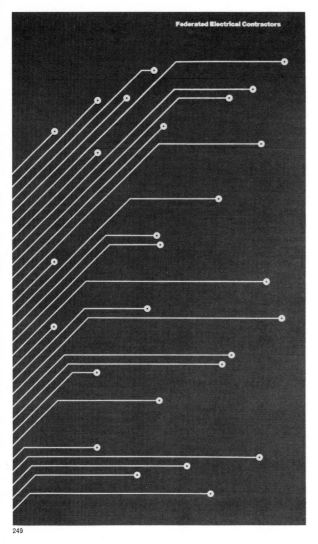

249

250

ARTIST / KÜNSTLER / ARTISTE:

247 Koren
251 Seymour Chwast
252 Design Center

DESIGNER / GESTALTER / MAQUETTISTE:

247 James Miho
248 Allan Hill
249 David Franek
250 Jon Craine
251 Toshiko Mori/Jeffrey Blonde
252 Design Center

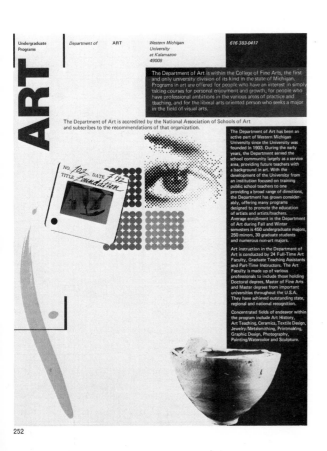

252

ART DIRECTOR / DIRECTEUR ARTISTIQUE:

247 James Miho
248 Allan Hill
249 David Franek
250 Jom Craine
251 Toshiko Mori/Jeffrey Blonde
252 Bruce Naftel

AGENCY / AGENTUR / AGENCE – STUDIO:

248 Mandala
249 Invisions, Ltd.
250 IBM
252 Design Center/Western Michigan University

247 Cover of a brochure of a paper manufacturer, showing how *Champion* coated papers are able to capture the imagination. (USA)
248 For a brochure highlighting *Sperry Univac* computer software systems. (USA)
249 Cover of a prospectus for Federated Electrical Contractors. (USA)
250 Inside spread of a leporello prospectus for the IBM Paris System, software solutions. (USA)
251 Folder with a well-known motif, for a consultancy company. (USA)
252 Cover of a folder about art undergraduate programmes of Western Michigan University. (USA)

247 Umschlag einer Broschüre des Papierherstellers *Champion*. Das englische Wort für Mantel – Thema der Illustrationen – bedeutet auch Beschichtungen, um die es hier geht. (USA)
248 Für eine Broschüre über Computer Software von *Sperry Univac*, mit einer Fallstudie. (USA)
249 Umschlag für einen Gemeinschaftsprospekt kooperierender Elektrizitätswerke. (USA)
250 Innenseite eines Leporello-Prospekts für ein IBM-Software-Programm für Einzelhändler. (USA)
251 Darstellung der unteren Hälfte Manhattans für den Faltprospekt eines Beratungsbüros. (USA)
252 Umschlag einer Mappe mit Informationen über das Studienprogramm einer Kunstschule. (USA)

247 Couverture d'une brochure du papetier *Champion*. Le mot anglais «coat» signifie à la fois manteau et revêtement de surface, d'où le jeu illustratif. (USA)
248 Pour une brochure de software de *Sperry Univac*, qui contient un exemple d'application. (USA)
249 Couverture du prospectus collectif d'une union de centrales électriques. (USA)
250 Page intérieure d'un prospectus en accordéon: programme software d'IBM pour détaillants. (USA)
251 Représentation du bas de Manhattan, pour le dépliant d'un bureau de consultants. (USA)
252 Couverture d'un dossier d'information sur le programme d'études de l'école d'art de la Western Michigan University. (USA)

253 Cover of a menu. In brown shades with a light green pear. (USA)
254–258 Double spreads with semi-circular index tabs and cover of a directory of specialities. Here the illustrations for an espresso offer, fruit drinks, milk-mix drinks and mixed drinks with a Vodka base. Green, ruby-red and black on cream-coloured stock. (USA)
259 Cover of a restaurant's wine list. Black and white on chamois. (USA)
260 Children's menu of a Mexican restaurant, in the shape of a "Mexican" robot that can be unfolded upwards. The menu-card is for children to take home. (USA)

253 Umschlag einer Speisekarte, in Brauntönen mit hellgrüner Birne. (USA)
254–258 Doppelseiten mit halbkreisförmig ausgestanztem Register und Umschlag einer Spezialitäten-karte. Hier die Illustrationen für das Espresso-Angebot, Fruchtgetränke, Milchmixgetränke und Wodka-Mixgetränke. Grün, Weinrot und Schwarz auf crèmefarbenem Papier. (USA)
259 Umschlag für eine Weinkarte des Restaurants «Sinclair's». Schwarzweiss auf Chamois. (USA)
260 Kinder-Speisekarte eines mexikanischen Restaurants, in Form eines «mexikanischen» Roboters, der sich nach oben aufklappen lässt. Die Karte ist zum Mitnehmen bestimmt. (USA)

253 Couverture d'un menu. Divers bruns, poire vert clair. (USA)
254–258 Doubles pages, index découpé en demi-cercle et couverture d'une carte des spécialités. On voit ici les illustrations pour l'espresso, les jus de fruits, les frappés, les cocktails à la vodka. Vert, bordeaux, noir sur papier crème. (USA)
259 Couverture d'une carte des vins d'un restaurant de la chaîne «Sinclair». Impression noir et blanc sur fond chamois. (USA)
260 Menu pour enfants d'un restaurant mexicain sous forme d'un robot «mexicain», qui s'ouvre vers le haut. Ce menu est laissé aux enfants en guise de souvenir. (USA)

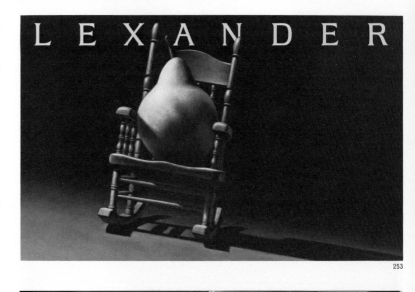

253

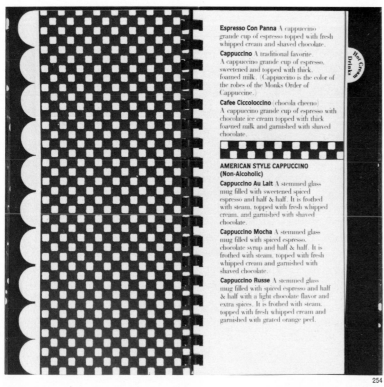

254

255

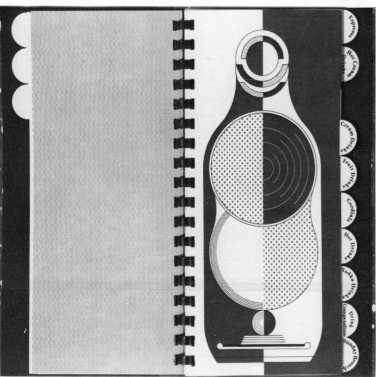

256

257

ARTIST / KÜNSTLER / ARTISTE:

253, 259 Greg MacNair
254–258 Luis Acevedo
260 Michael David Brown

DESIGNER / GESTALTER / MAQUETTISTE:

253 David Bartels
254–258 Woody Pirtle/Luis Acevedo
259 David Bartels/Michael Simpson
260 Michael David Brown/Kathleen Herring

ART DIRECTOR / DIRECTEUR ARTISTIQUE:

253, 259 David Bartels
254–258 Woody Pirtle/Luis Acevedo
260 Kathleen Wilmes Herring

AGENCY / AGENTUR / AGENCE – STUDIO:

253, 259 Bartels & Company
254–258 Pirtle Design
260 MDB Communications, Inc.

258

259

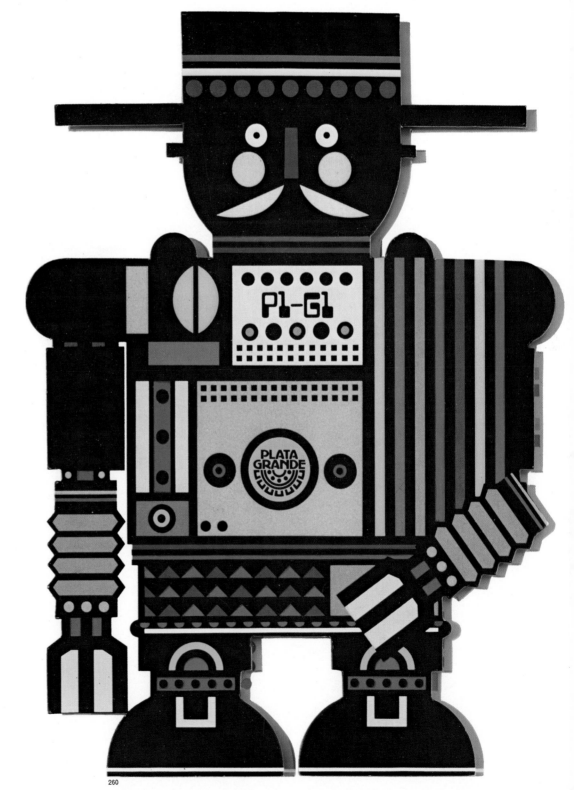

260

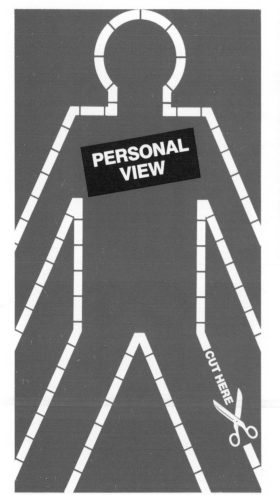

SCHAUSPIEL IM ZDF 1983
ELISABETH VON ENGLAND PEER
GYNT AGAMEMNON ARTURO
UI HEINRICH PENTHESILEA VON
KLEIST GALILEO DIE SPITZE DES
EISBERGES DIE NIRRERLÄNDER
MISTER Y IN AMSTERDAM LIVING
THEATRE EMPFINDLICHES GLEICH
GEWICHT DER WALZER
DER TOREROS WASSA
SCHELESNOWA DIE
SCHWÄRMER DER
NOBELPREIS SONNY
BOYS RUSSISCHES
DREIECK DER RAUB
DER SABINERINNEN

261

GESELLSCHAFTS
SPIELE

262

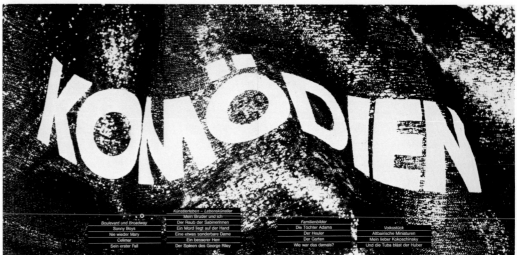

KOMÖDIEN

263

THEATER
WERKSTATT

264

PERSONAL
VIEW

CUT HERE

265

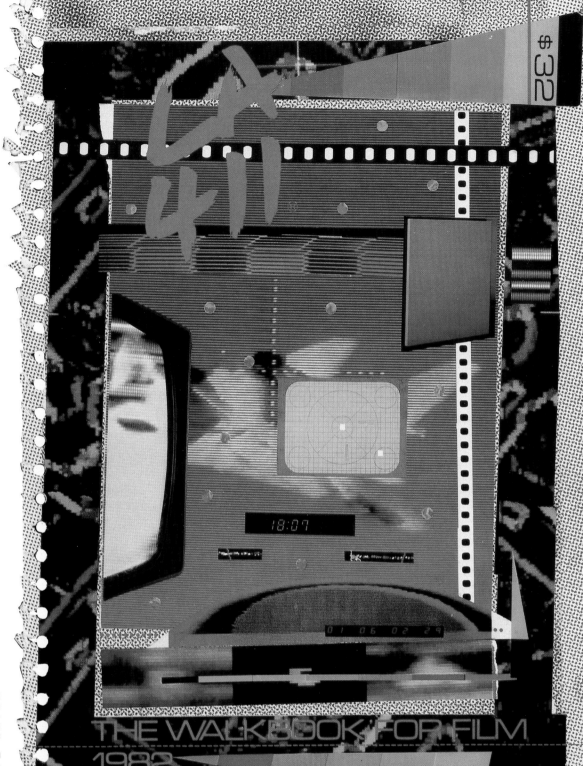

ARTIST / KÜNSTLER / ARTISTE:

266 Lou Beach

DESIGNER / GESTALTER / MAQUETTISTE:

261–264 Christof Gassner
265 Ian Pape
266 Lou Beach

ART DIRECTOR / DIRECTEUR ARTISTIQUE:

265 Peter Nutter
266 Lou Beach

AGENCY / AGENTUR / AGENCE – STUDIO:

265 Thumb Design Partnership
266 Lou Beach

261–264 Cover in black and white with gold, and introductory spreads in black and white, for the various chapters of a brochure containing the programme of German Television's Channel 2. Fig. 262: "Society Games"; Fig. 263: Comedies; Fig. 264: Theatre Workshop. (GER)
265 Recto of a leporello prospectus in red, blue and white, announcing a group exhibition entitled "Impressions on the Subject of People". (GBR)
266 Cover of a catalogue for a film festival held in Los Angeles. (USA)

261–264 Umschlag in Schwarzweiss mit Gold, und einleitende Doppelseiten in Schwarzweiss, zu den verschiedenen Kapiteln einer Broschüre mit dem Spielplan des ZDF. (GER)
265 Vorderseite eines Leporello-Prospekts in Rot, Blau und Weiss für die Ankündigung einer Gruppenausstellung unter dem Titel: «Impressionen zum Thema Mensch.» (GBR)
266 Umschlag eines Kataloges für ein Film-Festival in Los Angeles. (USA)

261–264 Couverture noir-blanc avec de l'or et pages doubles initiales noir et blanc de divers chapitres d'une brochure-programme de la 2e chaîne de télévision ouest-allemande. Fig. 262: «Jeux de société»; fig. 263: comédies; fig. 264: théâtre expérimental. (GER)
265 Recto d'un prospectus en accordéon en rouge, bleu, blanc, annonçant une exposition collective intitulée «Impressions au sujet de l'homme». (GBR)
266 Couverture du catalogue d'un festival du cinéma à Los Angeles. (USA)

266

Booklets / Prospekte / Brochures

Because each dark day of depression can feel like a month of misery...

267

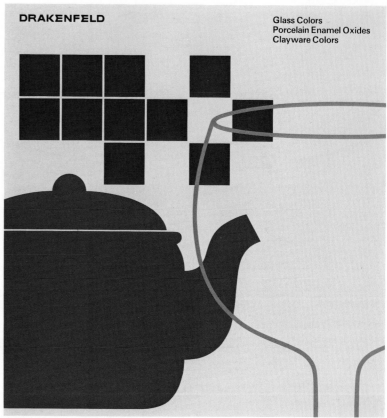

268

Amigdalitis

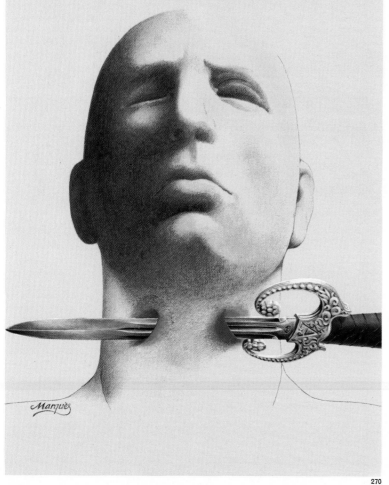

270

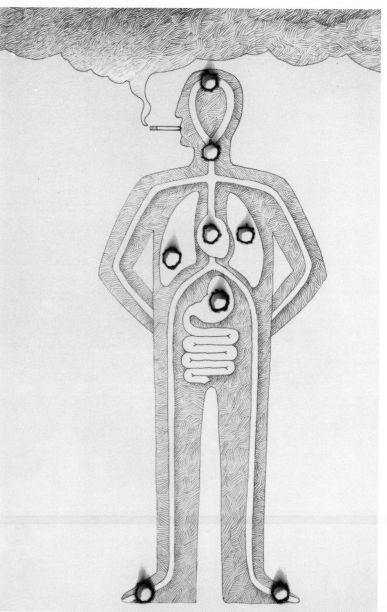

271

112

269

272

ARTIST / KÜNSTLER / ARTISTE:

267 Eugene Karlin
268 Paul Woods
269 Folon
270 Joan Marquès
271 Erich Maas
272 Christian Lang

DESIGNER / GESTALTER / MAQUETTISTE:

267 John Kashiwabara
268 Paul Woods
269 Charles Hively
270 Joan Marquès
271 Mihai Grosv
272 Christian Lang

ART DIRECTOR / DIRECTEUR ARTISTIQUE:

267 John Kashiwabara
268 Marcus Low
269 Charles Hively
270 Joan Marquès
271 Mihai Grosv
272 Christian Lang

AGENCY / AGENTUR / AGENCE – STUDIO:

267, 268 Ciba-Geigy
269 Metzdorf Advertising
270 Joan Marquès
271 Sudler & Hennessey
272 Werbung Ciba-Geigy

267 For a prospectus dealing with a *Ciba* anti-depressive. (USA)
268 Cover of a catalogue for *Ciba-Geigy* colours and oxides. In red, brown and blue on white. (USA)
269 Reproduction of a water-colour in blue and brown for a *Conoco* promotion folder. (USA)
270 Recto of a prospectus dealing with a *Uriach* medicament prescribed to combat tonsilitis. (SPA)
271 Cover of a brochure issued by Leo AG, for a chewing-gum which aids people in giving up smoking. (SWI)
272 Spread from a brochure issued by *Ciba-Geigy* for the *Ludiomil* anti-depressive medicament, in which the illustrator deals with the causes and symptoms of depression; here, in particular, with mechanization. (SWI)

267 Für einen Prospekt über ein Antidepressivum von *Ciba*. (USA)
268 Umschlag eines Katalogs für Glas-, Porzellan- und Tonfarben von *Ciba-Geigy*. In Rot, Braun und Blau auf Weiss. (USA)
269 Reproduktion eines Aquarells in Blau und Braun für eine Promotionsmappe des Chemieunternehmens *Conoco*. (USA)
270 Vorderseite eines Prospekts für ein Medikament gegen Mandelentzündungen. (SPA)
271 Umschlag einer Broschüre der Leo AG für ein Kaugummi zur Unterstützung der Raucherentwöhnung. (SWI)
272 Seite aus einer von *Ciba-Geigy* für das Antidepressivum *Ludiomil* herausgegebenen Broschüre, in der sich der Zeichner mit den Ursachen und Symptomen der Depression auseinandersetzt. Hier geht es um die Automatisierung. (SWI)

267 Pour un prospectus au sujet d'un antidépresseur *Ciba*. (USA)
268 Couverture d'un catalogue de couleurs et vernis pour verres, porcelaines et poteries fabriqués par *Ciba-Geigy*. Rouge, brun et bleu sur blanc. (USA)
269 Reproduction d'une aquarelle en bleu et brun pour un dossier promotionnel de la société de produits chimiques *Conoco*. (USA)
270 Recto d'un prospectus sur un remède des amygdalites. (SPA)
271 Couverture d'une brochure de Leo AG vantant les mérites d'un chewing-gum pour la désintoxication du fumeur. (SWI)
272 Page d'une brochure *Ciba-Geigy* sur l'antidépresseur *Ludiomil*, où le dessinateur retrace les causes et les symptômes de la dépression. Cette illustration traite du problème aigu de l'automatisation des tâches humaines. (SWI)

3

Newspaper Illustrations
Magazine Illustrations
Magazine Covers
Trade Magazines
House Organs
Corporate Publications
Annual Reports
Book Covers

Zeitungs-Illustrationen
Zeitschriften-Illustrationen
Zeitschriften-Umschläge
Fachzeitschriften
Hauszeitschriften
Firmenpublikationen
Jahresberichte
Buchumschläge

Illustrations de journaux
Illustrations de périodiques
Couvertures de périodiques
Revues professionnelles
Journaux d'entreprise
Publications d'entreprise
Rapports annuels
Couvertures de livres

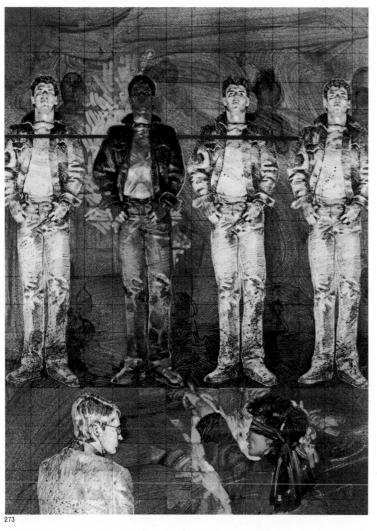

273

274

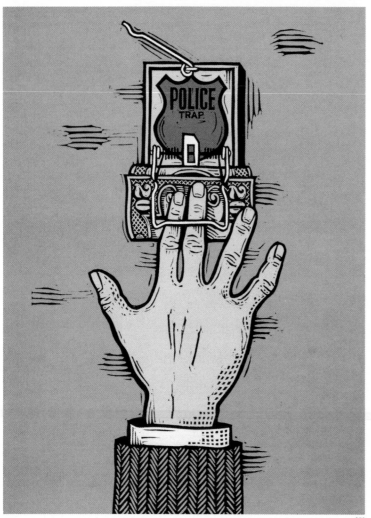

276

277

275

273, 274 Illustrations from *Science Magazine*. Fig. 273 refers to the inaccuracy of eyewitnesses; Fig. 274 to the origins of noises in our ears. (USA)
275 Illustration for a story published in *Saturday Night Magazine*. Green on a beige background. (CAN)
276 For an article about the undercover techniques of law enforcement agencies, taken from *Baltimore Magazine*. (USA)
277 Full-page illustration from *Chicago Magazine*. (USA)
278 Illustration for an article about how creativity can be encouraged in schoolchildren by means of visits by artists and writers. (USA)

273, 274 Illustrationen aus *Science Magazine*. Abb. 273: Über die Problematik des Erinnerungsvermögens von Augenzeugen. Abb. 273: «Der Klang der Stille», Artikel über die Ursachen von Geräuschen im Ohr. (USA)
275 Illustration zu einer Erzählung mit dem Titel «Der Chinesische Mantel», erschienen im *Saturday Night Magazine*. Grün auf beigem Hintergrund. (CAN)
276 Für einen Artikel über die Fragwürdigkeit von Polizeifallen, aus dem *Baltimore Magazine*. (USA)
277 «20 Fragen». Ganzseitige Illustration aus *Chicago Magazine*. (USA)
278 Illustration für einen Artikel über die Kreativität bei Kindern, gefördert durch Besuche von Künstlern und Schriftstellern in Schulen. (USA)

273, 274 Illustrations pour le *Science Magazine*. Fig. 273: le problème du témoignage des soi-disant témoins oculaires. Fig. 274: «Le son du silence», pour un article recherchant l'origine du son dans l'oreille. (USA)
275 Illustration pour un récit intitulé «Le manteau chinois», publié dans le *Saturday Night Magazine*. Vert sur fond beige. (CAN)
276 Pour un article jetant le doute sur la pratique policière de tendre des pièges aux suspects, paru dans le *Baltimore Magazine*. (USA)
277 «20 questions.» Illustration pleine page du *Chicago Magazine*. (USA)
278 Illustration d'un article sur la créativité des écoliers développée par la visite d'artistes et d'écrivains dans les écoles. (USA)

ARTIST / KÜNSTLER / ARTISTE:

273 Dean Williams
274 Brad Holland
275 Anita Kunz
276 David R. Street
277 Carl Kock
278 Wendell Minor

DESIGNER / GESTALTER / MAQUETTISTE:

273 Joyce L. Black
274 Rodney C. Williams
275 Bruce Ramsey
276 Paula Jaworski
277 Robert J. Post
278 Alice L. Degenhardt

ART DIRECTOR / DIRECTEUR ARTISTIQUE:

273, 274 Rodney C. Williams
275 Louis Fishauf
276 Paula Jaworski
277 Robert J. Post
278 Alice L. Degenhardt

AGENCY / AGENTUR / AGENCE – STUDIO:

276 Streetworks Studio
278 W. Minor Designs

PUBLISHER / VERLEGER / EDITEUR:

273, 274 AAAS
275 Saturday Night Magazine
276 Baltimore Magazine
277 WFMT, Inc.
278 Northwestern Mutual Life

·CHICKINOCEROS·

278

279

280

281

282

283

ARTIST / KÜNSTLER / ARTISTE:

279 Jill Karla Schwarz
280 Heinz Ita
281 Seymour Chwast
282 Michael Mathias Prechtl
283 Randall Enos

DESIGNER / GESTALTER / MAQUETTISTE:

281 Susan Rheinhardt

ART DIRECTOR / DIRECTEUR ARTISTIQUE:

280 Urs Husmann
281 Susan Rheinhardt
282 Günter Halden
283 Chris Austopcuck

AGENCY / AGENTUR / AGENCE – STUDIO:

281 Pushpin Lubalin Peckolick

PUBLISHER / VERLEGER / EDITEUR:

279 Inx, Inc.
280 Tages-Anzeiger AG
281 The Dial
282 Ringier Verlag
283 Rolling Stone

279 Black-and-white illustration for an article about Israel and the Lebanon that appeared in various newspapers. (USA)
280 Portrait of the writer Hermann Burger, taken from the report "Swiss authors under forty years of age" which appeared in the *Tages Anzeiger Magazin*. (SWI)
281 Illustration for an article on "Soap Operas", taken from *Dial Magazine*. (USA)
282 Illustration from Horst Stern's magazine *natur*, with the subtitle reading: "Mephisto or the 'quintessence' of the economic alchemy—the moneying of the world." (GER)
283 A caricature of the Rolling Stones pop group which appeared in *Rolling Stone* magazine under the title "Emotional rescue." (USA)

279 Illustration in Schwarzweiss zu einem Artikel mit dem Thema «Israel und Libanon», erschienen in verschiedenen Zeitungen. (USA)
280 Porträt des Schriftstellers Hermann Burger, aus dem Bericht «Schweizer Schriftsteller unter vierzig», erschienen im *Tages Anzeiger Magazin*. (SWI)
281 Illustration für einen Artikel über sentimentale Fernsehfilme, aus *Dial Magazine*. (USA)
282 Illustration aus Horst Sterns Umweltmagazin *natur*, mit dem Untertitel «Mephisto oder die ‹Quintessenz› der Wirtschafts-Alchemie – die Vergeldung der Welt». (GER)
283 «Emotionale Rettung.» Eine Karikatur der Gruppe Rolling Stones, die in der Zeitschrift *Rolling Stone* veröffentlicht wurde. (USA)

279 Illustration en noir et blanc pour un article intitulé «Israël et le Liban» publié simultanément dans plusieurs journaux. (USA)
280 Portrait de l'écrivain Hermann Burger illustrant le rapport sur «Les écrivains suisses de moins de 40 ans» publié dans le *Tages Anzeiger Magazin*. (SWI)
281 Illustration pour un article sur les films TV sentimentaux, dans *Dial Magazine*. (USA)
282 Illustration pour le magazine écologique *natur* de Horst Stern. La légende dit: «Méphist ou la ‹quintessence› de l'alchimie économique – la monétarisation de la planète.» (GER)
283 «Sauvetage émotionnel.» Caricature du groupe The Rolling Stones publiée dans le magazine *Rolling Stone*. (USA)

284

287

288

285

286

284 Cover illustration for *Temash* magazine. (IRN)
285 Illustration for the cover spread of *Liberty*, a magazine devoted to religious freedom. (USA)
286 Full-page illustration of the cover for *Amtn* magazine, the journal of all art, craft, engineering and drafting supplies. (USA)
287, 288 Complete double spread and illustration for an article that appeared in *Channels* magazine, concerning a new idea for sports fans to watch their favourite teams on pay television. (USA)
289 Illustration for an article about "Moonlighting", the making of illegal liquor in the USA. Taken from *Esquire Magazine*. (USA)

284 Umschlagillustration für das Magazin *Temash*. In Rottönen. (IRN)
285 Illustration der Umschlagseite von *Liberty*, ein Magazin für religiöse Freiheit. (USA)
286 Ganzseitige Illustration des Umschlages für die Zeitschrift *Amtn*, mit Informationen über Mal- und Zeichenbedarfsartikel. (USA)
287, 288 Vollständige Doppelseite und Illustration für einen Artikel über einen privaten Sportfernsehsender, der hohe Gebühren verlangt, erschienen in der Zeitschrift *Channels*. (USA)
289 Illustration zu einem Artikel über die illegale Herstellung von Alkohol in Amerika. Aus der Zeitschrift *Esquire*. (USA)

284 Illustration de couverture pour le magazine *Temash*. (IRN)
285 Illustration de couverture de *Liberty*, magazine qui défend la liberté religieuse. (USA)
286 Illustration de couverture pleine page du magazine *Amtn*: accessoires dessin, peinture. (USA)
287, 288 Double page complète et illustration d'un article du magazine *Channels* sur une station de télévision sportive privée dont les taxes sont jugées trop élevées. (USA)
289 Illustration pour un article sur les distilleries clandestines aux Etats-Unis paru dans *Esquire*. (USA)

289

290

291

290, 291 Introductory page and double spread for short stories published in *Grazia* magazine. Fig. 290: "Destiny in his hands", greyish-black and yellow on wrapping paper; Fig. 291: "The First Ball", magenta, blue and black on wrapping paper. (ITA)
292, 293 Complete double spread and illustration for a series about "The natural upbringing", which appeared in *Eltern* (Parents) magazine. (GER)
294 "Family reunion." Illustration for a work of fiction published in *Saturday Night Magazine*. (CAN)

290, 291 Einleitende Seite und Doppelseite für Kurzgeschichten in der Zeitschrift *Grazia*. Abb. 290: «Das Schicksal in seinen Händen»; Grauschwarz und Gelb auf Packpapier; Abb. 291: «Der erste Ball»; Magenta, Blau, Grün und Schwarz auf Packpapier. (ITA)
292, 293 Vollständige Doppelseite und Illustration zu einer Serie über «Die natürliche Erziehung» in der Zeitschrift *Eltern*. Die Illustration stellt das Verhalten des Kindes durch einen Vogel dar, und das Kind verkörpert den Erwachsenen. In zarten Farben. (GER)
294 «Familientreffen.» Illustration für eine Erzählung im *Saturday Night Magazine*. (CAN)

290, 291 Page initiale et double page de nouvelles parues dans le magazine *Grazia*. Noir, gris, jaune (fig. 290) resp. magenta, bleu, vert, noir (fig. 291) sur papier d'emballage. (ITA)
292, 293 Double page complète et illustration d'une série sur «l'éducation naturelle» publiée dans le magazine *Eltern*. Le comportement enfantin y figure sous forme d'oiseau, celui de l'adulte sous forme d'enfant. Couleurs tendres. (GER)
294 «Réunion de famille.» Illustration d'un récit paru dans le *Saturday Night Magazine*. (CAN)

292

293

294

ARTIST / KÜNSTLER / ARTISTE:

290, 291 Adelchi Galloni
292, 293 Edda Köchl
294 Gilbert Stone

DESIGNER / GESTALTER / MAQUETTISTE:

292, 293 Susanne Hoffmann
294 Bruce Ramsey

ART DIRECTOR / DIRECTEUR ARTISTIQUE:

290, 291 Adelchi Galloni
292, 293 Noelle Thieux
294 Derek Ungless

PUBLISHER / VERLEGER / EDITEUR:

290, 291 Arnoldo Mondadori
292, 293 Gruner & Jahr
294 Saturday Night Magazine

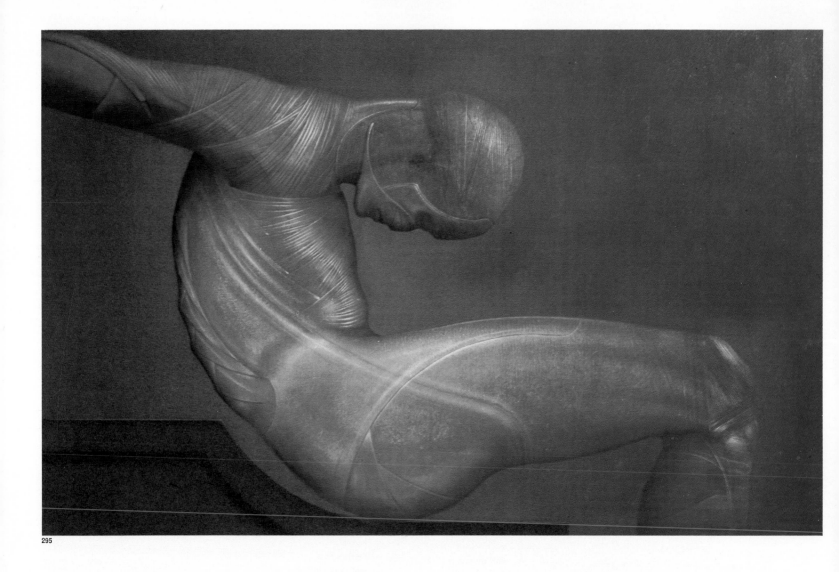

295

Magazine Illustrations
Zeitschriften-Illustrationen
Illustrations de périodiques

295 Double-spread illustration for the story "Augenblick", published in *Omni* magazine. (USA)
296 Full-colour illustration for the poem "Moving Day" which appeared in *Saturday Night Magazine*. (CAN)
297 Illustration for a far-out feature in *Omni* magazine. (USA)
298 Illustration for a feature entitled "In Praise of Women's Bodies", taken from the "Feminist Notes" section of *Ms* magazine. In soft shades of pink and light yellow. (USA)
299 Portrait of The Police rock group in *Rolling Stone*. (USA)

295 Doppelseitige Illustration für die Erzählung «Augenblick», aus der Zeitschrift *Omni*. (USA)
296 Mehrfarbige Illustration in der Zeitschrift *Saturday Night* für das Gedicht «Umzugstag». (CAN)
297 Illustration für eine Erzählung in der Zeitschrift *Omni*. (USA)
298 Illustration für einen Beitrag über die Prüderie von Frauen beim gemeinsamen Umkleiden, aus der Zeitschrift *Ms*. In zartem Rosa und Hellgelb. (USA)
299 Porträt der Rockgruppe The Police im *Rolling Stone*. (USA)

295 Illustration double page pour la nouvelle «Augenblick» publiée dans le magazine *Omni*. (USA)
296 Illustration polychrome accompagnant dans le magazine *Saturday Night* le poème «Jour de déménagement». (CAN)
297 Illustration d'un récit paru dans le magazine *Omni*. (USA)
298 «Eloge du corps féminin.» Illustration pour un article sur la fausse pudeur des femmes quand elles se déshabillent. Magazine *Ms*. Rose délicat et jaune clair. (USA)
299 Portrait du groupe rock The Police, dans *Rolling Stone*. (USA)

296

297

298

299

300

301

302

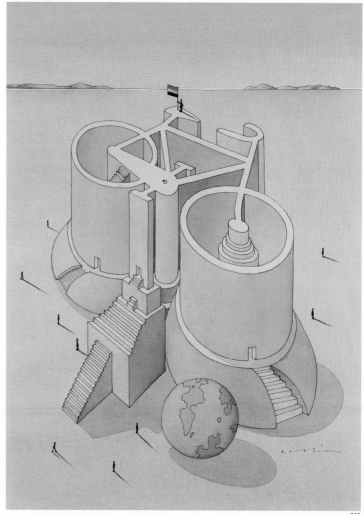

303

304

300 Illustration for the short story "The Blue Jacket", published in *Carina* magazine. In shades of blue and green. (GER)
301 Illustration for the story "The last Beauty of the South", published in *Freundin* magazine. (GER)
302 "The mirror exposes its secret." Illustration for a short story that appeared in *Carina* magazine. (GER)
303 Cover illustration for *Trans Atlantik* magazine. (GER)
304 Illustration for a *Time* article dealing with "what it means to be a woman". (USA)
305 "The Dead Woman of Beverly Hills." Illustration for a short story published in *Die Bunte* magazine. (GER)

300 Illustration für die Kurzgeschichte «Die blaue Jacke» aus der Zeitschrift *Carina*. In Blau- und Grüntönen. (GER)
301 Illustration für die Geschichte «Die letzte Schöne des Südens», veröffentlicht in der Zeitschrift *Freundin*. (GER)
302 «Der Spiegel gibt sein Geheimnis preis.» Illustration für eine Kurzgeschichte in der Zeitschrift *Carina*. (GER)
303 Umschlagillustration für die Zeitschrift *TransAtlantik*. (GER)
304 Illustration zu einem *Time*-Artikel über die Emanzipation: «Wie man sich als Frau fühlt.» (USA)
305 «Die Tote von Beverly Hills.» Illustration für eine Kurzgeschichte in der Zeitschrift *Die Bunte*. (GER)

300 Illustration pour la nouvelle «Le Veston bleu» publiée dans le magazine *Carina*. Divers bleus et verts. (GER)
301 Illustration pour le récit intitulé «La Dernière Beauté du Sud», paru dans le magazine *Freundin*. (GER)
302 «Le Miroir révèle son secret.» Illustration accompagnant une nouvelle parue dans le magazine *Carina*. (GER)
303 Illustration de couverture du magazine *Trans Atlantik*. (GER)
304 «Ce qu'on ressent en étant femme.» Illustration d'un article du magazine *Time* sur l'émancipation des femmes. (USA)
305 «La Morte de Beverly Hills.» Illustration pour une nouvelle publiée dans le magazine *Die Bunte*. (GER)

305

127

THE CHEAP AGONY OF UGLY GEORGE

personality

By D. KEITH MANO

*something inside him calls. his answer is to lure women
into hallways and convince them to strip for his camera*

306

sports **By Lee Green**

The Masochists' Marathon

*when you're facing
100 miles of
torture across
hellish terrain in
impossible
weather, winning
isn't the issue.
the question is,
will you survive?*

307

306–308 Double spreads taken from *Playboy* magazine. Fig. 306: Illustration in subdued shades for a story about the cheapness of a man who lures women into hallways to convince them to strip for his video camera; Fig. 307: Introductory double spread for an article about hundred-mile runs in extreme conditions, survival becoming the issue, not winning; Fig. 308: Sand-coloured and light-blue illustration for an essay about how managers could achieve near perfection if only they could eliminate human failure. (USA)
309, 310 Full-page illustrations from *Playboy* magazine. Fig. 309: in soft blue shades with violet, the body in white, floor and hair in black, for the story "Daphnes Melody"; Fig. 310: for a feature on the actor Peter O'Toole. In black-and-white. (USA)

306–308 Doppelseiten aus dem Magazin *Playboy*. Abb. 306: Illustration in düsteren Farben, für eine Geschichte über einen Unhold, der Frauen zwingt, sich vor seiner Video-Kamera auszuziehen; Abb. 307: Einleitende Doppelseite für einen Artikel über Marathon-Läufe unter extremen Bedingungen; Abb. 308: Illustration sandfarben und hellblau, für einen Essay über Management-Fragen mit dem Titel «Warum Dinge schiefgehen». (USA)
309, 310 Ganzseitige Illustrationen aus *Playboy*. Abb. 309: in sanften Blautönen mit Violett, der Körper in Weiss, Boden und Haare in Schwarz, für eine Erzählung mit dem Titel «Daphnes Melodie»; Abb. 310: zu einem Beitrag über «Das Doppelleben von Peter O'Toole». In Schwarzweiss. (USA)

306–308 Pages doubles du magazine *Playboy*. Fig. 306: Illustration aux couleurs sombres pour l'histoire d'un obsédé qui oblige les femmes à se déshabiller devant sa video caméra; fig. 307: Double page initiale d'un article sur les marathons organisés dans des conditions extrêmement dures; fig. 308: illustration sable et bleu clair pour un essai sur la gestion d'entreprises, «Pourquoi les choses ne fonctionnent pas». (USA)
309, 310 Illustrations pleine page du magazine *Playboy*. Fig. 309: aux tons bleus délicats, avec du violet, corps blanc, sol et chevelure noirs, pour un récit intitulé «La Mélodie de Daphné»; fig. 310: pour un article sur Peter O'Toole. Illustration noir-blanc. (USA)

america's managers could achieve near perfection—if only they could learn to cope with human mistakes

WHY THINGS DON'T WORK

essay
By JULES SIEGEL

308

309

310

311

Magazine Illustrations

312

313

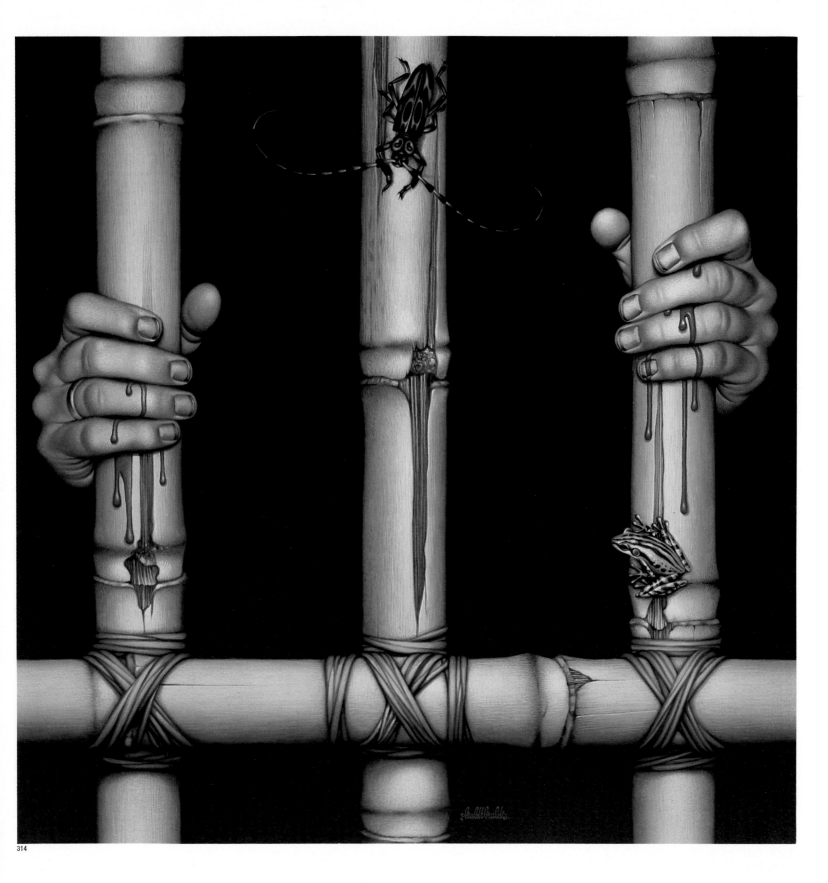

314

ARTIST / KÜNSTLER / ARTISTE:

311 Vincent Difate
312 Ralle
313 Etienne Sandorfi
314 Braldt Bralds

DESIGNER / GESTALTER / MAQUETTISTE:

311, 314 Claire Victor
312 Sheila A. Lynn
313 Paul Slutsky

ART DIRECTOR / DIRECTEUR ARTISTIQUE:

311, 314 Joe Brooks
312, 313 Richard Bleiweiss

PUBLISHER / VERLEGER / EDITEUR:

311–314 Penthouse International

311–314 Double spread and illustrations from *Penthouse* magazine. Fig. 311: for an article about the hopes of opening up the hitherto untapped resources of the outer space; Fig. 312: Reproduction of a picture for a science-fiction story; Fig. 313: Full-colour illustration for an article about the misuse of drugs and electroshock therapy; Fig. 314: for a story about a man who spent eleven years as a prisoner of war in Vietnam. (USA)

311–314 Doppelseite und Illustrationen aus dem Magazin *Penthouse*. Abb. 311: für einen Artikel mit dem Titel «Goldrausch zu den Sternen», in dem es um die Hoffnungen auf die unausgeschöpften Schätze des Weltalls geht; Abb. 312: Reproduktion eines Bildes für eine Science-Fiction-Geschichte; Abb. 313: mehrfarbige Illustration für einen Artikel über den Missbrauch von Drogen- und Elektroschocktherapien; Abb. 314: für eine Geschichte über einen Kriegsgefangenen in Vietnam. (USA)

311–314 Double page et illustrations du magazine *Penthouse*. Fig. 311: pour un article intitulé «La Ruée d'or vers les étoiles», exposant les espoirs placés dans les ressources inexploitées de l'espace; fig. 312: reproduction d'un tableau illustrant un récit de science-fiction; fig. 313: illustration polychrome pour un article sur les traitements abusifs par drogues psychotropes et électrochocs; fig. 314: pour l'histoire d'un prisonnier de guerre des Vietnamiens. (USA)

315

**Magazine Illustrations
Zeitschriften-Illustrationen
Illustrations de périodiques**

315 Illustration for a short story that appeared in *Penthouse* magazine, about a man on the verge of inheriting his father's newspaper empire and his long-suffering mistress. (USA)
316, 317 Complete introductory double spread and full-page illustration in actual size for a short story published in *Penthouse*. (USA)

315 Illustration für eine Erzählung im *Penthouse*, in der es um die Hinterlassenschaft eines mächtigen Mannes an seinen Sohn geht: ein Zeitungs-Imperium und eine frustrierte Geliebte. (USA)
316, 317 Vollständige, einleitende Doppelseite und ganzseitige Illustration in Originalgrösse zu einer Kurzgeschichte mit dem Titel «Doktor der Liebe», aus *Penthouse*. (USA)

315 Pour une nouvelle publiée dans *Penthouse* où un homme riche et puissant lègue à son fils son empire de la presse en même temps que sa sémillante, mais fort frustrée maîtresse. (USA)
316, 317 Double page initiale complète et illustration pleine page au format original d'une nouvelle intitulée «Docteur d'amour», dans *Penthouse*. (USA)

ARTIST / KÜNSTLER / ARTISTE:
315–317 Paul Wunderlich

DESIGNER / GESTALTER:
315 Sheila A. Lynn
316, 317 Richard Bleiweiss

ART DIRECTOR:
315–317 Richard Bleiweiss

PUBLISHER / VERLEGER:
315–317 Penthouse International

316

ARTIST / KÜNSTLER / ARTISTE:

318 Michel Henricot
319 Helene Guetary
320 H. R. Giger

DESIGNER / GESTALTER / MAQUETTISTE:

318, 319 Claire Victor
320 Sheila A. Lynn

ART DIRECTOR / DIRECTEUR ARTISTIQUE:

318, 319 Joe Brooks
320 Richard Bleiweiss

PUBLISHER / VERLEGER / EDITEUR:

318–320 Penthouse International

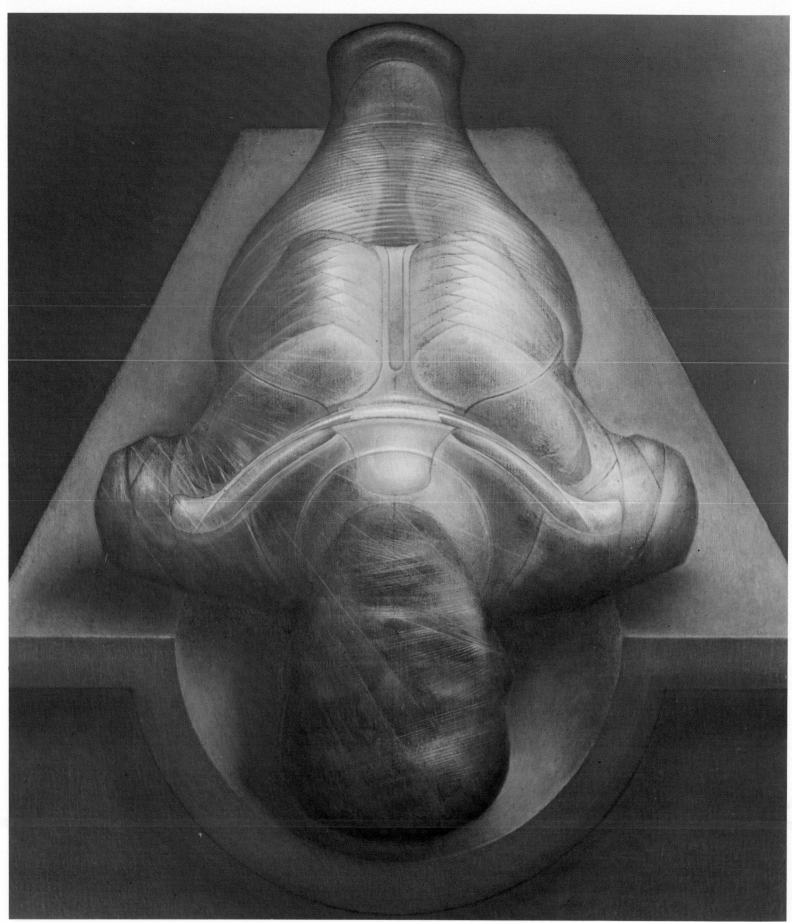

318

Magazine Illustrations / Zeitschriften-Illustrationen
Illustrations de périodiques

318 Illustration for a double spread opening a short story published in *Penthouse*. (USA)
319 Double-spread illustration in pastel shades as introduction to a story in *Penthouse* magazine about a gymnast who has mastered the most difficult of feats after months of intense training and who now basks in his own success. (USA)
320 Illustration for a short story published in *Penthouse*. In dark shades. (USA)

318 Illustration für die einleitende Doppelseite zu einer Kurzgeschichte mit dem Titel «Der Mann, der das ewige Leben erfand», veröffentlicht im Magazin *Penthouse*. (USA)
319 Doppelseitige Illustration in Pastellfarben als Einleitung zu einer Erzählung im *Penthouse*. Thema der Geschichte ist ein Sportstudent, der grosse gymnastische Leistungen erzielt hat und sich nun in seinem Erfolg sonnt. (USA)
320 Illustration zu einer Kurzgeschichte im Magazin *Penthouse*, in dunklen Farben. (USA)

318 Illustration pour la double page initiale d'une nouvelle intitulée «L'Homme qui inventa la vie éternelle», publiée dans le magazine *Penthouse*. (USA)
319 Illustration double page aux teintes pastel en tête d'un récit paru dans *Penthouse*. Il y est question d'un étudiant des sports qui a décroché la timbale dans des épreuves de gymnastique et se dore au soleil de sa gloire toute récente. (USA)
320 Illustration aux couleurs sombres pour une nouvelle parue dans le magazine *Penthouse*. (USA)

319

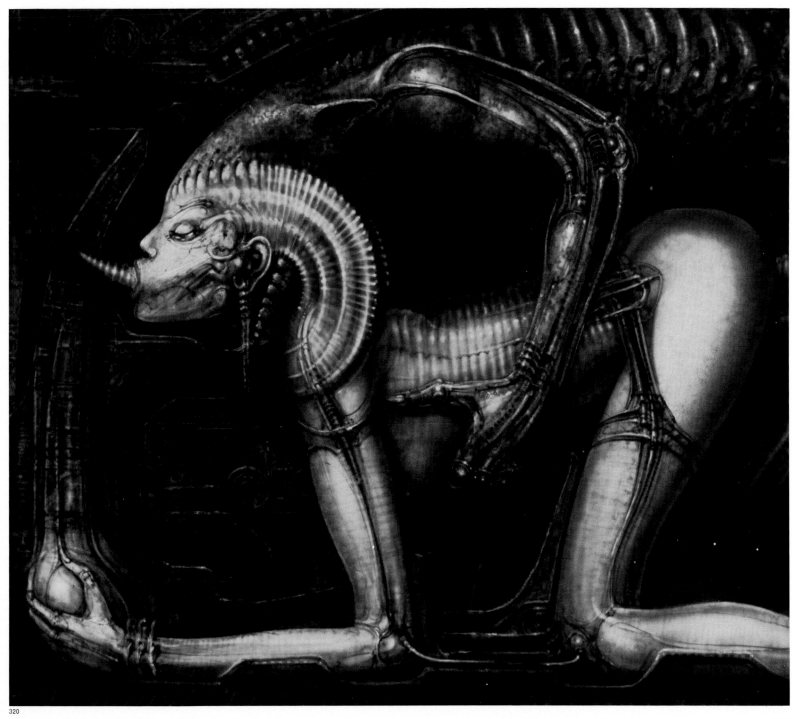

320

321

322

323

324

Magazine Illustrations
Zeitschriften-Illustrationen
Illustrations de périodiques

321–326 Examples of full-page illustrations and the complete cover (Fig. 325) of an issue of the humorous weekly magazine *Nebelspalter*, dealing with the twelve signs of the zodiac. On each page authors concentrate on their particular astrological sign, all the illustrations being by the Spanish artist Puig Rosado. With the exception of the portrayal of "Virgo", which is mainly in bluish shades of green and grey (Fig. 324), the illustrations shown here are all in warm brown, yellow, red and green shades. (SWI)

321–326 Beispiele der ganzseitigen Illustrationen und der vollständige Umschlag (Abb. 325) einer Ausgabe der humoristischen Wochenzeitschrift *Nebelspalter*, in der es um die zwölf Tierkreiszeichen geht. Auf je einer Seite setzen sich Autoren mit ihrem eigenen Sternbild auseinander; die Illustrationen stammen alle von dem spanischen Künstler Puig Rosado. Mit Ausnahme der vorwiegend in bläulichen Grün- und Grautönen gehaltenen Darstellung der «Jungfrau» (Abb. 324), herrschen in allen gezeigten Illustrationen warme Braun-, Gelb-, Rot- und Grüntöne vor. (SWI)

321–326 Exemples des illustrations pleine page et couverture complète (fig. 325) d'un numéro de l'hebdomadaire humoristique *Nebelspalter* consacré aux signes du zodiaque. Sur chaque page, des auteurs s'expliquent avec leur propre signe astrologique; les illustrations ont toutes été contribuées par l'artiste espagnol Puig Rosado. Les vert bleu et gris bleu prédominent dans les dessins de la Vierge (fig. 324), les bruns, les jaunes, les rouges et les verts chauds l'emportent dans les autres illustrations. (SWI)

ARTIST / KÜNSTLER / ARTISTE:
321–326 Fernando Puig Rosado

ART DIRECTOR / DIRECTEUR ARTISTIQUE:
141–326 Franz Mächler

PUBLISHER / VERLEGER / EDITEUR:
321–326 Nebelspalter-Verlag

325

326

328 Collage in brown shades with historical personalities from the World War II period, which appeared in the magazine *Boys Life*. (USA)
329 Illustration from *L'Espresso* for an article on Pietro Nenni, one of the Italien Socialist Party's leading politicians. Beige shades, tie and jacket in red. (ITA)
330 Illustration for an article by Umberto Eco entitled "In Praise of the Abridgement". (ITA)
331, 332 Double spread and illustration for an article on Bettino Craxi, dealing with the political standpoint of the leader of Italy's Socialist party. (ITA)

328 Collage in Brauntönen mit historischen Persönlichkeiten aus der Zeit des Zweiten Weltkrieges, erschienen in der amerikanischen Jugendzeitschrift *Boys Life*. (USA)
329 Illustration aus *L'Espresso* für einen Artikel über Pietro Nenni, einen der führenden Politiker der Sozialistischen Partei Italiens. Beigetöne, Kravatte und Jacke in Rot. (ITA)
330 Illustration für einen Artikel von Umberto Eco mit dem Titel «Lobrede auf die Kurzfassung», erschienen im *L'Espresso*. Vorwiegend in hellen und dunkeln Brauntönen. (ITA)
331, 332 Doppelseite und Illustration für einen Artikel über Bettino Craxi. Thema ist die politische Standortbestimmung des Generalsekretärs der Sozialistischen Partei. (ITA)

328 Collage en divers bruns réunissant des personnalités historiques de la Seconde Guerre mondiale et publié dans le magazine de jeunes américain *Boys Life*. (USA)
329 Illustration de *L'Espresso* pour un article consacré à Pietro Nenni, l'un des leaders du parti socialiste italien. Divers beiges, cravate et veston rouge. (ITA)
330 Illustration d'un article d'Umberto Eco intitulé «Eloge de la concision» paru dans *L'Espresso*. Tons brun clair et sombre prédominants. (ITA)
331, 332 Double page et illustration d'un article sur Bettino Craxi qui cherche à positionner sur l'échiquier politique le leader du parti socialiste italien. (ITA)

ARTIST / KÜNSTLER / ARTISTE:

328 Fred Otnes
329–332 Tullio Pericoli

ART DIRECTOR / DIRECTEUR ARTISTIQUE:

328 Joe Connolly

PUBLISHER / VERLEGER / EDITEUR:

328 Boys Life Magazine
329–332 L'Espresso

328

329

330

331

332

Magazine
Illustrations

333

334

140

335

333 Illustration for "Chronicle of a death foretold" by Gabriel Garcia Marquez, translated from the Spanish and published in *Vanity Fair*. (USA)
334 Illustration for an article entitled "The Death of Vigo", published in *Esquire*. In pastel shades. (USA)
335 Illustration for an article entitled "First Encounters: Frédéric Chopin and George Sand", published in *The Atlantic Monthly*. Pen and ink and watercolour. (USA)
336 Black-and-white illustration for the book section on the warring of the heirs of Alexander the Great. Taken from *Newsday* magazine. (USA)

333 Illustration zu einer aus dem Spanischen übersetzten Erzählung mit dem Titel: «Voraus-sage des Todes», erschienen in *Vanity Fair*. (USA)
334 «Vigos Tod.» Illustration für einen Artikel in der Zeitschrift *Esquire*. (USA)
335 Illustration für einen Artikel mit dem Titel «Erste Begegnungen: Frédéric Chopin und George Sand», veröffentlicht in der Zeitschrift *The Atlantic Monthly*. Kolorierte Tuschzeich-nung. (USA)
336 Schwarzweiss-Illustration aus dem Büchersektor der Zeitschrift *Newsday*. Thema: Der Kampf um das Erbe Alexander des Grossen. (USA)

333 Illustration pour un récit de G. G. Marquez traduit de l'espagnol sous le titre de «Prédiction de la mort» publié dans *Vanity Fair*. (USA)
334 «La Mort de Vigo.» Illustration d'un article paru dans le magazine *Esquire*. (USA)
335 Illustration pour un article du magazine *The Atlantic Monthly* publié sous le titre de «Premières rencontres: Frédéric Chopin et George Sand». Dessin à la plume et aquarelle. (USA)
336 Illustration noir et blanc pour la chronique des livres du magazine *Newsday*: la lutte des diadoques pour la succession d'Alexandre. (USA)

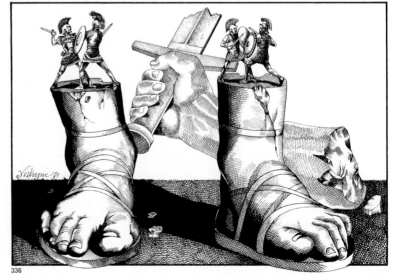

336

337

338

Magazine Illustrations
Zeitschriften-Illustrationen
Illustrations de périodiques

339

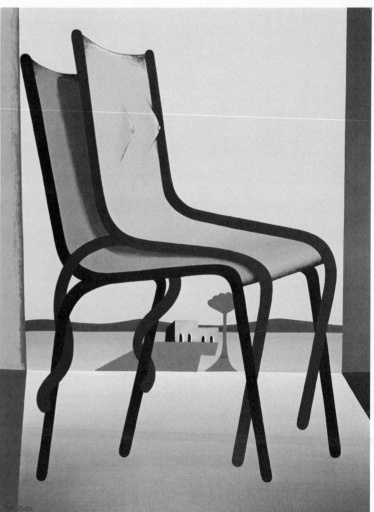

340

337 Cover illustration for *Vanity Fair* magazine. In full colour. (USA)
338 Illustration for a work of fiction by Paul Theroux, published in *Playboy*. (USA)
339 Illustration for an article about the Islamic revolution as seen by General Kaddafi, published in *Playboy* magazine. In brown shades. (ITA)
340 Illustration taken from *Penthouse* magazine. In pastel shades. (SWI)
341 Illustration in actual size for an article on the subject of meditation which appeared in *Homemaker's Magazine*. (CAN)
342 Full-colour illustration for a report in *Playboy* about gangsters in Hamburg. (GER)

337 Umschlagillustration für die amerikanische Zeitschrift *Vanity Fair*. In Farbe. (USA)
338 «Sex und seine Surrogate.» Illustration zu einer Erzählung im Magazin *Playboy*. (USA)
339 Illustration zu einem Artikel über die islamische Revolution unter der Führung des Obersten Kathafi. Veröffentlicht im Magazin *Playboy*. In Brauntönen. (ITA)
340 Illustration aus dem Magazin *Penthouse*. In Pastellfarben. (SWI)
341 «Kann der Geist helfen, den Körper zu heilen?» Illustration in Originalgrösse zu einem Artikel über Meditation, erschienen im *Homemaker's Magazine*. (CAN)
342 Mehrfarbige Illustration zu einem Bericht im *Playboy* über die Gangster in der Hansestadt. (GER)

337 Illustration de couverture pour le magazine américain *Vanity Fair*. En couleurs. (USA)
338 «Le Sexe et ses succédanés.» Illustration d'un récit dans le magazine *Playboy*. (USA)
339 Illustration pour un article sur la révolution islamique libyenne sous la direction du colonel Kadhafi paru dans le magazine *Playboy*. Divers bruns. (ITA)
340 Illustration pour le magazine *Penthouse*. Tons pastel. (SWI)
341 «L'Esprit peut-il aider à guérir le corps?» Illustration au format original pour un article sur les pouvoirs de la méditation publié dans *Homemaker's Magazine*. (CAN)
342 Illustration polychrome d'un rapport dans *Playboy* sur le gangstérisme hambourgeois. (GER)

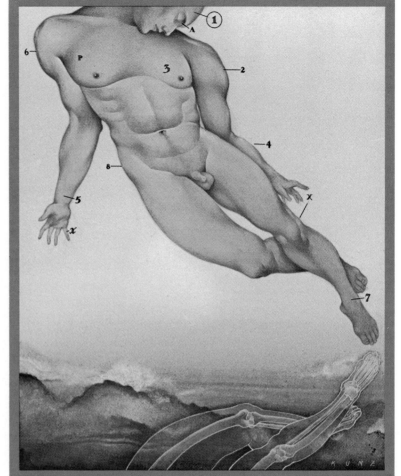

341

342

VOGUE

BRASIL

Nº 80 — Cr$ 350

POR IVO PITANGUY

TEXTOS: IGNÁCIO DE LOYOLA BRANDÃO, GIOVANNI DE BOURBON - SICILES, HÉLIO PELLEGRINO, PEDRO BLOCH, VIVI NABUCO, NORMA COURI E RUDI CRESPI. CRIAÇÃO: ZARAGOZA

343

Cathus Hull

344

345

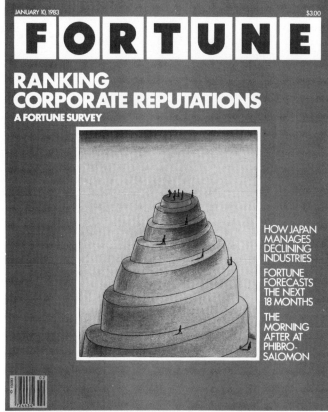

346

ARTIST / KÜNSTLER / ARTISTE:

343 José Zaragoza
344 Cathy Hull
345 Barth
346 Eugene Mihaesco
347 Pam Lefkowitz
348 Doug Taylor

DESIGNER / GESTALTER:

343 José Zaragoza
346, 348 Walter Bernard
347 Jack Lefkowitz

ART DIRECTOR:

343 José Zaragoza
344 Anthony Libardi
345 Franz Mächler
346, 348 Margery Peters/
Walter Bernard
347 Jack Lefkowitz

AGENCY / AGENTUR / AGENCE:

343 DPZ
347 Jack Lefkowitz, Inc.

PUBLISHER / VERLEGER:

343 Vogue Magazine
344 Time, Inc.
345 Nebelspalter-Verlag
346, 348 Fortune Magazine
347 Institute of
Industrial Launderers

347

348

343 Complete cover of *Vogue* on the subject of plastic surgery. (BRA)
344 Illustration for an article in *Time* about deficits and steep interest rates. (USA)
345 Cover spread of *Nebelspalter*, a satirical weekly. Full colour. (SWI)
346 Cover of *Fortune* magazine. In pastel shades. (USA)
347 Cover for the December 1982 issue of *Industrial Launderer* magazine, dealing with waste-water regulations. (USA)
348 Cover of *Fortune* magazine. In garish colours. (USA)

343 Vollständiger Umschlag für *Vogue* zum Thema plastische Chirurgie. (BRA)
344 Für einen Artikel über Verschuldung und Zinspolitik in *Time*. (USA)
345 Umschlagseite der satirischen Wochenzeitschrift *Nebelspalter*. In Farbe. (SWI)
346 Umschlag für das Wirtschaftsmagazin *Fortune*. Pastellfarben. (USA)
347 Umschlag für *Industrial Launderer*. Thema: «Die Probleme der amerikanischen Regierung mit den Vorschriften zur Kontrolle von Schmutzwasser.» (USA)
348 Umschlag für das Wirtschaftsmagazin *Fortune*. In grellen Farben. (USA)

343 Couverture complète de *Vogue* sur le sujet de la chirurgie plastique. (BRA)
344 Pour un article de *Time* sur l'endettement et les taux d'intérêt. (USA)
345 Page de couverture de l'hebdomadaire satirique *Nebelspalter*. En couleurs. (SWI)
346 Couverture du magazine économique *Fortune*. Tons pastel. (USA)
347 Couverture d'*Industrial Launderer*: la réglementation sur les eaux usées et la difficulté qu'il y a à mettre en application les contrôles officiels. (USA)
348 Couverture du magazine économique *Fortune*. Couleurs vives. (USA)

349

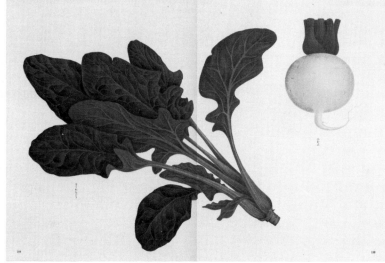

350

Magazine Covers
Zeitschriftenumschläge
Couvertures de périodiques

ARTIST / KÜNSTLER / ARTISTE:

349, 350 Tadashi Ohashi
351 Tom Curry
352, 354, 355 Dieter Wiesmüller
353 Peter Schössow

DESIGNER / GESTALTER / MAQUETTISTE:

349, 350 Tadashi Ohashi
351 Fred Woodward

349, 350 Double spreads from *Climat,* a Japanese magazine.
In shades of green and white. (JPN)
351 Cover of *Westward* magazine, devoted to the subject of
a store's Christmas catalogue. (USA)
352–355 Covers for four issues of Germany's Social Demo-
crat Party's magazine *Vorwärts* (Forwards). The illustrations
refer to articles about the changed situation in the question of
equal rights for women (Fig. 352), speculations about fluc-
tuations on the stock market (Fig. 353), the history of Saudi
Arabia (Fig. 354) and micro-electronics (Fig. 355). All
illustrations are in full colour. (GER)

349, 350 Doppelseiten aus der japanischen Zeitschrift *Climat.* In Grün- und Weisstönen. (JPN)
351 Umschlag des Magazins *Westward.* Thema ist der
Weihnachtskatalog eines Kaufhauses. (USA)
352–355 Umschläge für vier Ausgaben der Monatszeit-
schrift der Sozialdemokratischen Partei Deutschlands
(SPD) *Vorwärts.* Die Illustrationen beziehen sich auf Artikel
über die veränderte Situation auf dem Gebiet der Gleichstel-
lung der Frau (Abb. 352), Börsenspekulation (Abb. 353), die
Geschichte der Dynastie Saud (Abb. 354) und Mikroelek-
tronik (Abb. 355). Alle mehrfarbig. (GER)

349, 350 Doubles pages du magazine japonais *Climat.*
Divers verts et blancs cassés. (JPN)
351 Couverture du magazine *Westward* consacrée à l'analyse du catalogue de Noël d'un grand magasin. (USA)
352–355 Couvertures de quatre numéros du mensuel du
parti social-démocrate allemand *Vorwärts.* Les illustrations
ont trait aux obstacles qui empêchent les femmes d'être
mises sur un pied d'égalité avec les hommes (fig. 352), à la
spéculation boursière (fig. 353), à l'histoire de la dynastie
saoudite (fig. 354) et au pouvoir investi dans les microprocesseurs (fig. 355). En polychromie. (GER)

351

352

353

354

355

ART DIRECTOR / DIRECTEUR ARTISTIQUE:

349, 350 Tadashi Ohashi
351 Fred Woodward
352–355 Konrad Boch

PUBLISHER / VERLEGER / EDITEUR:

349, 350 Bungeishunju Co., Ltd.
351 Dallas Times Herald
352–355 Vorwärts Verlag

How to put your investment dollar back together again
Great tales from the city's jewelry center, by Alan Gross
Dining: Rohdes' burger boon • Kelsons' Manhattan marvels

Chicago
JULY 1982 $2.00

Stalking Charlie Swibel
The untold story of the move to oust the boss of the projects
by Steven Gittelson

356

Inside the artist's space, by Alan Gross
Down to the wire on cable TV, by Tom Panelas
Back in town at 25: The Joffrey Ballet

Chicago
APRIL 1982 $2.00

Who's buying Chicago?
by Alfredo Lanier

793929

357

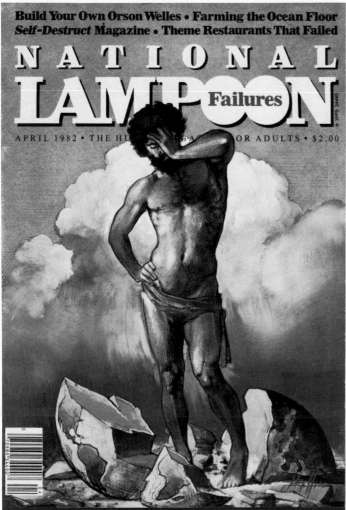

Build Your Own Orson Welles • Farming the Ocean Floor
Self-Destruct Magazine • Theme Restaurants That Failed

NATIONAL LAMPOON Failures
APRIL 1982 • THE HU͏͏͏A OR ADULTS • $2.00

358

A McGraw-Hill Publication

BusinessWeek

359

Magazine Covers
Zeitschriftenumschläge
Couvertures de périodiques

356, 357 Covers of *Chicago*, a monthly magazine. Fig. 356: red lettering on a bluish-grey ground; Fig. 357: yellow lettering, white, brown shades on lilac. (USA)
358 Cover for the humorous magazine *National Lampoon*. In full colour. (USA)
359 Cover of *Business Week*. Gold, grey and black on white. (USA)
360, 361 Complete cover and illustration for a feature on social security which appeared in *Time*, the American weekly magazine. (USA)

356, 357 Umschläge der monatlich erscheinenden Zeitschrift *Chicago*. Abb. 356: Rote Schrift auf blaugrauem Grund; Abb. 357: Gelbe Schrift, Weiss, Brauntöne auf Lila. (USA)
358 Umschlag für das humoristische Magazin *National Lampoon*: «Fehlschläge». In Farbe. (USA)
359 Umschlag für die Zeitschrift *Business Week*. Gold, Grau und Schwarz auf Weiss. (USA)
360, 361 «Sozialversicherungen: Was kann sich der Staat leisten?» Vollständiger Umschlag und Illustration für das Magazin *Time*. (USA)

356, 357 Couverture du mensuel *Chicago*. Fig. 356: texte en rouge sur fond gris bleu; fig. 357: texte en jaune, blanc et divers bruns sur fonds lilas. (USA)
358 Couverture du magazine d'humour *National Lampoon*: «Echecs». En couleurs. (USA)
359 Couverture du magazine *Business Week*. Or, gris, noir sur blanc. (USA)
360, 361 «La sécurité sociale: l'Etat en a-t-il les moyens?» Couverture complète et illustration pour le magazine *Time*. (USA)

360

ARTIST / KÜNSTLER / ARTISTE:

356 Eraldo Carugati
357 John Zielinski
358 Daniel Maffia
359 Stanislaw Fernandes
360, 361 Eugene Mihaesco

DESIGNER / GESTALTER:

356, 357 Robert J. Post
358 Michael Grossman
359 Stanislaw Fernandes

ART DIRECTOR:

356, 357 Robert J. Post
358 Michael Grossman
359 John Vogler
360, 361 Rudolph Hoglund

AGENCY / AGENTUR / AGENCE:

359 Stanislaw Fernandes Design

PUBLISHER / VERLEGER:

356, 357 WFMT, Inc.
358 National Lampoon
359 McGraw-Hill, Inc.
360, 361 Time, Inc.

361

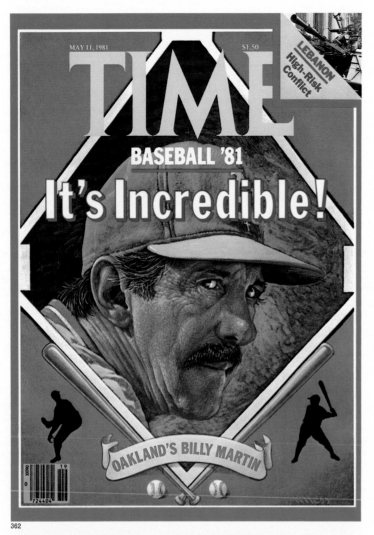

362

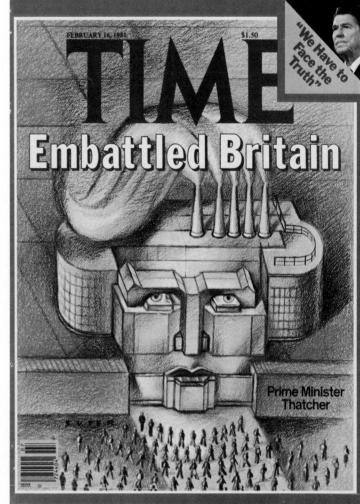

363

364

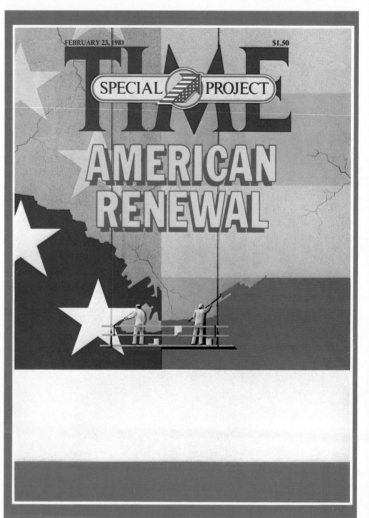

365

Magazine Covers
Zeitschriftenumschläge
Couvertures de périodiques

ARTIST / KÜNSTLER / ARTISTE:

362, 364 Richard Hess
363 David Suter
365 Robert Giusti
366 Regina Jolanta Pawlowska
367 André François
368 Eugene Mihaesco

DESIGNER / GESTALTER / MAQUETTISTE:

363 Nigel Holmes

367

366

ART DIRECTOR / DIRECTEUR ARTISTIQUE:

362–365 Rudolph Hoglund
366 Lech Zahorski
367, 368 Lee Lorenz

PUBLISHER / VERLEGER / EDITEUR:

362–365 Time, Inc.
366 Polish Interpress Agency
367, 368 The New Yorker Magazine, Inc.

362 Cover of *Time* magazine with the portrait of a successful baseball manager. (USA)
363 For an issue of *Time* magazine with a cover story about Prime Minister Margaret Thatcher. (USA)
364 Cover for an issue of *Time* magazine with an editorial on Wall Street and the economy. (USA)
365 Cover of *Time* on the subject of the introduction of reforms in the United States. (USA)
366 Complete cover of the magazine *Poland* which is published in a number of languages. (POL)
367 Cover of a summer issue of *The New Yorker*. Mainly in shades of green. (USA)
368 Another cover of *The New Yorker*. In warm yellow and rusty-red. (USA)

362 Umschlag des Magazins *Time* mit dem Porträt eines erfolgreichen Baseball-Spielers. (USA)
363 Für eine Ausgabe von *Time* mit einem Beitrag über Grossbritanniens Margaret Thatcher. (USA)
364 Wall Street und die Wirtschaft sind das Thema des Leitartikels dieser Ausgabe der *Time*. Der Bulle, Symbol optimistischer Tendenz der Börse, hier im Kampf mit den Kursinformationen. (USA)
365 Umschlag für *Time*. Thema ist die Diskussion um Reformen in den Vereinigten Staaten. (USA)
366 Vollständiger Umschlag der in mehreren Sprachen erscheinenden Zeitschrift *Polen*. (POL)
367 Umschlag für eine Sommerausgabe der Zeitschrift *The New Yorker*. Vorwiegend Grüntöne. (USA)
368 Ein weiterer Umschlag des Magazins *The New Yorker*. In warmem Gelb und Rostrot. (USA)

362 Couverture du magazine *Time* avec le portrait d'un joueur de base-ball renommé. (USA)
363 Pour un numéro de *Time* contenant un article sur le premier ministre Margaret Thatcher. (USA)
364 Wall Street et la situation économique sont les thèmes traités dans l'éditorial de ce numéro de *Time*. Le taureau symbolisant la tendance haussière de la Bourse est représenté se débattant dans un fouillis d'informations sur les cours. (USA)
365 Couverture de *Time*. Le sujet: la controverse autour des réformes en Amérique. (USA)
366 Couverture complète du magazine d'information *Pologne* publié en plusieurs langues. (POL)
367 Couverture d'un numéro d'été du magazine *New Yorker*, où prédominent les tons verts. (USA)
368 Une autre couverture du magazine *New Yorker*. Jaune chaud et rouille. (USA)

368

370

371

ARTIST / KÜNSTLER / ARTISTE:

369, 369a, 371 M. Arisman
370 Jerzy Kolacz
372 Stanislaw Fernandes

DESIGNER / GESTALTER:

370 Mary Opper
371 Theo Kouvatsos
372 Stanislaw Fernandes

Magazine Covers

369, 369a Illustration and cover for *Time* magazine on the subject of "The Curse of Crime". (USA)
370 Cover of *Quest* magazine on the subject of reading lessons. (CAN)
371 Illustration for an introductory double spread from an article in *Playboy* about Alexander Haig's rise to power. (USA)
372 Cover of *Madison Avenue Magazine*, a periodical specialising in the world of advertising. In full colour. (USA)

369, 369a Illustration und vollständiger Umschlag der Zeitschrift *Time* zum Thema «Der Fluch des Gewaltverbrechens». (USA)
370 «Warum unsere Kinder nicht lesen können.» Umschlag der Zeitschrift *Quest* mit einem Beitrag über den Schulunterricht im Lesen. (CAN)
371 Illustration für die einleitende Doppelseite zu einem Artikel im *Playboy* über Alexander Haigs Aufstieg an die Macht. (USA)
372 Umschlag des *Madison Avenue Magazine*, einer Zeitschrift für die Werbewelt. In Farbe. (USA)

369, 369a Illustration et couverture du magazine *Time*. Le sujet: «La malédiction du crime.» (USA)
370 «Pourquoi nos enfants ne savent pas lire.» Couverture du magazine *Quest*. Le numéro fait état d'une enquête sur la lecture à l'école. (CAN)
371 Illustration pour la page double en tête d'un article de *Playboy* qui analyse l'ascension d'Alexander Haig au faîte du pouvoir. (USA)
372 Couverture du *Madison Avenue Magazine*, une revue spécialisée dans le domaine publicitaire. En couleurs. (USA)

369a

ART DIRECTOR:

369, 369a Rudolph Hoglund
370 Arthur Niemi
371 Tom Staebler
372 Stanislaw Fernandes

PUBLISHER / VERLEGER / EDITEUR:

369, 369a Time, Inc.
370 Comac Communications
371 Playboy Enterprises, Inc.
372 Madison Avenue Magazine

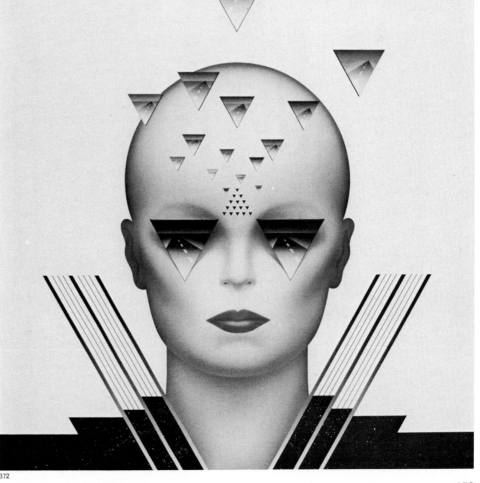

372

153

373

374

ARTIST / KÜNSTLER / ARTISTE:

373 Thomas Hunt
374 Anita Kunz
375 John Martin
376 Christine Bunny
377 Dennis Noble
378 Kim Lafave
379 Steven Guarnaccia
380 James Marsh

DESIGNER / GESTALTER:

373–378 B. J. Gailbraith
379 Michael Grossman
380 James Marsh

ART DIRECTOR:

373–378 B. J. Gailbraith
379 Michael Grossman
380 Jim Bunker

PUBLISHER / VERLEGER:

373–378 Saturday Night
Contract Publishing
379 National Lampoon
380 National Magazine Co.

376

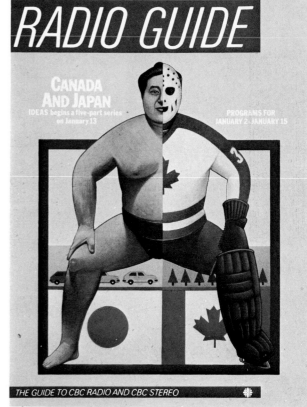

377

373–378 Covers of a Canadian radio-programme magazine. Fig. 373 deals with a "World Assembly of First Nations"; Fig. 374 refers to a debate pitting creationism against the evolution of man; Fig. 375 announces the transmission of the play *The Barber of Seville*, Fig. 376 deals with a programme devoted to James Joyce's genius on the occasion of what would have been his 100th birthday; Fig. 377: a series on the subject of Canada and Japan. Fig. 378 refers to a series of programmes centered on a drama series entitled "The Scales of Justice" dealing with court cases. All illustrations are in full colour. (CAN)
379 Full-page introductory illustration for a feature in *National Lampoon* entitled "How to Perform Hexmifacial Spasm Surgery on Yourself". Light green, light grey, light blue and brown shades. (USA)
380 Cover of the December issue of *The Connoisseur*, combining the spirit of Christmas with the contents of the magazine articles. In full colour. (GBR)

373–378 Umschläge einer kanadischen Radio-Programmzeitschrift. In Abb. 373 geht es um einen Bericht über die Weltversammlung der Urnationen; Abb. 374 bezieht sich auf eine Debatte über den Ursprung der Menschheit – Schöpfungsakt Gottes kontra Evolution; Abb. 375 kündigt eine Übertragung des *Barbier von Sevilla* an; Abb. 376 weist auf eine Sendung anlässlich des hundertsten Geburtstages von James Joyce hin; Abb. 377 betrifft eine Reihe zum Thema Kanada und Japan; Abb. 378 eine Unterhaltungsreihe über Gerichtsfälle. Alle Illustrationen sind mehrfarbig. (CAN)
379 Einleitende, ganzseitige Illustration für einen Beitrag über medizinische Selbsthilfe, erschienen in der humoristischen Zeitschrift *National Lampoon*. (USA)
380 Umschlag einer Dezemberausgabe von *The Connoisseur*, wobei die Themen der Ausgabe und die weihnachtliche Sitte des Schenkens in der Illustration zum Ausdruck kommen sollten. Mehrfarbig. (GBR)

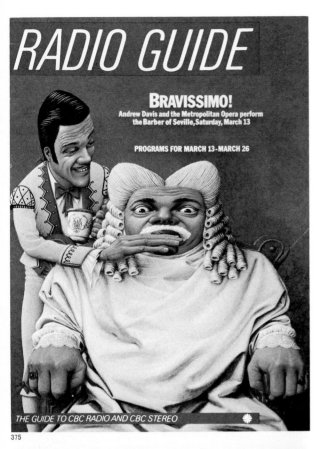

375

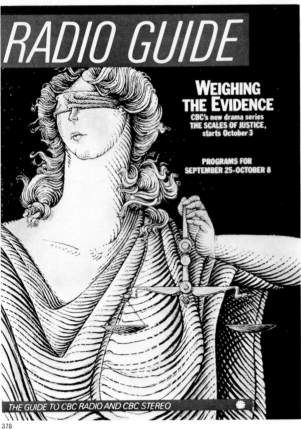

378

379

373–378 Couvertures d'un journal de radio-TV canadien. La fig. 373 se rapporte à une conférence mondiale des nations primitives; la fig. 374 évoque le débat sur l'origine de l'Homme – créationnisme contre évolutionnisme; la fig. 375 annonce une représentation du *Barbier de Séville*; la fig. 376 illustre une émission commémorant le centième anniversaire de James Joyce; la fig. 377 introduit une série d'émissions consacrées à la fois au Japon et au Canada; la fig. 378 annonce une série dramatique évoquant des causes judiciaires. Toutes les illustrations en polychromie. (CAN)
379 Illustration pleine page en tête d'un article sur le do-it-yourself médical paru dans la revue satirique *National Lampoon*. (USA)
380 Couverture d'un numéro de décembre du *Connoisseur*. Les sujets des divers articles y sont combinés avec une évocation réussie de l'esprit de générosité qui prévaut à Noël. En polychromie. (GBR)

380

382

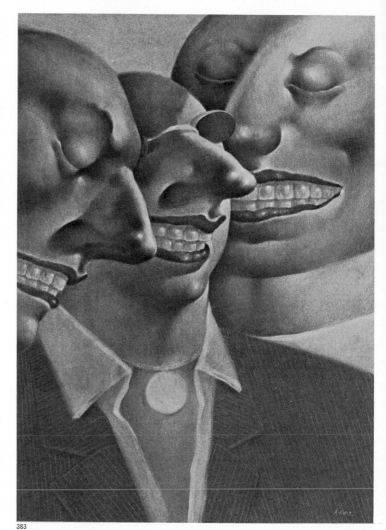

383

384

ARTIST / KÜNSTLER / ARTISTE:

382, 383 Anita Kunz
384 Kent Smith
385 Blair Drawson

DESIGNER / GESTALTER / MAQUETTISTE:

382, 383, 385 Bruce Ramsay
384 Louis Fishauf

ART DIRECTOR / DIRECTEUR ARTISTIQUE:

382, 383 Derek Ungless
384, 385 Louis Fishauf

PUBLISHER / VERLEGER / EDITEUR:

382–385 Saturday Night Magazine

382, 383 Full-page illustrations from *Saturday Night* magazine, belonging to an article about Jews in Canada—from a working-class, left-wing, immigrant minority, Canadian Jews have evolved into a community preoccupied with the middle-class ideal. (CAN)
384 Illustration for an article about the power of judges in Canada which appeared in *Saturday Night* magazine. Mainly in subdued green and brown. (CAN)
385 Illustration of the introductory double spread of a short story in *Saturday Night* about the mysterious circumstances of a man suffering from amnesia. (CAN)

382, 383 Ganzseitige Illustrationen aus *Saturday Night*. In dem dazugehörigen Artikel geht es um die Wandlung des Juden in Kanada: vom linksstehenden Arbeiter in einer Minorität von Immigranten zum Angehörigen des Mittelstands. (CAN)
384 Illustration für einen Artikel über die Macht der Richter in Kanada, erschienen in *Saturday Night*. Vorwiegend in mattem Grün und Braun. (CAN)
385 Illustration der einleitenden Doppelseite zu einer Kurzgeschichte über einen Mann, der sein Gedächtnis verloren hat. Aus *Saturday Night*. (CAN)

382, 383 Illustrations pleine page dans *Saturday Night*. L'article qu'elles visent débat de l'ascension socioprofessionnelle des juifs canadiens, jadis ouvriers engagés à gauche et appartenant à une minorité d'immigrants, aujourd'hui dans la bourgeoisie. (CAN)
384 Illustration du pouvoir des juges au Canada, pour un article paru dans *Saturday Night*. Teintes: surtout du vert et du brun mats. (CAN)
385 Illustration de la double page initiale d'une nouvelle qui met en scène un homme ayant perdu la mémoire dans des circonstances troubles. Dans *Saturday Night*. (CAN)

385

387

386

386–392 Illustrations and covers for *The Atlantic*. The black-and-white drawing in Fig. 386 refers to DIVAD, an expensive weapon; Fig. 387 deals with the memories of a young man growing up in Chicago; black and white with grey; Fig. 388 in light ruby-red with brown shades and yellow, for a story about musicians' performance anxiety; Fig. 389 in reddish-brown with bluish-grey and green, belongs to a story about Texas; and a report about the police and neighbourhood safety and "The Politics of Crime" are the themes of the covers shown in Figs. 390 and 391 (black on cream); Fig. 392 illustrates the recollections of a former marine soldier. (USA)

ARTIST / KÜNSTLER / ARTISTE:

386, 387 J. C. Suarès
388 Alexa Grace
389, 392 Robert Giusti
390 Seymour Chwast
391 R. O. Blechman

DESIGNER / GESTALTER / MAQUETTISTE:

386–392 Judy Garlan

390

391

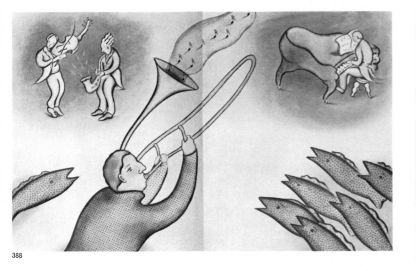

388

389

386–392 Illustrationen und Umschläge für die Zeitschrift *The Atlantic Monthly*. Thema der Zeichnung (Schwarzweiss) in Abb. 386 sind die Probleme mit einem Panzertyp; in Abb. 387 (Schwarzweiss mit Grau) geht es um die Erinnerungen eines Mannes an seine Jugend in Chicago; Abb. 388 (helles Bordeaurot mit Brauntönen und Gelb) illustriert eine Geschichte über das Lampenfieber von Musikern; Abb. 389 (Rotbraun mit Blaugrau und Grün) gehört zu einer Geschichte über Texas; «Die Polizei und die Sicherheit in Wohnquartieren» und «Politik der Kriminalität» sind die Themen der Umschläge in Abb. 390 und 391 (Schwarz auf Crème); Abb. 392 illustriert die Erinnerungen eines Marinesoldaten. (USA)

386–392 Illustrations et couvertures du magazine *The Atlantic*. Le sujet du dessin noir et blanc de la fig. 386, ce sont les problèmes que cause un certain type de blindé; dans la fig. 387 (noir, blanc avec du gris), un homme se rappelle sa jeunesse à Chicago; la fig. 388 (bordeaux clair avec divers bruns et du jaune) est une illustration sur double page qui évoque le trac des musiciens; la fig. 389 (brun roux avec du gris bleu et du vert) accompagne un récit texan; les fig. 390 et 391 reproduisent des couvertures (noir sur crème) qui illustrent les thèmes «la police et la sécurité dans les quartiers résidentiels», d'une part, «la politique de la criminalité», de l'autre; la fig. 392 interprète les souvenirs d'un ancien marine américain. (USA)

ART DIRECTOR / DIRECTEUR ARTISTIQUE:
386–392 Judy Garlan

AGENCY / AGENTUR / AGENCE – STUDIO:
390 Pushpin Lubalin Peckolick

PUBLISHER / VERLEGER / ÉDITEUR:
386–392 The Atlantic Monthly

392

393

394

395

396

Magazine
Illustrations

397

ARTIST / KÜNSTLER:

393–398 Guy Billout

DESIGNER / GESTALTER:

393–396 Judy Garlan

ART DIRECTOR:

393–396 Judy Garlan
397, 398 Rudolph Hoglund

AGENCY / AGENTUR:

393–396 Atlantic Monthly
397, 398 Time, Inc.

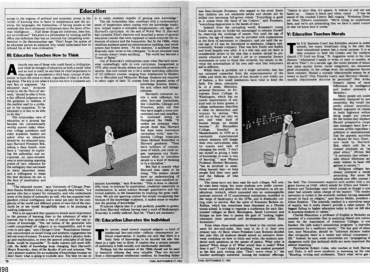

398

393–396 Examples of humorous, full-page illustrations, all containing an unexpected point, from a series published in *The Atlantic Monthly*. The subjects, which the artist can choose himself, are as follows in the examples shown here: Jungle, Gravity, Detour, Intersection. All the illustrations shown here are in full colour. (USA)

397, 398 Illustration and double spread from an article entitled "Five Ways to Wisdom" which appeared in *Time*. The question asked here is: "as US colleges open their doors, how can they also open minds?" Fig. 398 is from the introductory double spread, its illustrations are in pink with black arrow (left) and black, pink and grey (right). (USA)

393–396 Vier Beispiele von humorvollen, ganzseitigen Illustrationen aus einer in der Zeitschrift *The Atlantic Monthly* veröffentlichten Serie. Die Themen, die der Künstler selbst wählen kann, sind hier folgende: «Dschungel», «Schwerkraft», «Umleitung», «Strassenkreuzung». Alle Illustrationen sind mehrfarbig. (USA)

397, 398 Illustration und Doppelseite aus einem Artikel mit dem Titel «Fünf Wege zur Weisheit», erschienen in der Zeitschrift *Time*. Es geht vor allem um die Ausbildung an den amerikanischen Universitäten und den Sinn und Wert der Erziehung. Abb. 398 Rosa mit schwarzem Pfeil (linke Abbildung) und Schwarz, Rosa und Grau (rechte Abbildung). (USA)

393–396 Quatre exemples des illustrations pleines d'humour sur page entière qui composent une série publiée dans le magazine *The Atlantic Monthly*. L'artiste a pu choisir ses sujets lui-même. Nous montrons ici «Jungle», «Gravitation», «Déviation», «Intersection». Toutes ces illustrations sont exécutées en polychromie. (USA)

397, 398 Illustration et double page d'un article intitulé «Les Cinq Chemins de la sagesse» et publié dans le magazine *Time*. Il s'agit de l'éducation que dispensent les universités américaines: on y admet généreusement des jeunes gens, mais est-on aussi en mesure de leur ouvrir l'esprit sur les réalités du monde? C'est une question de philosophie de l'éducation. (USA)

399

400

401

402

ARTIST / KÜNSTLER / ARTISTE:

399 Renee Klein
400 Alexa Grace
401 Dagmar Frinta
402 Seymour Chwast
403 Vivienne Flesher

DESIGNER / GESTALTER / MAQUETTISTE:

399 Catherine Aldrich
400–402 Ronn Campisi
403 Lynn Staley

ART DIRECTOR / DIRECTEUR ARTISTIQUE:

399–402 Ronn Campisi
403 Lynn Staley

AGENCY / AGENTUR / AGENCE – STUDIO:

402 Pushpin Lubalin Peckolick

PUBLISHER / VERLEGER / EDITEUR:

399–403 The Boston Globe

162

Magazine Illustrations
Zeitschriften-Illustrationen
Illustrations de périodiques

399–401 Full-page illustration from the *Boston Globe Magazine*. Fig.399 is taken from the "garden" section of the magazine; Fig. 400 is devoted to folk tales from the Caribbean, and Fig. 401 belongs to an article about a dangerous habit, bulimia, particularly among young women who deliberately vomit after meals. (USA)
402 Cover illustration from the *Boston Globe Magazine*. The article in question deals with the training of a new breed of veterinary surgeon. (USA)
403 Black-and-white illustration taken from a double spread in *The Boston Globe* dealing with theatre tours. (USA)

399–401 Ganzseitige Illustration aus dem *Boston Globe Magazine*. Abb. 399 gehört zu einem Beitrag aus dem Sektor «Garten», Abb. 400 zu «Volksmärchen aus der Karibik» und Abb. 401 zu einem Artikel über die gefährliche Sucht vor allem junger Frauen, durch absichtlich herbeigeführtes Erbrechen nach dem Essen schlank zu werden bzw. zu bleiben. (USA)
402 Umschlagillustration des *Boston Globe Magazine*. Sie bezieht sich auf einen Artikel über eine besondere Ausbildung der Veterinäre. (USA)
403 Schwarzweiss-Illustration einer Doppelseite aus der Zeitung *The Boston Globe* mit einem Beitrag über Theater-Tourneen. (USA)

399–401 Illustration pleine page pour le *Boston Globe Magazine*. La fig. 399 fait partie d'un article dans la section «Jardinage», la fig. 400 illustre des «contes des Caraïbes», la fig. 401 une habitude alimentaire fâcheuse répandue parmi les jeunes femmes et qui consiste à rester svelte en s'obligeant à vomir après les repas. (USA)
402 Illustration de couverture du *Boston Globe Magazine*. L'article qu'elle concerne explique un principe de formation nouveau pour les vétérinaires. (USA)
403 Illustration noir et blanc pour une double page du journal *The Boston Globe* où il est question des tournées de théâtre. (USA)

403

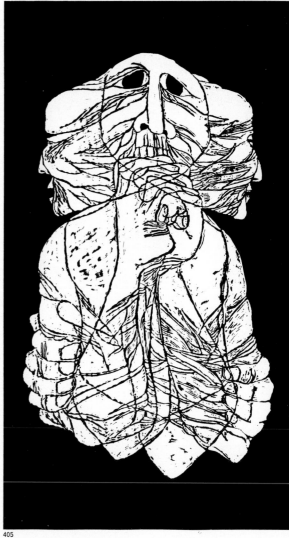

404

405

407

404 "Taming monsterous energy costs" is the subject of this illustration which belongs to a feature published in the *St. Louis Business Journal*. (USA)
405 Woodcut in black and white from *Ramparts Magazine*, dealing with the conflict between Israel and neighbouring countries. (USA)
406 Illustration for an article about the women's movement. Mainly in soft shades of blue and red, with brown. (USA)
407 Illustration for a fiction story in *Omni* magazine. (USA)
408 Drawing from the humorous magazine *Szpilki*, commenting on the fascination of television. (POL)

404 «Monströse Energiekosten» und deren Bewältigung sind Thema dieser Illustration, die zu einem im *St. Louis Business Journal* erschienenen Beitrag gehört. (USA)
405 Holzschnitt in Schwarzweiss aus *Ramparts Magazine* zum Konflikt Israels mit seinen Nachbarstaaten. (USA)
406 Illustration für einen Artikel über die Frauenbewegung. Vorwiegend in sanften Blau- und Rottönen, mit Braun. (USA)
407 Illustration zu einer Geschichte mit dem Titel «Die weisse Pest» erschienen in der Zeitschrift *Omni*. (USA)
408 Kommentar zur Faszination des Fernsehens, aus dem humoristischen Magazin *Szpilki*. (POL)

404 «Le coût monstrueux de l'énergie» et comment en venir à bout, voilà le thème de cette illustration pour un article publié dans le *St. Louis Business Journal*. (USA)
405 Gravure sur bois, en noir et blanc, pour *Ramparts Magazine*. Il s'agit du conflit entre Israël et ses voisins. (USA)
406 Illustration pour un article sur les mouvements féministes. Divers bleus et rouges atténués, avec du brun. (USA)
407 Illustration pour l'histoire parue dans le journal *Omni* avec le titre «La Peste blanche». (USA)
408 Commentaire de la fascination qu'éprouvent les téléspectateurs face au petit écran. Magazine satirique *Szpilki*. (POL)

406

408

ARTIST / KÜNSTLER / ARTISTE:

404 Greg MacNair
405 Stephen Osborn
406 Dagmar Frinta
407 Charles Pfahl
408 Andrzej Czeczot

DESIGNER / GESTALTER:

404 Greg MacNair
405 Stephen Osborn
407 Margaret Richichi

ART DIRECTOR:

404 David Bartels
406 Bob Eichinger
407 Elizabeth Woodson

AGENCY / AGENTUR / AGENCE:

404 Bartels & Company

PUBLISHER / VERLEGER / EDITEUR:

404 St. Louis Business Journal
405 Ramparts Magazine
406 At&T Telephone Co.
407 Omni Publications International
408 Szpilki

409

410

411

412

Magazine Illustrations
Zeitschriften-Illustrationen
Illustrations de périodiques

166

413

Night duty

The danger is always there

By Laura Philips
Special to The Globe

At midnight the night shift turns over from the "first half" to the "last half," called "morning watch," and the District 4 police force — whose boundaries run from Arlington street to the BU Bridge and Camden street to Boston City Hospital to Back street behind Beacon street just before Storrow drive — shrinks with the passing of day. Each of the cruisers carries two officers. The streets are cold and barren, with no officers mounted or on foot on morning watch.

"We have patrol supervisors out there — there's always a sergeant on the street, at least one — and he's instructed to go answer the calls and make sure the officers respond fast," says District 4 Capt. James McDonald. "Sleeping on duty certainly hasn't been a problem in this district."

The night-calls are more of a criminal nature, and hence more dangerous, than the day-calls, which tend to be more service-oriented, such as lockouts or breaking-and-enterings (B&Es) when people are at work. Male and female prostitute activity abounds at night in all seasons. Street-crimes occur more often in summer when people are out walking, and a street-robber is more apt to show a weapon at night than in daylight. Wintertime fires proliferate in the poorer sections of the city from the use of space heaters and the habit of leaving oven doors open. Domestic quarrels occur more frequently in summer, when people are drinking and temperaments are on edge from the heat, but the incidence picks up again near the Christmas season as families push to make ends meet for the holidays. While the crime-figures rise and the dangers to police and citizens increase at night, so does the number of arrests, due to easier maneuvering through empty streets.

"The people who are out at 3 or 4 in the morning, you know they're up to ill-doings. You get a certain element of people walking the streets," says McDonald. "Night-duty is a young man's job."

POLICE, Page 84

414

ARTIST / KÜNSTLER / ARTISTE:

409 Alexa Grace
410 Andrzej Dudzinski
411, 414 Mel Williges
412 Mark Fisher
413 Steve Guarniccia
415 Karen Watson

DESIGNER / GESTALTER:

409–414 Ronn Campisi
415 Catherine Aldrich

ART DIRECTOR:

409–415 Ronn Campisi

PUBLISHER / VERLEGER:

409–415 The Boston Globe

409 Illustration from the *Boston Globe Magazine* for a short story. Pastel shades. (USA)
410 Full-colour cover illustration from the *Boston Globe Magazine*. (USA)
411, 412 Full-page colour illustrations from *The Boston Globe Magazine* relating to articles about Christmas and moral education in schools. (USA)
413 Full-colour illustration for an article that appeared in the *Boston Globe Magazine*. (USA)
414 Illustration for an article about police night duty. Taken from *The Boston Globe*. (USA)
415 Full-page illustration from the recipes section in *The Boston Globe Magazine*. (USA)

409 Illustration zu einer Kurzgeschichte im *Boston Globe Magazine*. Pastelltöne. (USA)
410 Umschlagillustration des *Boston Globe Magazine*: Die Macher der – konservativen – Ideologie in Washington. Mehrfarbig. (USA)
411, 412 Farbillustrationen aus dem *Boston Globe Magazine*. Die Themen: Weihnachten und moralische Erziehung als neues Unterrichtsfach. (USA)
413 Mehrfarbige Illustration für einen Artikel über die Zulässigkeit von Zeugenaussagen, die durch Hypnose entstanden. *Boston Globe Magazine*. (USA)
414 Illustration für einen Artikel über den Nachtdienst der Polizei. Aus *The Boston Globe*. (USA)
415 Ganzseitige Illustration aus dem Rezeptteil, hier für Geräuchertes. *Boston Globe Magazine*. (USA)

409 Illustration d'une nouvelle parue dans le *Boston Globe Magazine*. Tons pastel. (USA)
410 Illustration de couverture du *Boston Globe Magazine*: comment se forge l'idéologie conservatrice aux Etats-Unis. En polychromie. (USA)
411, 412 Illustrations couleur du *Boston Globe Magazine*. Il s'agit des fêtes de Noël et d'une nouvelle discipline scolaire: l'éducation morale. (USA)
413 Illustration polychrome d'un article où l'on met en cause les témoignages obtenus sous hypnose. *Boston Globe Magazine*. (USA)
414 Illustration d'un article sur le service de nuit des policiers. Tiré du *Boston Globe*. (USA)
415 Illustration pour la section Recettes de cuisine du *Boston Globe Magazine*: les mets fumés. (USA)

415

416

417

420

416 Full-page illustration from a story published in *Plain Dealer Magazine*. (USA)
417 Cover of the *Plain Dealer Magazine*. In full colour. (USA)
418 Full-page illustration from the *Dallas Times Herald* for a story about football. (USA)
419 Illustration from a feature entitled "Transsexuals—Inhabitants of an Inbetween World" that appeared in *Plain Dealer Magazine*. In shades of brownish-red and beige. (USA)
420, 421 Covers of *Plain Dealer Magazine*. In green, yellow, blue and pink. (USA)
422 One man's experience in advertising. Full-page illustration from the *Dallas Times Herald*. (USA)

416 «Ein Abend im Zirkus.» Ganzseitige Illustration zu einer Geschichte im *Plain Dealer Magazine*. (USA)
417 Umschlag des *Plain Dealer Magazine*. Das Thema: Zahnspangen für Erwachsene. In Farbe. (USA)
418 Ganzseitige Illustration aus *Dallas Times Herald* zu einer Geschichte über Football. (USA)
419 Illustration zu einem Beitrag über Transsexualität, erschienen im *Plain Dealer Magazine*. In bräunlichen Rot- und Beigetönen. (USA)
420, 421 Umschläge des *Plain Dealer Magazine*. Abb. 420: eine Diskussion über das Verlieben; Abb. 421: Das geteilte Image der Lehrer in Cleveland, in Grün, Gelb, Blau und Rosa. (USA)
422 Ganzseitige Illustration aus *Dallas Times Herald* zu einem Beitrag über das Werbegeschäft. (USA)

416 «Une Soirée au cirque.» Illustration pleine page d'un récit du *Plain Dealer Magazine*. (USA)
417 Couverture du *Plain Dealer Magazine*. On y parle des «sourires métalliques» que provoquent les appareils d'orthodontie que l'on met aux adultes. En couleurs. (USA)
418 Illustration pleine page du *Dallas Times Herald* pour une histoire de footballeur. (USA)
419 «Les transsexuels – habitants d'un monde intermédiaire»: illustration sur le transsexualisme, dans le *Plain Dealer Magazine*. Divers rouge brun et beiges. (USA)
420, 421 Couvertures du *Plain Dealer Magazine*. Fig. 420: le problème du coup de foudre. Fig. 421: L'image ambivalente des professeurs de Cleveland; vert, jaune, bleu, rose. (USA)
422 Illustration pleine page du *Dallas Time Herald* pour le récit d'un publicitaire. (USA)

ART DIRECTOR / DIRECTEUR ARTISTIQUE:

416, 417, 419–421 Greg Paul
418, 422 Fred Woodward

PUBLISHER / VERLEGER / EDITEUR:

416, 417, 419–421 The Plain Dealer Publishing Co.
418, 422 Dallas Times Herald

418

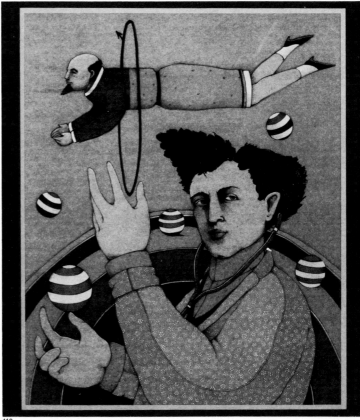

419

THE SPLIT
IMAGE
OF CLEVELAND
TEACHERS

America's
Jazziest Artist
Page 32

THE PLAIN DEALER *Magazine*
SUNDAY, NOV. 14, 1982

421

422

423

424

425

426

Weekend Supplements / Wochenendbeilagen
Suppléments dominicaux

ARTIST / KÜNSTLER / ARTISTE:

423, 425 Dora Wespi
424 Gary Viskupic
426 Lynn Staley
427 Buddy Hickerson
428 George F. Kocar
429 Elwood H. Smith

DESIGNER / GESTALTER / MAQUETTISTE:

424 Miriam Smith
426 Lynn Staley
427 Buddy Hickerson
428 Sam Capuano
429 Fred Woodward

ART DIRECTOR / DIRECTEUR ARTISTIQUE:

423, 425 Albert Kaelin
424 Miriam Smith
426 Lynn Staley
427 Randy Bishop
428 Greg Paul
429 Fred Woodward

428

PUBLISHER / VERLEGER / EDITEUR:

423, 425 Tages-Anzeiger AG
424 Newsday Inc.
426 The Boston Globe
427, 429 Dallas Times Herald
428 The Plain Dealer Publishing Co.

423, 425 Full-page illustration from the "well seasoned" column in the *Tages Anzeiger Magazine*. Cardamon and nutmeg the themes here. (SWI)
424 "Why Can't Men Be True Friends?" Illustration for a feature in *Newsday*. (USA)
426 From the "Calendar", a supplement of *The Boston Globe*. (USA)
427 Illustration from an article about the 50's in the *Dallas Times Herald*. (USA)
428 Double-spread illustration from a report on Cleveland Radio that appeared in *Plain Dealer Magazine*. In full colour. (USA)
429 Full-page, full-colour illustration for an article on Nashville's "Fan Fair", which appeared in the magazine of the *Dallas Times Herald*. (USA)

423, 425 Ganzseitige Illustration zu der Rubrik «Gut gewürzt» im *Tages Anzeiger Magazin*. Kardamon und Muskat sind hier die Themen. (SWI)
424 Für einen Beitrag über Männerfreundschaften, erschienen in *Newsday*. (USA)
426 Ganzseitiges Porträt des Rock-Musikers George Thorogood für einen Bericht über einen Auftritt in Boston. Aus dem «Calendar», einer Beilage des *Boston Globe*. (USA)
427 Illustration zu einem Artikel über die 50er Jahre im *Dallas Times Herald*. (USA)
428 «Schock-Wellen.» Doppelseitige Illustration zu einem Bericht im *Plain Dealer Magazine* über Sex und Brutalität als Zugpferd für einen Radio-Sender. In Farbe. (USA)
429 Ganzseitige Illustration aus dem Magazin des *Dallas Times Herald*. Es geht hier um «Fan Fair», eine Veranstaltung, bei welcher bekannte und weniger bekannte Stars der Country-Musik die Autogrammwünsche ihrer Fans erfüllen. Mehrfarbig. (USA)

423, 425 Illustration pleine page pour la rubrique «Bien épicé» du *Tages Anzeiger Magazin*. On y montre la cardamome et le muscat. (SWI)
424 Pour un article sur l'amitié difficile entre hommes paru dans *Newsday*. (USA)
426 Portrait pleine page du musicien rock George Thorogood accompagnant un reportage sur un concert. Dans «Calendar», un supplément du *Boston Globe*. (USA)
427 Illustration d'un article sur les années 50 dans le *Dallas Time Herald*. (USA)
428 «Ondes de choc.» Illustration double page d'un rapport du *Plain Dealer Magazine* sur le sexe et la brutalité utilisés comme locomotives par une radio. Couleurs. (USA)
429 Illustration pleine page pour le magazine du *Dallas Time Herald*. Il y est question de la foire aux vedettes de la country music à Nashville, qui permet aux musiciens célèbres et moins connus de signer des autographes. En polychromie. (USA)

427

429

ARTIST / KÜNSTLER / ARTISTE:

430–432 Alan E. Cober
433, 434 Peter Krämer

ART DIRECTOR / DIRECTEUR ARTISTIQUE:

430, 431 Fred Woodward
432 Don Owens
433, 434 Willy Fleckhaus

PUBLISHER / VERLEGER / EDITEUR:

430–432 Dallas Times Herald
433, 434 Frankfurter Allgemeine Zeitung

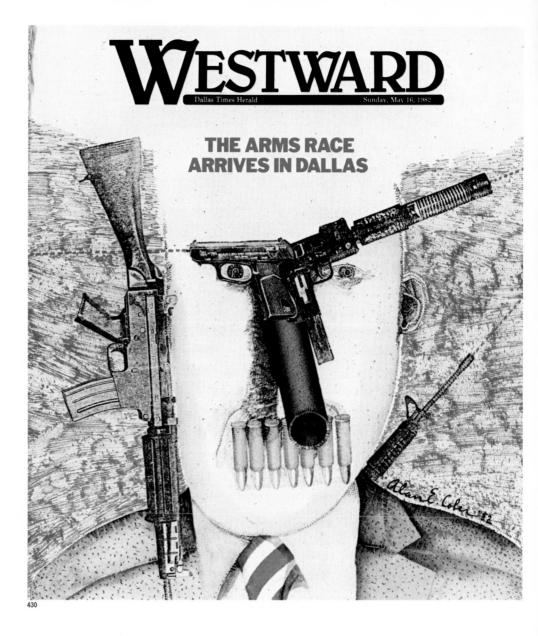

430

430, 432 Cover and illustration for an article in *Westward* about the disturbing fact that the arms race has now arrived in Dallas: too many guns and other weapons are in private hands. (USA)
431 Illustration for a feature in *Westward,* the magazine of the *Dallas Times Herald.* Memories are re-awakened at the Vietnam War Memorial in Washington. (USA)
433, 434 Cover of the *Frankfurter Allgemeine Magazin* and double spread for a feature on the colour red. (GER)

430, 432 Umschlag und Illustration zu einem Artikel in *Westward* über den beängstigenden Waffenbesitz von Privatleuten: «Der Rüstungs-wettkampf hat Dallas erreicht.» (USA)
431 «Harte Wahrheit.» Illustration zu einem Beitrag in *Westward,* Magazin des *Dallas Times Herald.* Es geht um Erinnerungen, die das Vietnam-Kriegsdenkmal in Washington wachruft. (USA)
433, 434 Umschlag des *Frankfurter Allgemeine Magazins* und Doppel-seite zu einem Beitrag über die Farbe Rot. (GER)

430, 432 Couverture et illustration d'un article de *Westward* où il est question de la multiplication des armes dans la population: «La course aux armements a atteint Dallas.» (USA)
431 «Dure vérité.» Illustration pour un article de *Westward,* le magazine du *Dallas Times Herald,* à l'occasion de l'inauguration à Washington du monument aux soldats tombés au Viêt-nam. (USA)
433, 434 Couverture du *Frankfurter Allgemeine Magazin* et page double d'un article consacré à la couleur rouge. (GER)

432

172

431

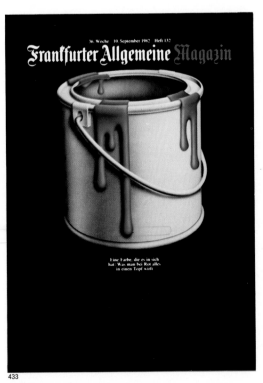

Frankfurter Allgemeine Magazin

36. Woche · 10. September 1982 · Heft 132

Eine Farbe, die es in sich
hat: Was man bei Rot alles
in einen Topf wirft

433

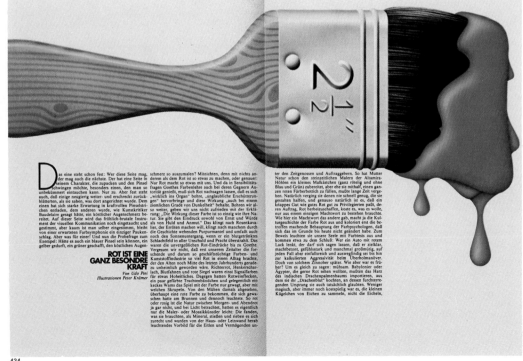

434

D as eine steht schon fest: Wer diese Seite mag, der mag auch die nächste. Der hat eine Seite in seinem Charakter, die zupacken und den Pinsel schwingen möchte, besonders einen, den man so unbekümmert eintauchen kann. Nur zu. Aber fest steht auch, daß einige neugierig weiter- und erschreckt zurückblätterten, als sie sahen, was dort angerichtet wurde. Dem einen hat sich starke Erwartung in kraftvollen Pinselstrichen entladen, dem anderen wurde, wie Kunstkritiker Baudelaire gesagt hätte, ein köstlicher Augenschmerz bereitet. Auf dieser Seite wird das fröhlich-brutale Instrument der visuellen Kommunikation noch eingetaucht und gestimmt, aber kaum ist man selber eingestimmt, bleibt von einer erwarteten Farbsymphonie ein einziger Paukenschlag. Aber was für einer! Und nun die Probefrage zum Exempel: Hätte es auch ein blauer Pinsel sein können, ein gelber gedurft, ein grüner geschafft, den köstlichen Augen-

schmerz so auszumalen? Mitnichten, denn mit nichts anderem als dem Rot ist so etwas zu machen, oder genauer: Nur Rot macht so etwas mit uns. Und da in Sensibilitätsfragen Goethes Farbenlehre auch bei deren Gewarnten Autorität genießt, muß ich Rot nachsagen lassen, daß es sich "wirklich ins Organ" bohre, "ungläubliche Erschütterungen" hervorbringe und diese Wirkung "auch bei einem ziemlichen Grade von Dunkelheit" behalte. Bohren wir also weiter, geben wir uns nicht zufrieden mit der Erklärung: "Die Wirkung dieser Farbe ist so einzig wie ihre Natur. Sie gibt den Eindruck sowohl von Ernst und Würde als von Huld und Anmut." Das klingt nach Rosenkavalier, der Erröten machen wir, klingt nach manchem durch die Geschichte wehenden Purpurmantel und umfaßt auch noch die Sonnenuntergang, wenn er ein blutgetränktes Schlachtfeld in aller Unschuld und Pracht überstrahlt. Das waren die unvergeßlichen Rot-Eindrücke bis zu Goethe. Vergessen wir nicht, daß wir unserem Zeitalter die forschende und darum so geschäftstüchtige Farbes- und Kunststoffindustrie so viel Rot in einen Alltag brachte, der den Alten noch Mitte des letzten Jahrhunderts geradezu unheimlich gewesen wäre. Richterrot, Henkerscharlach, Blutfahnen und rote Siegel waren einst Signalfarben für etwas Hoheitliches. Dagegen hatten Rotweinflecken, ein paar gefärbte Trachtenbändchen und gelegentlich ein keckes Wams nur das Spiel mit der Farbe nur gewagt, aber mit welchen Skrupeln. Von den Mühen damals abgesehen, überhaupt eine rote Farbe zu bekommen, die sich gewaschen hatte am Brunnen und dennoch leuchtete. So rot oder rosig ist die Natur zwischen Morgen- und Abendrot ja gar nicht, und bei Licht betrachtet, hatten es eigentlich nur die Maler- oder Mosaikkünstler leicht: Die fanden, was sie brauchten, als Mineral, stießen und rieben es sich zurecht und wurden von der Haus- oder Leinwand herab leuchtendes Vorbild für die Eitlen und Vermögenden un-

ter den Zeitgenossen und Auftraggebern. So hat Mutter Natur schon den steinzeitlichen Malern der Altamira-Höhlen ein kleines Malkästchen (ganz rötelig und ohne Blau und Grün) abbereitet, aber ehe sie mithalf, einen ganzen roten Färberbottich zu füllen, mußte lange Zeit vergehen. Natürlich verging sie denen nie schnell genug, die sie gestalten halfen, um jeden Preis. Und genauso natürlich ist es, daß knapps Gut wie gutes Rot gut zu Privilegierten paßt, deren Auftrag, Rot herbeizuschaffen, koste es, was es wolle, nur aus einem einzigen Machtwort zu bestehen brauchte. Wie hier ein Machtwort das andere gab, macht ja die Kulturgeschichte der Farbe Rot aus und koloriert erst die bis sich als im Grunde bis heute nicht geändert hat. Zum Beweis leuchten uns unsere Seele mit Farbtests aus und kommen etwa zu dem Schluß: Wer ein Auto mit rotem Lack lenkt, der darf sich sagen lassen, daß er zielklar, machthetoig, gefühlreich und auswegfindig sei bis hin zur kalkulierten Aggressivität beim Überholmanöver. Doch von solchem Zinnober später. Wie aber war es früher? Um es gleich zu sagen: mühsam. Babylonien oder Ägypter, die gerne Rot sehen wollten, mußten das Harz des indischen Drachenpalmbaums importieren, aus dem sie die "Drachenblut" kochten, an dessen furchterregenden Ursprung sie erst tatsächlich glaubten. Weniger magisch, aber immer noch kostspielig war es, die kleinen Kügelchen von Eichen zu sammeln, nicht die Eichen,

ROT IST EINE GANZ BESONDRE KRAFT

Von Udo Pini
Illustrationen Peter Krämer

173

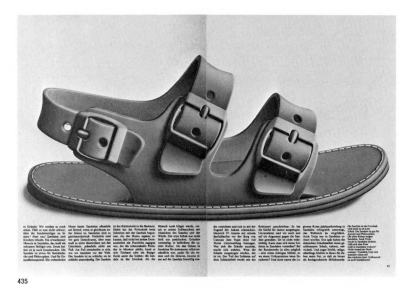

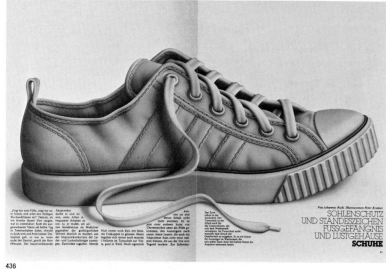

Von Johannes Ruth. Illustrationen Peter Krämer

SOHLENSCHUTZ
UND STANDESZEICHEN
FUSSGEFÄNGNIS
UND LUSTGEHÄUSE
SCHUHE

435

436

Weekend Supplements
Wochenendbeilagen
Suppléments dominicaux

435, 436 Double spreads from the *Frankfurter Allgemeine Magazin* for a feature on shoes and the people who wear them. (GER)
437 Full-page illustration for a story in *Newsday* dealing with an undercover policeman in a radical group of the 60's. (USA)
438 Full-colour illustration for an article that appeared in the *Financial Post Magazine* about rewards paid for helping to catch a thief or for relevant information passed on to the police. (CAN)
439 Black-and-white illustration for a short story in the *Boston Globe Magazine* about a mentally disturbed child. (USA)

435, 436 Doppelseiten aus dem *Frankfurter Allgemeine Magazin* zu einem Beitrag über Schuhe und die Menschen, die sie tragen. (GER)
437 Ganzseitige Illustration zu einer Geschichte in *Newsday*, in der es um einen Polizeiagenten in einer radikalen Gruppe der 60er Jahre geht. (USA)
438 Mehrfarbige Illustration zu einem Artikel über Belohnungen für das Ergreifen von Verbrechern oder entsprechende Hinweise an die Polizei. Erschienen im *Financial Post Magazine*. (CAN)
439 Schwarzweiss-Illustration zu einer Kurzgeschichte im *Boston Globe Magazine*. Thema ist ein seelisch gestörtes Kind. (USA)

435, 436 Doubles pages du *Frankfurter Allgemeine Magazin*. Article consacré aux types de chaussures et aux gens qui les portent. (GER)
437 Illustration pleine page pour un récit paru dans *Newsday* au sujet d'un policier qui s'est insinué dans un groupe radical dans les années 60. (USA)
438 Illustration polychrome d'un article étudiant le système des primes accordées pour l'identification d'un malfaiteur et paru dans le *Financial Post Magazine*. (CAN)
439 Illustration noir et blanc pour une nouvelle publiée dans le *Boston Globe Magazine*. Le sujet: un enfant perturbé émotionnellement. (USA)

437

438

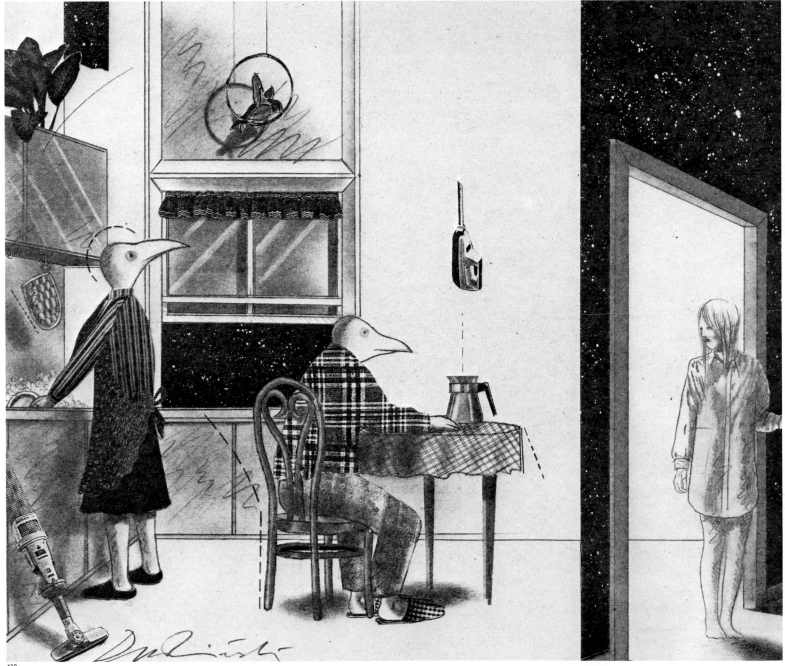

439

175

440

440 Illustration for the introductory double spread of a feature in *Quest* about the problem of settling the visiting times for children of divorced parents. In soft colours. (CAN)
441, 442 "Hard Choices." Two facing illustrations in black and white from an article about the situation and problems of unions. Taken from *The Progressive*. (USA)
443 Illustration from the dummy-issue of *Issues*, a magazine devoted to anti-nuclear subjects. (USA)
444 Illustration in black and white for a feature in *New Jersey Monthly*. The subject dealt with here is bribes cases of two Senators. (USA)
445 Illustration in actual size from an article taken from *Spiegel* and re-published in *Saturday Night*. It claims that in its justification and depiction of the annual seal hunt the federal government has deliberately deceived the Canadian public. (CAN)

440 Illustration für die einleitende Doppelseite zu einem Beitrag in *Quest* über das Problem der Besuchsregelung für Kinder geschiedener Eltern. In sanften Farbtönen. (CAN)
441, 442 Zwei gegenüberliegende Illustrationen in Schwarzweiss aus einem Artikel über die Situation und Probleme der Gewerkschaften. Aus *The Progressive*. (USA)
443 Aus der Null-Nummer von *Issues*, einer Zeitschrift, die sich gegen die Nuklearrüstung richtet. (USA)
444 Illustration in Schwarzweiss zu einem Beitrag in *New Jersey Monthly*. Es geht darin um Bestechungsaffairen zweier Senatoren. (USA)
445 «Blutige Lügen.» Illustration in Originalgrösse zu einem aus dem *Spiegel* übernommenen Artikel in *Saturday Night*. Die kanadische Regierung wird darin beschuldigt, gegenüber der Öffentlichkeit bewusst falsche Angaben über die Robbenjagd gemacht zu haben. (CAN)

441

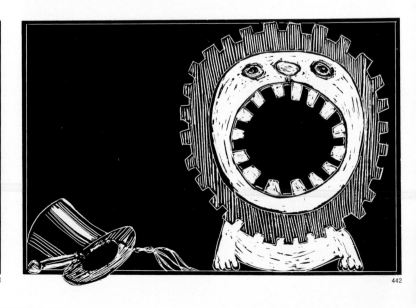

442

444

ARTIST / KÜNSTLER / ARTISTE:

440 Blair Drawson
441–444 Frances Jetter
445 Bill Russell

DESIGNER / GESTALTER / MAQUETTISTE:

440 Mary Opper
441, 442 Patrick Flynn
444 Kati Korpijaako
445 Bruce Ramsay

ART DIRECTOR / DIRECTEUR ARTISTIQUE:

440 Arthur Niemi
441, 442 Patrick Flynn
443 Steve Heller/Martin Fox/Andrew Kner
444 Kati Korpijaako
445 Louis Fishauf

PUBLISHER / VERLEGER / EDITEUR:

440 Comac Communications
441, 442 The Progressive
443 Issues Magazine
444 New Jersey Monthly
445 Saturday Night Magazine

440 Illustration pour la page double initiale d'un article de *Quest* sur le problème des visites d'un parent divorcé à l'enfant resté chez son conjoint. Couleurs adoucies. (CAN)
441, 442 Ces deux illustrations noir et blanc se font face pour documenter les problèmes et la situation des syndicats. Dans *The Progressive*. (USA)
443 Illustration pour le numéro pilote d'*Issues*, un magazine résolument anti-nucléaire. (USA)
444 Illustration noir-blanc pour un article du *New Jersey Monthly* évoquant des affaires de corruption où sont impliqués deux sénateurs. (USA)
445 «Mensonges sanglants.» Illustration au format original pour un article de *Saturday Night* repris du *Spiegel*. On y accuse le gouvernement canadien d'avoir menti à l'opinion publique au sujet de la chasse aux bébés-phoques. (CAN)

443

445

446

446 "The Mountain Men—A Lifestyle of Challenge." Introductory illustration in shades of brown and green for a feature in *Westward*, the week-end magazine of the *Dallas Times Herald*. (USA)
447 Black-and-white illustration for an espionage story in *Washington Post Magazine*, excerpted from a book by a retired CIA intelligence officer. (USA)
448 "The Deadly Legacy of Hiroshima and Nagasaki." Illustration for a feature in *Plain Dealer Magazine* about the danger of the atomic armaments race. (USA)

446 «Die Männer der Berge.» Einleitende Illustration in Braun- und Grüntönen zu einem Artikel über einen Führer in Kanadas Wildnis. Aus *Westward*, Wochenend-Magazin des *Dallas Times Herald*. (USA)
447 Schwarzweiss-Illustration für einen Beitrag im *Washington Post Magazine*, in dem es um eine Spionage-Affaire im besetzten Wien nach dem Kriege geht. (USA)
448 «Tödliches Vermächtnis von Hiroshima und Nagasaki.» Illustration für einen Beitrag im *Plain Dealer Magazine* über die Gefahr des atomaren Wettrüstens. (USA)

446 «Les Hommes de la montagne.» Illustration en tête d'un article consacré à un guide de la vie sauvage au Canada. Divers bruns et verts. Dans *Westward*, le magazine dominical du *Dallas Time Herald*. (USA)
447 Illustration en noir et blanc pour un article du *Washington Post Magazine* décrivant une affaire d'espionnage dans la Vienne occupée de l'après-guerre. (USA)
448 «L'héritage mortel d'Hiroshima et de Nagasaki.» Illustration pour un article du *Plain Dealer Magazine* dénonçant les dangers de la course aux armements. (USA)

447

448

ARTIST/KÜNSTLER/ARTISTE:

446 James Noel Smith
447 Brad Holland
448 Marshall Arismann

ART DIRECTOR/DIRECTEUR ARTISTIQUE:

446 Fred Woodward
447 Ed Schneider
448 Greg Paul

PUBLISHER/VERLEGER/EDITEUR:

446 Dallas Times Herald
447 The Washington Post
448 The Plain Dealer Publishing Co.

449

ARTIST / KÜNSTLER / ARTISTE:

449, 452, 453 J.C. Suarès
450 Barbara Nessim
451 Dale Brubaker

DESIGNER / GESTALTER / MAQUETTISTE:

449 Nicky Kalish
450 Pam Vassil
451 Dale Brubaker

ART DIRECTOR / DIRECTEUR ARTISTIQUE:

449 Nicky Kalish
450 Pam Vassil
452 Steven Heller
453 George Delmerico

AGENCY / AGENTUR / AGENCE – STUDIO:

450 Nessim & Associates

PUBLISHER / VERLEGER / EDITEUR:

449, 450, 452, 453 The New York Times
451 The Miami News

449 Illustration for the "Art and Leisure" section in the *New York Times* on the subject of trends in art seen in the perspective of art history. (USA)
450 Pen-and-ink drawing for "A Guide to Summer Dance Festivals" in the *New York Times*. (USA)
451 Black-and-white illustration for a feature on reincarnation published in the *Miami News*. (USA)
452, 453 Two pen-and-ink drawings as illustrations for the Op-Ed page of *The New York Times*. The drawings accompanied the following texts: Fig. 452 an article on productivity; Fig. 453 an article entitled "Chicken". (USA)

449 Illustration für den Sektor «Kunst und Freizeit» in der *New York Times*, hier im Zusammenhang mit einer Betrachtung der neusten Kunsttrends unter kunstgeschichtlichen Aspekten. (USA)
450 Federzeichnung für einen «Führer zu Sommer-Tanzfestivals» in der *New York Times*. (USA)
451 Schwarzweiss-Illustration für einen Beitrag zum Thema Reinkarnation, aus *Miami News*. (USA)
452, 453 Tuschzeichnungen zur Illustration von Artikeln in der *New York Times*. Abb. 452 war für das Thema Produktivität, Abb. 453 für einen Beitrag mit dem Titel «Chicken» (Umgangssprache für «junges Mädchen») bestimmt. (USA)

449 Illustration pour la section «Art et Loisirs» du *New York Times*. Elle se rapporte à la comparaison de tendances artistiques récentes avec l'histoire de l'art tout entière. (USA)
450 Dessin à la plume. «Guide des festivals de danse de l'été» du *New York Times*. (USA)
451 Illustration noir-blanc d'un article sur la réincarnation publié dans *Miami News*. (USA)
452, 453 Dessins à la plume illustrant deux articles du *New York Times*. La fig. 452 traite de la productivité, la fig. 453 concerne un article intitulé «Chicken» (qui veut dire «poulet», mais aussi «jeune fille»). (USA)

450

451

452

453

454

455

456

Newspaper Illustrations
Zeitungs-Illustrationen
Illustrations de journaux

ARTIST / KÜNSTLER / ARTISTE:

454 David Johnson
455–457 Randall Enos

DESIGNER / GESTALTER / MAQUETTISTE:

454 Steven Heller

ART DIRECTOR / DIRECTEUR ARTISTIQUE:

454 Steven Heller
455, 456 Nancy Kent
457 Jerelle Kraus

PUBLISHER / VERLEGER / EDITEUR:

454–457 The New York Times

454–457 Illustrations taken from *The New York Times*. Fig. 454 belongs
to a discussion on books, showing the writers Henry James, Stephen
Crane, H. G. Wells, Ford Madox Ford and Joseph Conrad; Fig. 455 refers
to menu suggestions as alternatives to the traditional turkey dinner on
Thanksgiving Day; Fig. 456 illustrates a reader's question concerning
deviled bones; Fig. 457 is an illustration in actual size for a feature in
which two union bosses are compared. (USA)

454–457 Illustrationen aus der *New York Times*. Abb. 454 gehört zu einer
Buchbesprechung: «Gruppenporträt» (der Schriftsteller Henry James,
Stephen Crane, H. G. Wells, Ford Madox Ford und Joseph Conrad) von
Nicholas Delbanco; Abb. 455 betrifft Menu-Vorschläge zum Erntedank-
fest, als Alternative zu dem traditionellen amerikanischen Truthahnes-
sen; Abb. 456 illustriert eine Anfrage zu dem Gericht «Teufelsknochen»;
Abb. 457 zeigt eine Illustration in Originalgrösse zu einem Beitrag, in dem
zwei Gewerkschafts-Führer miteinander verglichen werden. (USA)

454–457 Illustrations du *New York Times*. La fig. 454 se réfère à un
compte rendu de «Portrait de groupe» (des écrivains Henry James,
Stephen Crane, H. G. Wells, Ford Madox Ford et Joseph Conrad) par
Nicholas Delbanco; la fig. 455 illustre des menus de Thanksgiving
permettant d'éviter la dinde traditionnelle; la fig. 456 interprète une
question de lectrice au sujet de la préparation d'osso-bucco «à la diable»;
quant à la fig. 457, elle représente, reproduite en grandeur originale, les
similarités existant entre deux leaders syndicaux. (USA)

457

458

459

Newspaper Illustrations
Zeitungs-Illustrationen
Illustrations de journaux

462

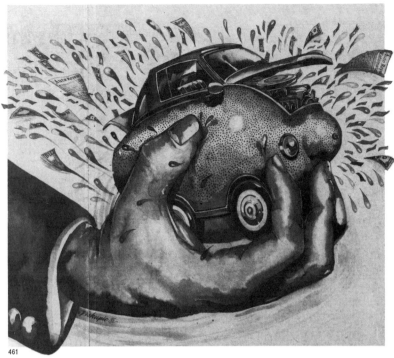

460

461

458 Ein «Mord im Dom». Der entsprechende Beitrag im *Miami Herald* basiert auf einer Predigt zum Gedenken an den ermordeten Erzbischof von San Salvador, Oscar Romero. (USA)
459 Aus *Denver Post*. Das Thema: Väter, die das Sorgerecht für ihre Kinder haben. (USA)
460 Aus *Haagsche Courant* für einen Artikel über Eltern seelisch kranker Kinder. (NLD)
461 Für einen Beitrag in *Newsday* über skrupellose Autowerkstätten, die ständig Reparaturen an hoffnungslos defekten Autos vornehmen und berechnen, sie also wie Zitronen ausquetschen. (USA)
462 «Mittelamerika: Ein Kessel sozialen Verfalls.» Illustration für die Besprechung von Büchern über die Situation in Mittelamerika, erschienen im *Dallas Times Herald*. (USA)
463 Denkende Maschinen sind das Thema des hier illustrierten Artikels aus der *New York Times*. (USA)
464 Aus *Miami Herald*: Die iranische Geiselaffäre und ihre Konsequenzen für die USA. (USA)

458 Un «meurtre dans la cathédrale» (par analogie avec l'œuvre de T. S. Eliot): évocation de l'assassinat de l'archevêque du Salvador Oscar Romero dans le *Miami Herald*. (USA)
459 Illustration du *Denver Post*: quand les pères se voient confier la garde des enfants. (USA)
460 Pour un article du *Haagsche Courant* sur les parents d'enfants perturbés. (NLD)
461 Pour un article de *Newsday* où l'on stigmatise les garagistes sans scrupules qui font payer de grosses factures de réparation sur des autos délabrées et pressent donc «le citron». (USA)
462 «L'Amérique centrale: le chaudron du délabrement social.» Illustration pour un compte rendu d'ouvrages décrivant la situation dans cette région pour le *Dallas Time Herald*. (USA)
463 Le penseur de Balzac relayé par le robot: «l'affaire du siècle». (USA)
464 Dans le *Miami Herald*: l'affaire des otages de Téhéran et les conséquences. (USA)

Machines Who Think:
The Big Business Around the Corner

By BARNABY J. FEDER

SOME people say that, strictly speaking, machines that "think" are unimaginable. A few say that such artificial intelligence is conceivable, but should never be built. But most people seem to feel that, by any reasonable definition, artificial intelligence is already a reality and that one day its manufacture will become a big business.

Scientists have programmed computers to store so much information and use the data so well that the machines perform as if they are in fact thinking. Laboratory models can make medical diagnoses, serve as skilled chemical laboratory assistants, propose and evaluate military tactics, play such games as chess at expert levels and teach mathematics.

Many programs involve some capacity to learn from experience, and industrial robots equipped with camera vision are being given an increasing capacity to adjust to unexpected changes on the factory floor.

"It is developing slowly, and by degree," said Frederic Withington, vice president in charge of information systems at the Cambridge, Mass., consulting firm of Arthur D. Little Inc. "There have been no breakthroughs, but in principle there are some very large markets."

Experts in artificial intelligence envision machines serving as lawyers, doctors, stock analysts, weather forecasters, production workers — and as computer programmers. It is hard to predict how much job displacement such developments might involve. But most experts believe intelligent machines will serve as assistants to humans, instead of as replacements, except in production jobs.

"There is no clear dividing line between computer programming and artificial-intelligence work," said S. Jerrold Kaplan, director of technical marketing for Teknowledge Inc. of Palo Alto, Calif. "It is an attitude toward the structure of your problem and your intellectual lineage. You could say that an artificial-intelligence program can be incorrect without being invalid. That is, you are dealing with artificial intelligence when the program can operate correctly but make a bad judgment."

Mr. Kaplan, whose company was founded last July by 20 computer scientists to provide consulting, training and research services on artificial intelligence, said that he saw an "enormous potential" for the development of "A.I.," the widely recognized initials for the field.

Those working in the field can almost write their own economic ticket. The lowest paid A.I. assistants — those who write the programs and those with masters' degrees in computer science who are involved in a variety of jobs — start at $27,000 to $30,000 a year, according to Mr. Kaplan.

"At the top end, it is meaningless to talk about salary," he said, explaining that top researchers typically had to be offered shares of stock of the company employing them or some other monetary inducement.

In fact, he said, one person holding a doc-

'It has been developing slowly, and by degree. There have been no breakthroughs, but in principle there are some very large markets.'

torate from the Massachusetts Institute of Technology's artificial-intelligence program reportedly turned down a starting salary of $100,000 for a less remunerative position that apparently offered more personal rewards.

Experts on artificial intelligence who attended the annual robotics trade show in Detroit this month dismissed the story, but said that experienced A.I. researchers could easily find offers in the $50,000 to $70,000 range.

"I have never seen a field with so much beating of the bushes to find warm bodies," said Pamela McCorduck, author of "Machines Who Think." "The problem is that you need so much training."

That training starts with a solid grounding in computer science, a field that goes well beyond basic programming skills. In essence, the researcher in artificial intelligence needs to learn how computers accumulate and manipulate information in general, not just how to get a certain model to perform a particular task.

Most of the work is done with a computer language known as List Processing, or LISP, developed in the late 1950's by John McCarthy of the Massachusetts Institute of Technology. According to artificial-intelligence experts, familiarity with the language, which now has splintered into "dia-

lects," paves the way for involvement in any of three major research and development areas.

The two more general areas are natural language processing and knowledge representation. Language skills have often been singled out as a characteristic that separates humans from less intelligent creatures and inanimate machines. Thus, endowing machines with the capacity to analyze and respond to nonmathematical language has been a major goal for artificial-intelligence scientists.

Similarly, the problem of how to represent information so that it becomes accessible to the machine in different situations and can be used in various ways has attracted many leading artificial-intelligence researchers.

Beyond that, much work in artificial intelligence requires expertise in a particular "problem domain." Thus, if the intelligent machine is to serve as an assistant for a chemistry laboratory, its creators need to know a great deal about what chemists think about in addition to how a computer "thinks."

At the same time, industrial robot designers need to understand the kinds of decisions and judgments a worker on the typical assembly line makes.

"In any particular intellectual area," Daniel Bobrow, a Xerox Corporation researcher who is a leading industrial expert in the A.I. field, told The New York Times Magazine in a 1980 interview, "we can probably formalize the knowledge sufficiently so that the computer will do as well or better than most people can do in that area. It turns out that consistency of judgment is at least as important as the knowledge."

The rapidly growing research into artificial intelligence has resulted in the creation of many new university programs beyond the four usually cited as leaders in the field — M.I.T., Yale, Carnegie-Mellon and Stanford.

In the last two years, business interest has expanded beyond the use of such "think tanks" like the MITRE Corporation, SRI International, and the RAND Corporation and industrial pioneers like Schlumberger Ltd., the New York- and Paris-based oilservices giant.

A host of well-known information industry companies, including I.B.M., and numerous start-up companies with inventive-buying names such as Machine Intelligence Corporation, Artificial Intelligence Corporation, and Cognitive Systems Inc. have entered the field.

"So far many of the best young Ph.D.'s are still being absorbed into universities," said Carl Engelman, head of knowledge-based systems studies at MITRE.

"But artificial-intelligence experts say that the demand is so strong that attempts by businesses to raid university programs or one another are common. And, following the pattern established in biotechnology, many academics are also getting involved in companies that allow them to invest in the field without abandoning their campus careers.

463

464

185

465 Portrait of the Brazilian poet V. de Morais. (BRA)
466 Pen-and-ink drawing taken from *The New York Times* for an article about the Shiits in the Lebanon. (USA)
467 Woodcut in black and white for an illustration of a political feature published in *Folhetim*. (BRA)
468 Another black-and-white woodcut from the newspaper *Folhetim* on the subject of behavioural research. (BRA)

465 Porträt des brasilianischen Dichters V. de Morais. (BRA)
466 Federzeichnung aus der *New York Times*, für einen Artikel über die Schiiten im Libanon. (USA)
467 Holzschnitt in Schwarzweiss für die Illustration eines politischen Beitrags in *Folhetim*. (BRA)
468 Ein weiterer Holzschnitt aus der Zeitung *Folhetim*, hier zum Thema der Verhaltensforschung. Schwarzweiss. (BRA)

465 Portrait du poète brésilien V. de Morais. (BRA)
466 Dessin à la plume pour le *New York Times*, dont un article évoque la communauté chi'ite au Liban. (USA)
467 Gravure sur bois, noir et blanc, illustrant un article politique de *Folhetim*. (BRA)
468 Une autre gravure sur bois publiée dans le journal *Folhetim*. Le sujet: l'éthologie (science du comportement). Noir, blanc. (BRA)

465

466

ARTIST / KÜNSTLER / ARTISTE:

465 João Abel Manta
466 Ardeshir Mohasses
467, 468 Rubem Campos Grilo

ART DIRECTOR / DIRECTEUR ARTISTIQUE:

465 João Abel Manta
466 Jerelle Kraus

PUBLISHER / VERLEGER / EDITEUR:

465 Projornal Ltd.
466 The New York Times
467, 468 Folha de São Paulo

467

468

187

469–480 Spreads with illustrations by Miran taken from the humorous graphics magazine *Raposa* which is made up like a newspaper. Fig. 469: title spread of the first issue of the magazine's newly designed edition; Fig. 470: a satirical feature about the "abortion of creativity"; Fig. 471: a special page with a list of bars; Fig. 472: portrait of a Brazilian from Parana, "Export Type"; Fig. 473: a black-and-white collage for an article about Yoko Ono, taken from *Baton* (lipstick), the special section for women; Fig. 474: opening page of a story entitled "Exile"; Figs. 476–478: double spreads containing commentaries ("Pros and cons") and poems; Fig. 479: a full-page illustration for a corresponding "true story"; Fig. 480: a feature on the subject of democracy. (BRA)

469–480 Seiten mit Illustrationen von Miran aus der humoristischen Graphikerzeitschrift *Raposa*, die wie eine Zeitung aufgemacht ist. Abb. 469: Titelseite der ersten Nummer der neugestalteten Ausgabe des Magazins; Abb. 470: ein satirischer Beitrag über «Abtreibung der Kreativität»; Abb. 471: spezielle Seite mit einer Liste von Bars; Abb. 472 Porträt eines Brasilianers aus Paraná, «Typ Export»; Abb. 473: Collage in Schwarzweiss für einen Artikel über Yoko Ono, aus dem Sonderteil für Frauen, *Baton* (Lippenstift); Abb. 474: «Geschichte aus dem Exil»; Abb. 475: für einen politischen Beitrag; Abb. 476–478: Doppelseiten mit Kommentaren («Pro und Kontra») und Gedichten; Abb. 479: ganzseitige Illustration zu einer «wahren Geschichte»; Abb. 480: ein Beitrag über die Demokratie. (BRA)

469–480 Pages, illustrées par Miran, de la revue graphique humoristique *Raposa* présentée comme un journal. Fig. 469: page de titre du premier numéro de la nouvelle série de la revue; fig. 470: «l'avortement de la créativité» vu sous un jour satirique; fig. 471: page spéciale avec une liste de bars; fig. 472: portrait d'un Brésilien du Paraná «type exportation»; fig. 473: collage noir et blanc pour un article sur Yoko Ono dans la section féminine intitulée *Baton* (rouge à lèvres); fig. 474: «histoire d'un exil»; fig. 475: illustration d'un article politique; fig. 476–478: doubles pages agrémentées de commentaires («pour et contre») et de poèmes; fig. 479: illustration pleine page pour une «histoire vraie»; fig. 480: pour un article sur le difficile sujet de la démocratie. (BRA)

House Organs
Hauszeitschriften
Journaux d'entreprise

ARTIST / KÜNSTLER / ARTISTE:
469–480 Oswaldo Miranda (Miran)

DESIGNER / GESTALTER / MAQUETTISTE:
469–480 Oswaldo Miranda

ART DIRECTOR / DIRECTEUR ARTISTIQUE:
469–480 Oswaldo Miranda

AGENCY / AGENTUR / AGENCE:
469–480 Miran Estudio

PUBLISHER / VERLEGER / EDITEUR:
469–480 Raposa Magazine

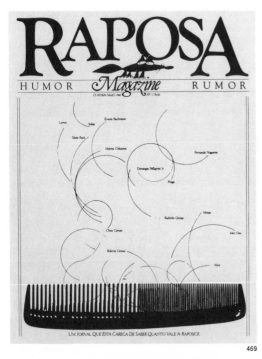

469

470

471

472

473

474

475

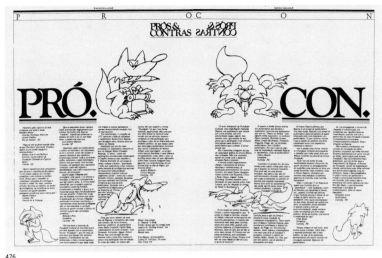

476

477

478

479

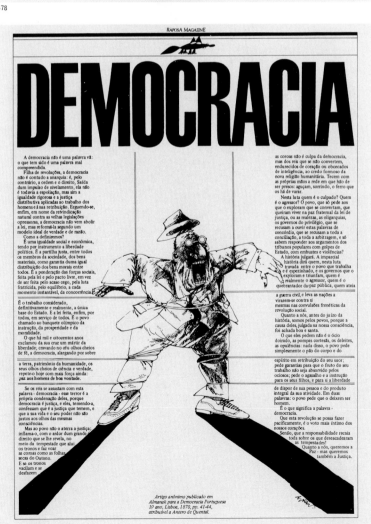

480

482

483

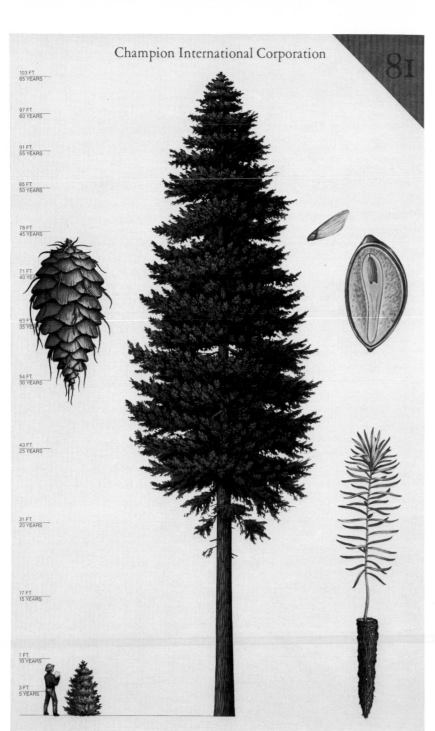

Champion International Corporation

81

103 FT.
65 YEARS

97 FT.
60 YEARS

91 FT.
55 YEARS

85 FT.
50 YEARS

78 FT.
45 YEARS

71 FT.
40 YEARS

63 FT.
35 YEARS

54 FT.
30 YEARS

43 FT.
25 YEARS

31 FT.
20 YEARS

17 FT.
15 YEARS

7 FT.
10 YEARS

3 FT.
5 YEARS

481

ARTIST / KÜNSTLER / ARTISTE:

481 Mark Hess
482–484 Peter Good

DESIGNER / GESTALTER / MAQUETTISTE:

481 Richard Hess
482–484 Jerry Pavey

ART DIRECTOR / DIRECTEUR ARTISTIQUE:

481 Richard Hess
482–484 Jerry Pavey

AGENCY / AGENTUR / AGENCE – STUDIO:

482–484 Jerry Pavey Design Studio, Inc.

481 Cover for the 1981 annual report of the paper manufacturer *Champion International*. The presentation of a tree along with details of its characteristics shown on the verso, is an integral part of a uniform style chosen by this company for its annual reports which have all been designed and illustrated by Richard and Mark Hess. (USA)
482–484 Taken from the Farm Credit Banks' Report to Investors. All illustrations are photographs of textile work—here a double spread with patchwork in green shades with blue and yellow, and an illustration in actual size. (USA)

481 Umschlag für den Jahresbericht 1981 des Papierherstellers *Champion International*. Die Darstellung eines Baumes mit Einzelheiten über seine Eigenschaften auf der Rückseite gehört zu dem einheitlichen Stil, den das Unternehmen für die Präsentation seiner Jahresberichte gewählt hat: alle von Richard und Mark Hess gestaltet und illustriert. (USA)
482–484 Aus dem Geschäftsbericht einer landwirtschaftlichen Kreditanstalt. Alle Illustrationen sind Aufnahmen textiler Arbeiten; hier eine Doppelseite mit Patchwork in Grüntönen mit Blau und Gelb und eine Illustration in Originalgrösse. (USA)

481 Couverture du rapport annuel pour 1981 du papetier *Champion International*. La représentation d'un arbre avec descriptif détaillé au dos est le type même du style uniforme adopté pour la présentation des rapports annuels de cette entreprise par Richard et Mark Hess, qui en signent la conception et l'illustration. (USA)
482–484 Extraits du rapport annuel d'un Crédit Agricole. Toutes les illustrations consistent en photos de travaux textiles; on voit ici une double page de patchwork en divers verts avec du bleu et du jaune et une illustration grandeur originale. (USA)

485 Presentation of research and development expenses for existing products, new products, basic and other, and new investments. Taken from the 1981 annual report of *W. R. Grace & Company*. (USA)
486–488 Diagrams of the leasing receivables (Fig. 486) and bank-related finance companies by net receivables (Fig. 487), taken from a report of *Manufacturers Hanover*. The inserted diagram section is on orange paper and the larger text section on beige paper. (USA)
489–493 From the report concerning the research and development programme of *Nestlé S.A.* The areas presented are as follows: two research programmes (Fig. 489); the percentages of essential fatty acids in foodstuffs (Fig. 490); a person's daily nutritional requirements, etc. (Fig. 491); the company's various spheres of research (Fig. 492) and technical documentation (Fig. 493). (SWI)

485 Darstellung der Ausgaben für Forschung und Entwicklung in vier Bereichen, aus dem Jahresbericht 1981 des Industrieunternehmens *W. R. Grace & Company*. (USA)
486–488 Diagramme aus einem Bericht der Bank *Manufacturers Hanover* zur Darstellung des Umlaufvermögens aus zwei Bereichen und vollständige Präsentation des eingehefteten Diagrammteils. (USA)
489–493 Aus dem Bericht über das Forschungs- und Entwicklungsprogramm der *Nestlé S.A.* Die dargestellten Gebiete: Zwei Forschungsprogramme (Abb. 489); Anteile essentieller Fettsäuren in Nahrungsmitteln (Abb. 490); Tagesbedarf des Menschen an Nährstoffen etc. (Abb. 491); die verschiedenen Forschungsbereiche (Abb. 492); die technische Dokumentation (Abb. 493). (SWI)

485 Interprétation graphique des quatre tranches de dépenses au titre de la recherche et du développement, dans le rapport annuel pour 1981 du groupe industriel *W. R. Grace & Co*. (USA)
486–488 Diagrammes des comptes débiteurs de la banque *Manufacturers Hanover* dans deux secteurs d'activité et présentation complète de la section diagrammes du rapport annuel. (USA)
489–493 Pages d'un rapport sur le programme de recherche et de développement de *Nestlé S.A.* Sujets représentés: deux programmes de recherche (fig. 489); les pourcentages d'acides gras essentiels dans l'alimentation (fig. 490); les besoins quotidiens en substances nutritives (fig. 491); les domaines de recherche (fig. 492); la documentation technique (fig. 493). (SWI)

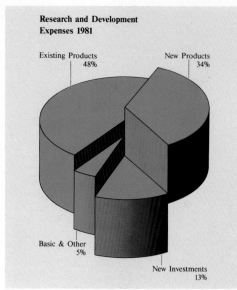

485

486

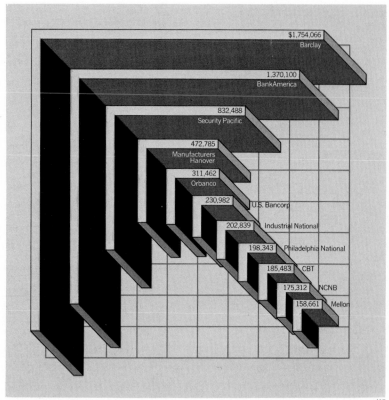

487

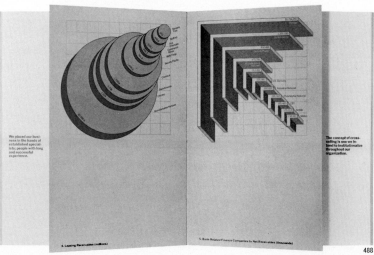

488

489

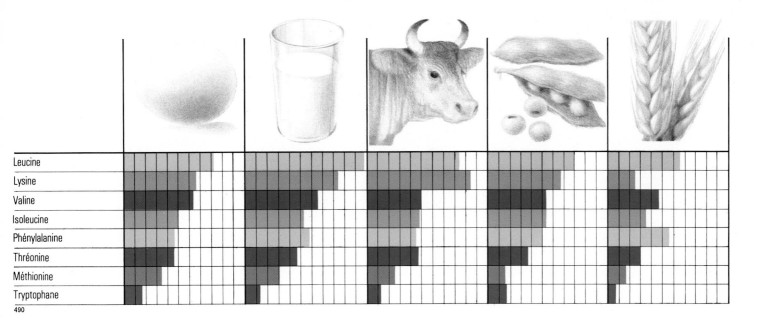

	Leucine																											
Leucine																												
Lysine																												
Valine																												
Isoleucine																												
Phénylalanine																												
Thréonine																												
Méthionine																												
Tryptophane																												

490

DESIGNER / GESTALTER / MAQUETTISTE:

485 George Tscherny/Elizabeth Coburn Ball
486–488 Peg Patterson
489–493 Blumenstein, Plancherel, Krügel

ART DIRECTOR / DIRECTEUR ARTISTIQUE:

485 George Tscherny
486–488 Anthony Russell

AGENCY / AGENTUR / AGENCE – STUDIO:

485 George Tscherny, Inc.
486–488 Anthony Russell, Inc.
489–493 Nestec, Abt. Grafik und Druck

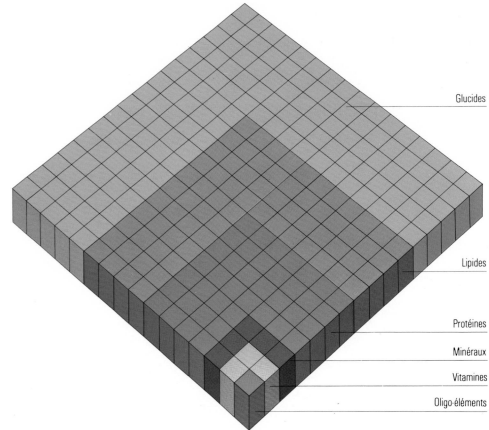

Glucides

Lipides

Protéines

Minéraux

Vitamines

Oligo-éléments

491

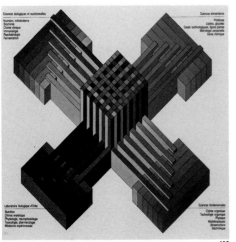

492

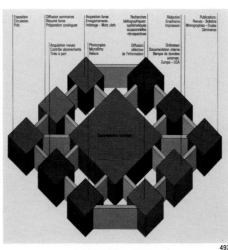

493

Annual Reports
Jahresberichte
Rapports annuels

494

496

495

497

498

ARTIST / KÜNSTLER / ARTISTE:

494, 495 Lonnie Sue Johnson
496 Robert Weaver
497 David Wilcox
499 Jim Butcher/Robert J. Jones
500, 501 Michael Mabry

DESIGNER / GESTALTER / MAQUETTISTE:

494, 495 Tom Laidlaw
496–498 Bennett Robinson/Paula Zographos
499 Joel Katz/Jerome Cloud
500, 501 Michael Mabry

ART DIRECTOR / DIRECTEUR ARTISTIQUE:

494, 495 Michael Weymouth
496–498 Bennett Robinson
499 Anthony V. Leone
500, 501 Nicolas Sidjakov

AGENCY / AGENTUR / AGENCE – STUDIO:

494, 495 Weymouth Design, Inc.
496–498 Corporate Graphics Inc.
499 Katz Weeler Design/Lewis & Gilman
500, 501 Hill & Knowlton/Sidjakov Berman & Gomez

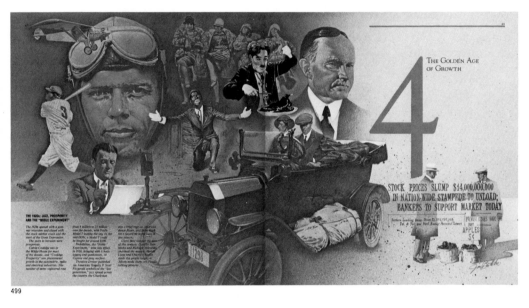

499

494, 495 Full-colour illustrations from the annual report of *Chelsea*, a diversified company. Fig. 494: the careful exploration of many avenues and alternatives; Fig. 495: responding to the challenge of the future. (USA)
496–498 Illustrations and cover of the 1982 annual report of the *H. J. Heinz* company. Ten *Heinz* employees responded notably well when challenged to express themselves by way of poetry, and these poems were then interpreted by ten leading illustrators. (USA)
499 Full-colour double spread from a brochure issued on the occasion of the 100th anniversary of UGI corporation. (USA)
500, 501 Double spread and page from the 1981 annual report of the *Highlands Energy Corporation*. The illustrations, in pastel shades, show a travelling block (a component of the drilling rig) and a truck-mounted light-duty rig for exploration drilling. (USA)

494, 495 Mehrfarbige Illustrationen aus einem Jahresbericht des diversifizierten Unternehmens *Chelsea*. Abb. 494: die sorgfältige Wahl der Wege und Alternativen; Abb. 495: wie man den Anforderungen der Zukunft gerecht werden will. (USA)
496–498 Illustrationen und Umschlag des *Heinz*-Jahresberichtes 1982. Zehn Angestellte des Unternehmens schrieben Gedichte, die dann von zehn bekannten Illustratoren für den Bericht interpretiert wurden. (USA)
499 Mehrfarbige Doppelseite aus einer Broschüre anlässlich des hundertjährigen Bestehens eines Energiekonzerns. (USA)
500, 501 Doppelseite und Seite aus dem Jahresbericht 1981 der *Highlands Energy Corporation*. Die Illustrationen zeigen ein auf einen Lastwagen montiertes Leichtbohrgerät für Probebohrungen und einen Bohrkopf (Bestandteil eines Bohrgerätes). (USA)

494, 495 Illustrations polychromes dans un rapport annuel du groupe diversifié *Chelsea*. Fig. 494: le choix circonspect des orientations et alternatives; fig. 495: comment répondre aux exigences de l'avenir «avec une résolution inchangée». (USA)
496–498 Illustrations et couverture du rapport annuel de la société H. J. *Heinz* pour 1982. Dix employés du groupe se sont mués en poètes dans cette publication, et leurs productions ont été confiées pour illustration à dix artistes réputés. (USA)
499 Double page polychrome d'une brochure publiée à l'occasion du centenaire d'un groupe producteur d'énergie. (USA)
500, 501 Double page et page simple du rapport annuel pour 1981 de la *Highlands Energy Corporation*. On y voit un équipement de forage léger sur camion faisant sonde mobile et une tête de sonde pour forage rotary. (USA)

500

501

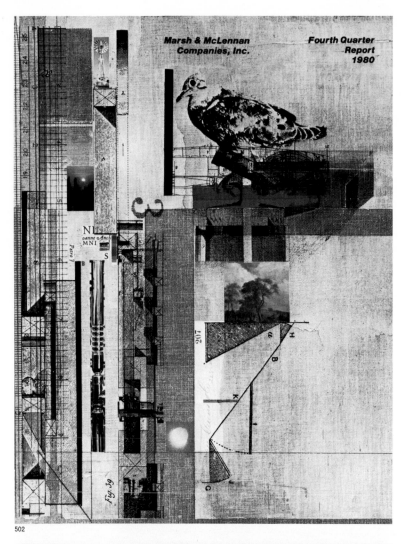

Marsh & McLennan
Companies, Inc.

*Fourth Quarter
Report
1980*

502

Marsh & McLennan
Companies, Inc.

*First Quarter Report
1980*

503

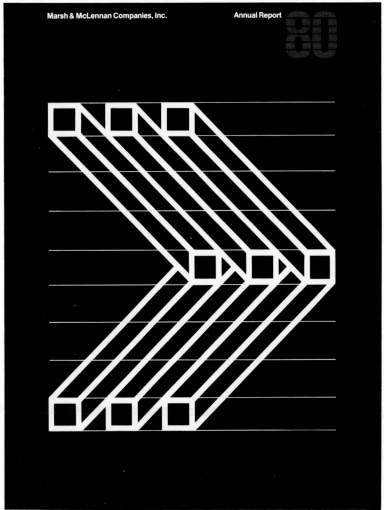

Marsh & McLennan Companies, Inc.   Annual Report   80

504

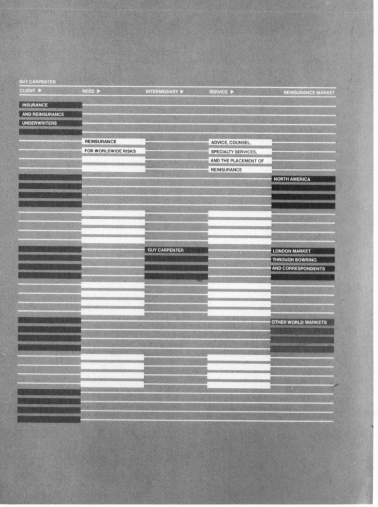

GUY CARPENTER

CLIENT ▶   NEED ▶   INTERMEDIARY ▶   SERVICE ▶   REINSURANCE MARKET

INSURANCE
AND REINSURANCE
UNDERWRITERS

REINSURANCE   ADVICE, COUNSEL,
FOR WORLDWIDE RISKS   SPECIALTY SERVICES,
                              AND THE PLACEMENT OF
                              REINSURANCE

                                                         NORTH AMERICA

                GUY CARPENTER   LONDON MARKET
                                                         THROUGH BOWRING
                                                         AND CORRESPONDENTS

                                                         OTHER WORLD MARKETS

505

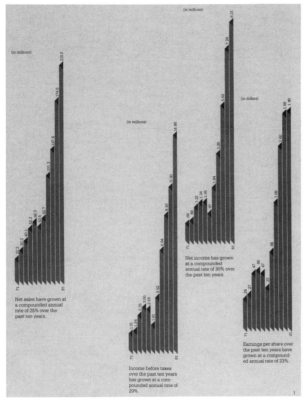

506

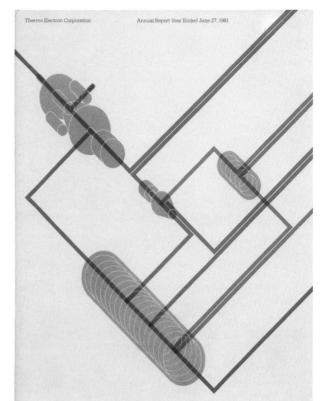

507

ARTIST / KÜNSTLER / ARTISTE:

502, 503 Fred Otnes
506, 507 Michael Weymouth/
Tom Laidlaw
509 Michael Garland

DESIGNER / GESTALTER:

504, 505 Karen Katinas
506, 507 Tom Laidlaw
508 H. A. Wyler

ART DIRECTOR:

502, 503 Karen Katinas
504, 505 Leslie A. Segal
506, 507 Michael Weymouth
508 H. A. Wyler
509 Lee Ann Jaffee

AGENCY / AGENTUR / AGENCE:

504, 505 Corporate Annual
Reports, Inc.
506, 507 Weymouth Design, Inc.
508 SHW Werbeberatung

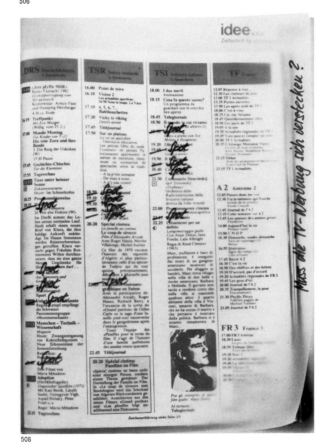

508

509

502–505 Umschläge von zwei Quartalsberichten, Umschlag des Jahresberichtes 1980 und Seite daraus, für die Versicherungsgruppe *Marsh & McLennan*. (USA)
506, 507 Seite mit Säulendiagramm des Einkommens und Umschlag des Jahresberichtes 1981 der *Thermo Electron Corporation*. (USA)
508 Pergamentpapier mit blauer Handschrift über Fernsehprogrammseite als Umschlag für *Idee*, eine Werbefachzeitschrift. (SWI)
509 Umschlag für *View*, eine Zeitschrift für Kabelfernsehen. (USA)

502–505 Covers of two quarterly reports and cover of the 1980 annual report with one of its pages, for the *Marsh & McLennan* insurance group. Figs. 502 and 503 in full colour; Fig. 504 white on dark blue, red numbers. (USA)
506, 507 Page with a diagram of the income and cover of the 1981 annual report of *Thermo Electron Corporation*. (USA)
508 Vellum paper with blue handwriting over page with television programmes as a cover for *Idee* (Idea), a magazine for the advertising world. (SWI)
509 Cover for *View*, the magazine of cable television programming. Designed in typical comic-strip colours. (USA)

502–505 Couvertures de deux rapports trimestriels, couverture du rapport annuel pour 1980 et page extraite de ce dernier, pour la compagnie d'assurances *Marsh & McLennan*. (USA)
506, 507 Page où les revenus de la *Thermo Electron Corporation* figurent sous forme de diagrammes en barres, et couverture du rapport pour 1981. (USA)
508 Programme TV avec griffonnage sur papier parcheminé: c'est là une couverture du magazine publicitaire *Idee*. (SWI)
509 Couverture de *View*, magazine de la télévision par câble. Les couleurs utilisées sont typiques de la bande dessinée. (USA)

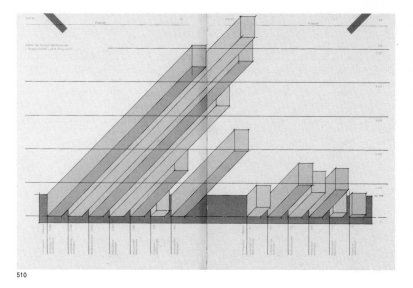

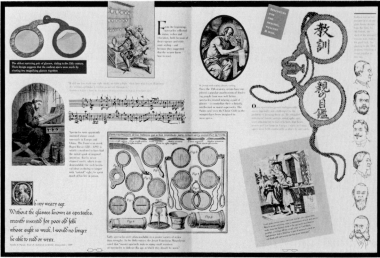

510

511

510 Doppelseite aus einem Jahres- und Geschäftsbericht des Südwestfunks mit einer Darstellung der Fernseh-Sendeminutenkosten. Säulen in Violett- und Grüntönen. (GER)
511, 512 Doppelseite und Umschlag eines Jahresberichts der *Omega Optical Company.* (USA)
513–515 Doppelseiten und auf Pergamentpapier gedruckter Schutzumschlag eines in Buchform erschienenen Geschäftsberichtes einer Gruppe von acht arabischen Firmen. Abb. 513: Wiederholung des Diagramms auf dem Umschlag (Abb. 515), hier mit Angabe der Besitzverteilung; Abb. 514: einleitende Doppelseite zum ersten Kapitel. «Die Wahrheit, wie das Oel, kommt immer an die Oberfläche.» (KUW)
516 Eine der Illustrationen aus einem Buch über die Dachgärten New Yorks. (USA)

510 Double spread from an annual- and business report of Germany's south-west broadcasting corporation, showing television's costs per minute. Columns in violet and green shades. (GER)
511, 512 Double spread and cover of an annual report of the *Omega Optical Company.* (USA)
513–515 Double spreads and a dust jacket printed on vellum of a large-format corporate publication designed to act as a coordinating vehicle and annual report for a group of eight varied Arab companies owned by Al Marzook. Fig. 513: a repetition of the diagram on the cover (Fig. 515); Fig. 514: the introductory double spread to the first chapter. (KUW)
516 One of the illustrations taken from a book about New York's roof gardens. (USA)

510 Double page d'un rapport annuel de la chaîne de radio-télévision du sud-ouest de l'Allemagne Südwestfunk indiquant les frais d'émissions à la minute. Barres violets, verts. (GER)
511, 512 Double page et couverture d'un rapport annuel de l'*Omega Optical Company.* (USA)
513–515 Doubles pages et jaquette sur papier parcheminé d'un rapport annuel publié en volume par un groupe de huit sociétés arabes. Fig. 513: répétition du diagramme de la couverture (fig. 515), assorti de la répartition des actifs; fig. 514: double page initiale du premier chapitre: «La vérité, tout comme le pétrole, finit toujours par faire surface.» (KUW)
516 Illustration tirée d'un ouvrage consacré aux jardins-terrasses des toits de New York. (USA)

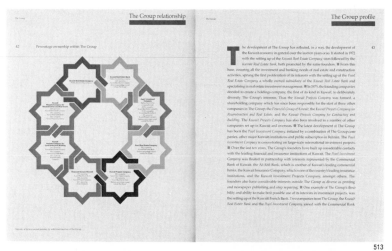

513

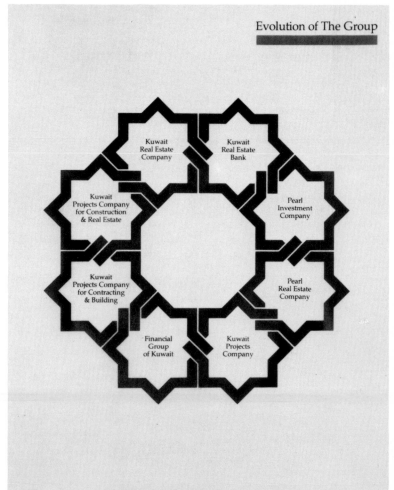

514

515

512

516

ARTIST / KÜNSTLER / ARTISTE:

510 Heinz Bähr
511, 512 Woody Pirtle/Frank Nichols/
    Luis Acevedo/Mike Schroeder
514 Ahmed Moustafa
516 André François

DESIGNER / GESTALTER / MAQUETTISTE:

510 Heinz Bähr
511, 512 Woody Pirtle
513–515 Alan Fletcher/Paul Anthony/
    Gill Davis

ART DIRECTOR / DIRECTEUR ARTISTIQUE:

510 Heinz Bähr
511, 512 Woody Pirtle
513–515 Alan Fletcher
516 Chermayeff & Geismar Assoc.

AGENCY / AGENTUR / AGENCE – STUDIO:

511, 512 Pirtle Design
513–515 Pentagram
516 Chermayeff & Geismar Assoc.

517–522 Illustrations from a specialised magazine for young doctors, *Postgraduate Medicine*. Fig. 517: Bacterial skin infections; Fig. 518: The child with impaired consciousness; Fig. 519: Unresolved bereavement—medical reenactment of a loved one's terminal illness; Fig. 520: Acute upper airway obstruction in the adult (illustration in actual size); Fig. 521: Jaw repositioning and strength testing after this treatment; Fig. 522: How useful is the intensive care unit? (USA)

517–522 Illustrationen aus der Fachzeitschrift für junge Ärzte, *Postgraduate Medicine*, zu folgenden Themen. Abb. 517: Infektionskrankheiten der Haut; Abb. 518: Bewusstseinsstörungen bei Kindern; Abb. 519: Unüberwundener Verlust eines geliebten Menschen und die häufig vom Verstorbenen übernommenen Krankheitssymptome; Abb. 520: akute Verstopfung der oberen Luftwege bei Erwachsenen (Illustration in Originalgrösse); Abb. 521: Kieferkorrekturen mit einem orthopädischen Kinnbackengerät und ihr – umstrittener – Einfluss auf die Körperkraft und Ausdauer; Abb. 522: Intensivstationen und die in manchen Fällen übertriebene Ausnutzung. (USA)

517–522 Illustrations pour la revue *Postgraduate Medicine* destinée aux jeunes médecins. Les sujets traités sont: fig. 518, les troubles de la conscience chez les enfants; fig. 519: les conséquences de la perte d'un être cher sous forme d'un revécu des symptômes morbides du défunt ou de la défunte; fig. 520: l'obstruction aiguë des voies respiratoires supérieures chez l'adulte (illustration au format original); fig. 521: les corrections de mâchoires à l'aide d'appareils orthodontiques et l'influence qu'elles sont censées avoir sur la force et la résistance de l'individu; fig. 522: les unités de soins intensifs et l'utilisation abusive qui en est parfois faite. (USA)

Trade Magazines
Fachzeitschriften
Revues professionnelles

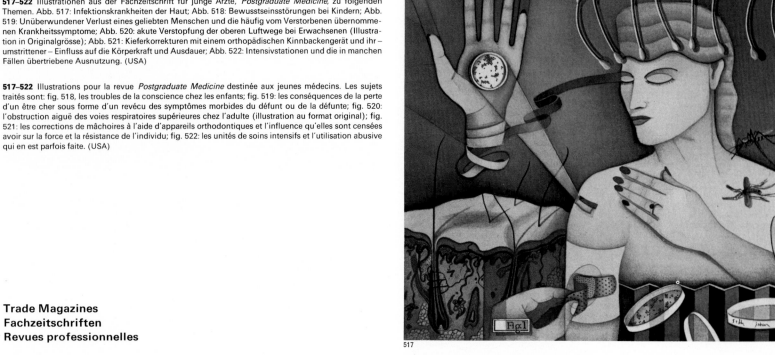

517

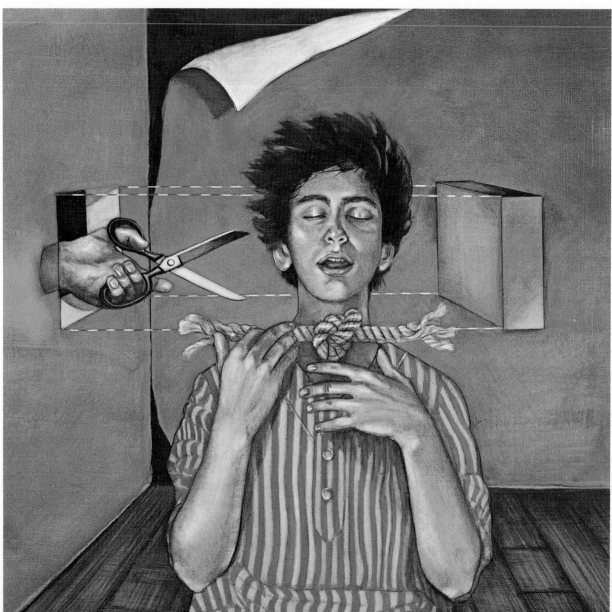

520

ARTIST / KÜNSTLER / ARTISTE:

517 Seth Jaben
518 Peter Bono
519 Sandra Filippucci
520 Anne Kobayashi
521 Terry Boles
522 Geoffrey Moss

ART DIRECTOR:

517–522 Tina Adamek

PUBLISHER / VERLEGER / EDITEUR:

517–522 McGraw-Hill, Inc.

518

519

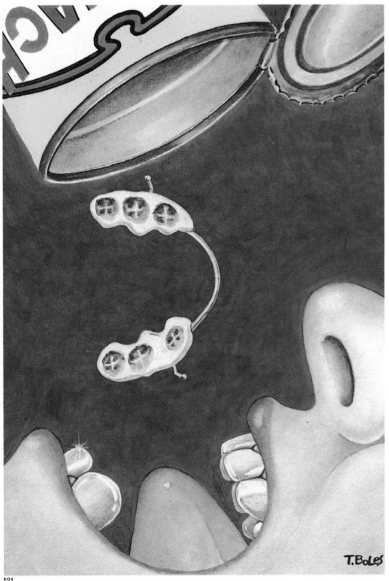

521

522

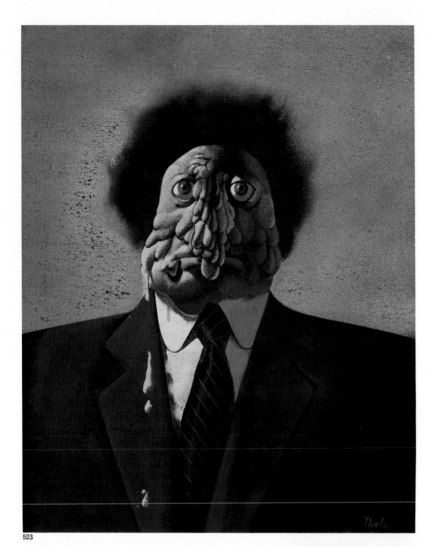

523

524

527

523, 524 Illustration and complete cover of *Portfolio Illustratori*. In green shades. (ITA)
525 Cover of the medical periodical *RN Magazine*. Bright blue, white and red. (USA)
526 Black-and-white illustration for an article in *Postgraduate Medicine* about mild hypertension. (USA)
527, 528 Covers of *Print*, a graphic-design magazine. Fig. 528: reddish brown, ruby red, blue. (USA)
529 Cover for an issue of *Adweek* which shows the founder of CBS, William Paley. (USA)

523, 524 Illustration und vollständiger Umschlag von *Portfolio Illustratori*. In Grüntönen. (ITA)
525 Umschlag der medizinischen Fachzeitschrift *RN Magazine*. Leuchtendes Blau, Weiss und Rot. (USA)
526 Schwarzweiss-Illustration zu einem Artikel in *Postgraduate Medicine* über hohen Blutdruck. (USA)
527, 528 Umschläge der Graphik-Design-Fachzeitschrift *Print*. Abb. 528: Rotbraun, Weinrot, Blau. (USA)
529 Umschlag für eine Ausgabe von *Adweek* mit einem Porträt von William Paley, Gründer von CBS. (USA)

523, 524 Illustration et couverture complète du *Portfolio Illustratori*. Divers tons verts. (ITA)
525 Couverture du magazine médical *RN Magazine*. Bleu lumineux, blanc, rouge. (USA)
526 Illustration noir et blanc d'un article de *Postgraduate Medicine* sur l'hypertension. (USA)
527, 528 Couvertures du magazine d'art graphique *Print*. Fig. 528: brun roux, bordeaux, bleu. (USA)
529 Couverture pour un numéro d'*Adweek*, un magazine publicitaire avec un portrait de William Paley, fondateur de CBS. (USA)

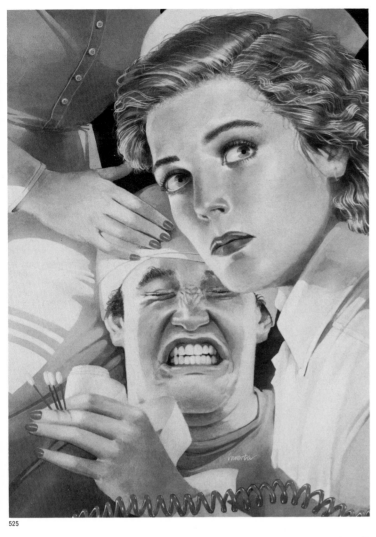

525

526

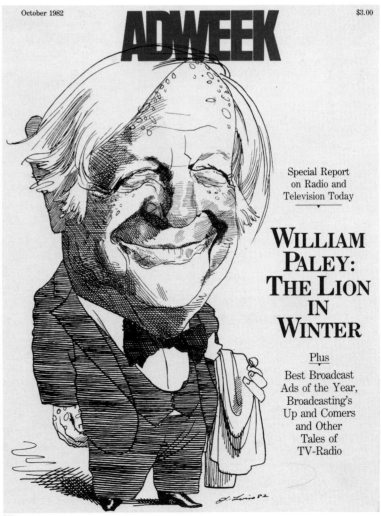

$5 **Print**
AMERICA'S GRAPHIC DESIGN MAGAZINE
MARCH/APRIL 1982
PRINT XXXVI:II

528

October 1982   **ADWEEK** $3.00

Special Report
on Radio and
Television Today

**WILLIAM
PALEY:
THE LION
IN
WINTER**

Plus

Best Broadcast
Ads of the Year,
Broadcasting's
Up and Comers
and Other
Tales of
TV-Radio

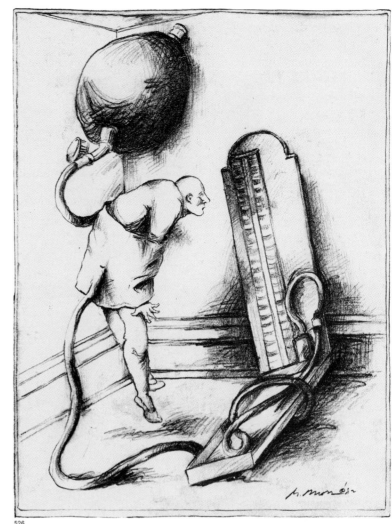

529

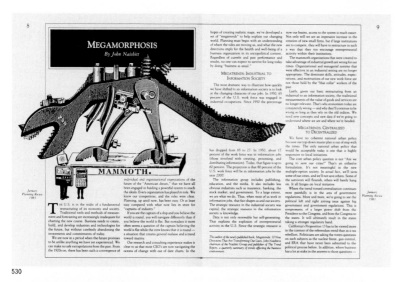

530

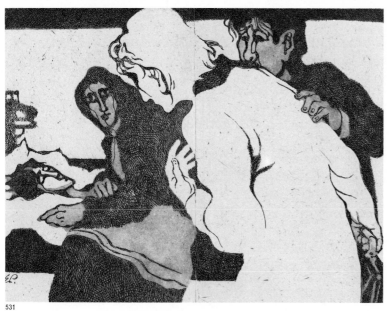

531

532

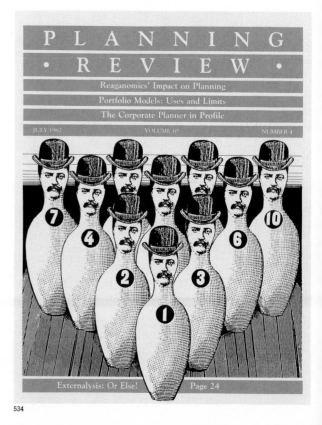

533

534

530, 532 Double spread and an illustration from *Planning Review*, a magazine for corporate planners. Dealt with here is the change in US business from industrial to an informational society and the risks involved in international business. (USA)
531 For a story in the magazine *Medizin heute*. (GER)
533 Cover of *Score*, a news magazine for golf. (GER)
534 Cover of *Planning Review*, a specialised magazine for corporate planners. The theme of the illustration is the dangers of companies that put too much emphasis on internal strategic planning. In black and white with reddish brown beams. (USA)
535, 536 Illustration and complete cover of *Chip*, a specialised magazine for the microcomputer business. (GER)

530, 532 Doppelseite und eine Illustration aus *Planning Review*, einer Fachzeitschrift für Unternehmensplaner. Es geht hier um den Wechsel von einer Industrie- zu einer Informatik-Gesellschaft und um Risiken im internationalen Geschäft. (USA)
531 Für eine Geschichte in der Zeitschrift *Medizin heute*. (GER)
533 Umschlag der Stuttgarter Golf-Nachrichten *Score*. (GER)
534 Umschlag von *Planning Review*, einer Fachzeitschrift für Unternehmensplaner. Thema der Illustration ist die Gefahr, die durch Überbewertung geschäftsinterner Strategien entsteht. In Schwarzweiss mit rotbraunen Balken. (USA)
535, 536 Illustration und vollständiger Umschlag von *Chip*, einem Mikrocomputer Fachmagazin. (GER)

530, 532 Double page et une illustration de *Planning Review*, un magazine d'organisation d'entreprises. Il s'agit ici du passage de la société industrielle à une société informatisée et des risques inhérents aux affaires internationales. (USA)
531 Pour un récit paru dans le magazine *Medizin heute*. (GER)
533 Couverture de *Score*, périodique du golf. (GER)
534 Couverture de *Planning Review*, un magazine d'organisation d'entreprises. L'illustration interprète le danger qu'il y a à surévaluer les stratégies internes de l'entreprise. Illustration en noir et blanc, barre brun roux. (USA)
535, 536 Illustration et couverture complète de *Chip*, un magazine spécialisé dans le domaine des microprocesseurs. (GER)

536

535

ARTIST / KÜNSTLER / ARTISTE:

530, 532, 534 Ner Beck
531 Edward Prüssen
533 Wolfgang M. Dehm
535, 536 Ernst Jünger

DESIGNER / GESTALTER:

530, 532, 534 Ner Beck
533 Wolfgang M. Dehm

ART DIRECTOR:

530, 532, 534 Ner Beck/
Robert Randall
531 Helmut Hagen
533 Wolfgang M. Dehm
535, 536 Hans Kur

AGENCY / AGENTUR / AGENCE:

530, 532, 534 Beck Graphics
533 Art & Concept Studio

PUBLISHER / VERLEGER / EDITEUR:

530, 532, 534 Robert J. Allio
531 Deutscher Aerzte-Verlag
533 Stuttgarter Golf Club Solitude
535, 536 Vogel-Verlag KG

Trade Magazines

IN THE WAKE OF A BLAST

By Harold F. Hamit, M.D.

Scientific interest in blast injury usually increases during wartime and declines during times of peace. As a result, physicians tend to become less familiar with the nature and mechanisms of these injuries and lose a clear sense of the special treatment considerations they involve. The importance of blast injury is by no means limited to wartime, however. Many of the *(continued*

EMERGENCY MEDICINE / JANUARY 30, 1983

537

ILLUSTRATION BY PATRICK BLACKWELL

538

539

ARTIST / KÜNSTLER / ARTISTE:

537 Eric Fowler
538 Patrick Blackwell
539 Yoji Kuri
540 Bill Sanderson
541 Richard B. Farrell
542 Diz Wallis

DESIGNER / GESTALTER / MAQUETTISTE:

538 Terry Ross Koppel
541 Tom Sizemore
542 Patrick Deffenbaugh

ART DIRECTOR / DIRECTEUR ARTISTIQUE:

537 James Walsh
538 Terry Ross Koppel
539 Yoji Kuri
540 Tony Stanford
541 Wayne Burkart
542 Elizabeth Woodson

AGENCY / AGENTUR / AGENCE – STUDIO:

538 T. Ross Koppel Graphics
539 Gallery Art Kuri Jikken Kobo

PUBLISHER / VERLEGER / EDITEUR:

537 Fischer Medical Publications
538 The Boston Globe
539 Upjohn
540 Unilever PLC
541 Deere & Company
542 Omni Publications International Ltd.

537 Introductory double spread for a feature in the medical magazine *Emergency Medicine* dealing with injuries caused by catastrophes. (USA)
538 Cover of the house magazine of *The Boston Globe*. Vermilion, brown and black on beige. (USA)
539 For *Scope*, house magazine of the Japanese *Up-John* firm. Mat olive green, light blue, brown. (JPN)
540 "Money to burn?" Full-page illustration from *Unilever Magazine* on the subject of energy. (USA)
541 Full-page illustration from *JD Journal*, house organ of the *John Deere* company. (USA)
542 Illustration for an article in *Omni* magazine on future forms of life. (USA)

537 Einleitende Doppelseite für einen Beitrag in der medizinischen Fachzeitschrift *Emergency Medicine*. Thema sind die durch Katastrophen verursachten Verletzungen. (USA)
538 Umschlag der Hauszeitschrift des *Boston Globe*. Ziegelrot, Braun und Schwarz auf Beige. (USA)
539 Für *Scope*, Hauszeitschrift der japanischen *Up-John*. Mattes Olivgrün, Hellblau und Braun. (JPN)
540 «Geld zum Verbrennen?» Ganzseitige Illustration aus dem *Unilever Magazine* zum Thema Energie. (USA)
541 Ganzseitige Illustration aus dem *JD Journal*, Hauszeitschrift von *John Deere*, für einen Beitrag mit dem Titel «Ich mag meinen Chef, aber ...». (USA)
542 Illustration zu einem Artikel aus der Zeitschrift *Omni* über zukünftige Lebensformen. (USA)

537 Double page initiale d'un article du magazine médical *Emergency Medicine*, sur le sujet des blessures dues à des catastrophes accidentelles ou non. (USA)
538 Couverture de la revue d'entreprise du *Boston Globe*. Vermillon, brun, noir sur beige. (USA)
539 Pour *Scope*, la revue d'entreprise d'*Up-John* Japon. Olive mat, bleu clair, brun. (JPN)
540 «De l'argent à brûler?» Illustration pleine page d'*Unilever Magazine*. Thème: l'énergie. (USA)
541 Illustration pleine page pour le *JD Journal*, revue d'entreprise de *John Deere*. L'article en question s'intitule «J'aime bien mon chef, mais ...». (USA)
542 Illustration d'un article d'*Omni* au sujet de formes de vie futures. (USA)

House Organs
Hauszeitschriften
Journaux d'entreprise

540

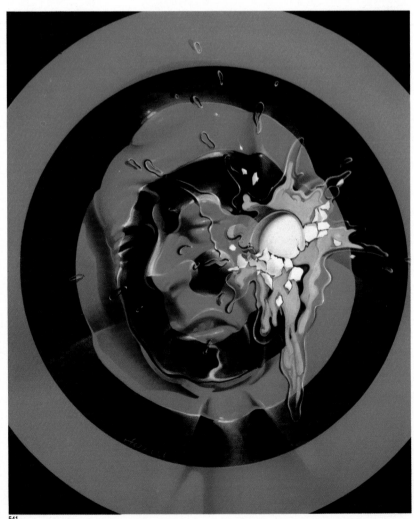

541

542

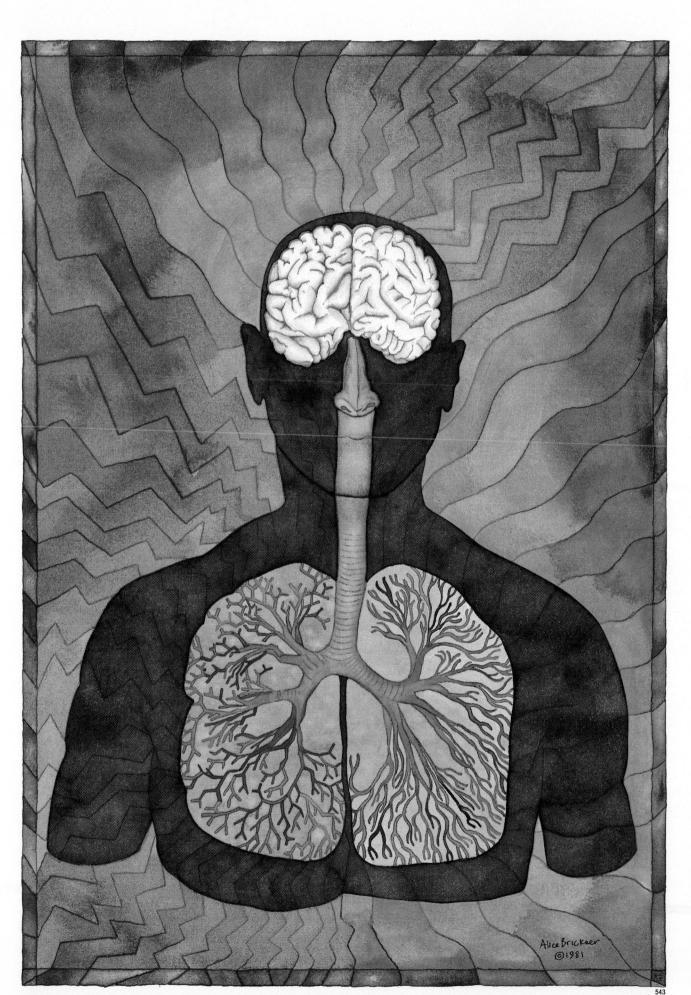

543

ARTIST / KÜNSTLER:

543 Alice Brickner
546 Lonnie Sue Johnson
547 Terry Boles
548 Tom Lungstrom

DESIGNER / GESTALTER:

543 Mary Zisk
544, 545 Michael Bierut
546 Barbara Morris

ART DIRECTOR:

543 Mary Zisk
544, 545 Massimo Vignelli
546 Barbara Groenteman
547, 548 Tina Adamek

AGENCY / AGENTUR:

544, 545 Vignelli Assoc.

PUBLISHER / VERLEGER:

543 Hearst Corp.
544, 545 Institute for
Architecture and
Urban Studies
546 Medical Economics
547, 548 McGraw-Hill

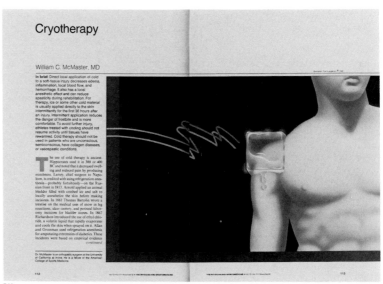

543 Full-page illustration for a feature on breathing, published in *Science Digest*, a specialised magazine relating to the sciences. (USA)
544, 545 Double spreads from *Skyline*, a magazine devoted to architecture and design. (USA)
546 Double spread from *Medical Economics*. Illustration in blue, red and white. (USA)
547, 548 Illustration and a double spread from the magazine for sports medicine *The Physician and Sportsmedicine*. Fig. 547 deals with injuries that can be caused by weight-lifting in the pre-puberty years; Fig. 548 deals with the local application of cold to a soft-tissue injury. (USA)

543 Ganzseitige Illustration für einen Beitrag über das Atmen, erschienen in der wissenschaftlichen Fachzeitschrift *Science Digest*. (USA)
544, 545 Doppelseiten aus *Skyline*, Fachzeitschrift für Architektur und Design. (USA)
546 Doppelseite aus *Medical Economics* für einen Beitrag, in dem es um das Problem des Vorgehens gegen unqualifizierte Ärzte geht. Illustration in Blau, Rot und Weiss. (USA)
547, 548 Illustration und eine Doppelseite aus der Fachzeitschrift für Sportmedizin, *The Physician and Sportsmedicine*. In Abb. 547 geht es um gesundheitliche Schäden durch Gewichtheben im vorpubertären Alter, in Abb. 548 um die Heilung von Oberflächenverletzungen mit Eis. (USA)

543 Illustration pleine page pour un article sur la respiration publié dans le magazine scientifique *Science Digest*. (USA)
544, 545 Doubles pages de *Skyline*, revue d'architecture et de design. (USA)
546 Double page de *Medical Economics* pour un article où l'on discute des mesures à prendre contre les médecins non qualifiés. Illustration bleu, rouge, blanc. (USA)
547, 548 Illustration et une double page de la revue de médecine du sport *The Physician and Sportsmedicine*. Fig. 547: les dangers qu'implique l'haltérophilie prépubertaire; fig. 548: la guérison de blessures superficielles au moyen d'applications de glace. (USA)

209

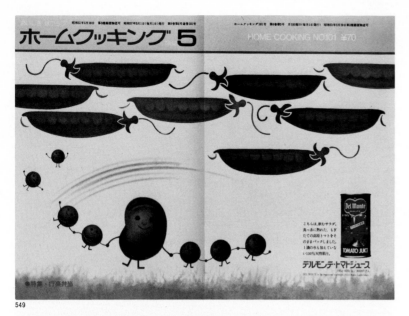

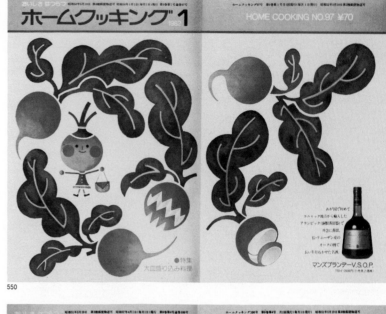

549

550

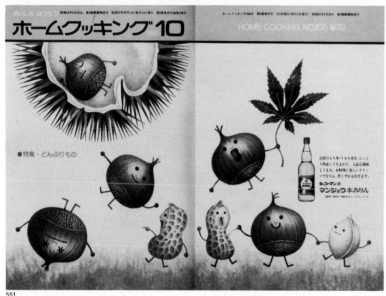

551

552

House Organs
Hauszeitschriften
Journaux d'entreprise

ARTIST / KÜNSTLER / ARTISTE:

549–552 Tadashi Ohashi
553 Geoffrey Moss
554 Frans van der Wiel
555 Seymour Chwast

DESIGNER / GESTALTER / MAQUETTISTE:

549–552 Tadashi Ohashi
553 Dennis DiVincenzo
554 Jan Lepair
555 Seymour Chwast

ART DIRECTOR / DIRECTEUR ARTISTIQUE:

549–552 Tadashi Ohashi
553 Jerry Demoney
554 Jan Lepair
555 Seymour Chwast

AGENCY / AGENTUR / AGENCE – STUDIO:

554 Lepair Design

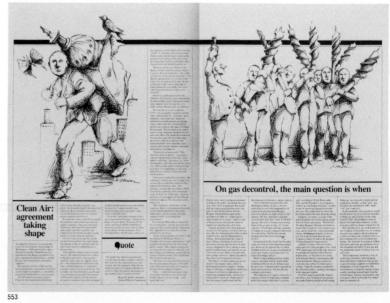

553

549–552 Complete covers of *Home Cooking*, a house magazine devoted to cooking, issued by *Kikkoman*, makers of spiced sauces. In each case the left half is the recto, and all illustrations are in full colour. (JPN)
553 Inside spreads of *Re:Cap*, the *Mobil* house newspaper which informs the company's employees on matters concerning the oil industry. Here the revision of the Clean Air Act and the decontrolling of petrol prices. Illustrations are in black on a yellowish paper. (USA)
554 Cover with a pen-and-ink and water-colour drawing for *Partner*, issued by *Honeywell Bull*. (NLD)
555 Double spread taken from *Push Pin Graphic*, house organ of the former Push Pin Studios (now Pushpin Lubalin Peckolick, Inc.). (USA)

549–552 Vollständige Umschläge von *Home Cooking*, eine dem Kochen gewidmete Hauszeitschrift von *Kikkoman*, Hersteller von Gewürzsaucen. Die linke Hälfte ist jeweils die Vorderseite; alle Illustrationen sind mehrfarbig. (JPN)
553 Innenseiten von *Re:Cap*, Hauszeitung von *Mobil*, welche die Angestellten über Themen informiert, die für die Ölindustrie von Bedeutung sind: hier die Gesetzgebung gegen Luftverschmutzung und die Freigabe des Gaspreises. Illustrationen in Schwarz auf gelblichem Papier. (USA)
554 Umschlag mit Farbstiftzeichnung für *Partner*, Hauszeitschrift von *Honeywell Bull*. (NLD)
555 «Das Leben auf Noahs Arche am vierzigsten Tag.» Doppelseite aus *Push Pin Graphic*, Hauszeitschrift der ehemaligen Push Pin Studios (jetzt Pushpin Lubalin Peckolick, Inc.). (USA)

549–552 Couvertures complètes de *Home Cooking*, revue d'entreprise de *Kikkoman*, le fabricant de sauces épicées, consacrée à la cuisine. La partie gauche est dans chaque cas le recto; toutes les illustrations sont en polychromie. (JPN)
553 Pages intérieures de *Re:Cap*, la revue d'entreprise de *Mobil*, où les employés se voient livrer des informations sur des sujets d'importance pour l'industrie pétrolière, ici sur la législation antipollution et la libération du prix du gaz. Noir sur papier jaunâtre. (USA)
554 Couverture (dessin au crayon couleur) de *Partner*, le house organ de *Honeywell Bull*. (NLD)
555 «La vie sur l'arche de Noé le 40e jour.» Double page de *Push Pin Graphic*. (USA)

PUBLISHER / VERLEGER / EDITEUR:

549–552 Kikkoman Corp.
553 Mobil Corporation
554 Honeywell Bull
555 Push Pin Graphic, Inc.

554

LIFE ABOARD NOAH'S ARK ON THE FORTIETH DAY.

555

556

557

Trade Magazines

ARTIST / KÜNSTLER / ARTISTE:

556, 557 Andrzej Sieragowski
558 Marshall Arisman
559 Leszek Wisniewski
560 Andrzej Dudzinski

ART DIRECTOR:

556, 557 Gernot Lauffer/
      Gerald Brettschuh
558 Lester Goodman
559 Ernst Pavlovic
560 Andrea DaRif

PUBLISHER / VERLEGER:

556, 557 Verlag Sterz
558 Ziff-Davis Publishing
559 Zeitschriftenverlagsges. mbH
560 Heather & Pine International, Inc.

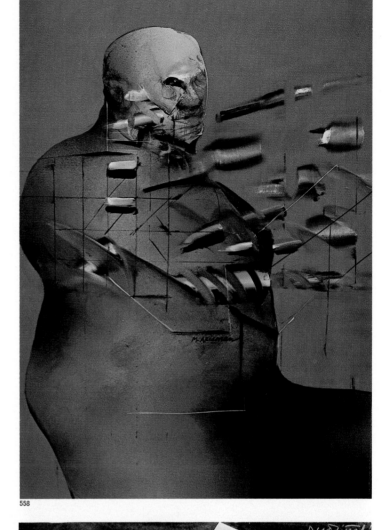

558

556, 557 "Moloch, the God of Machines." Illustration and complete spread from *Sterz* magazine. (AUT)
558 Full-page illustration taken from *Psychology Today*: "How the Mind Heals." (USA)
559 From a series of illustrations for an article about bankruptcies in Austria. (AUT)
560 For a feature on the rôle of the mind in tennis, taken from *Racquet Quarterly*. (USA

556, 557 Illustration und vollständige Seite aus *Sterz*, einer Kulturzeitschrift. (AUT)
558 Ganzseitige Illustration aus *Psychology Today*: Wie das Gehirn Krankheiten heilt. (USA)
559 Aus einer Serie von Illustrationen für einen Artikel über die Pleiten in Österreich. (AUT)
560 Für einen Beitrag über die Rolle des Verstandes beim Tennisspielen, aus *Racquet Quarterly*. (USA)

556, 557 Illustration et page complète de *Sterz*, une revue culturelle. (AUT)
558 Illustration pleine page de *Psychology Today*: «Comment le cerveau répare le corps». (USA)
559 Exemple d'une série d'illustrations pour un article sur les faillites en Autriche. (AUT)
560 Pour un article sur la mobilisation du cerveau dans le tennis. *Racquet Quarterly*. (USA)

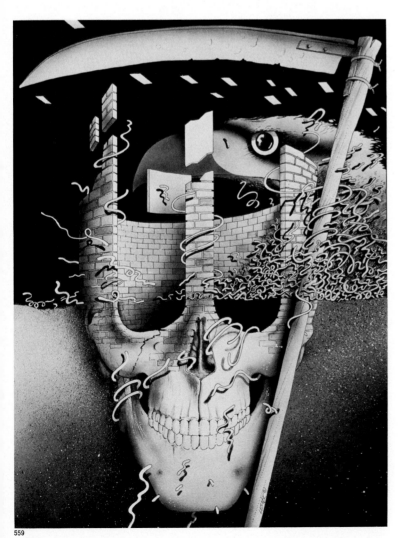

559

560

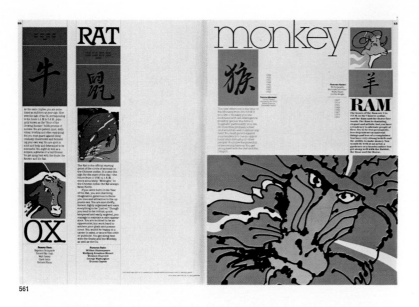

561

ARTIST / KÜNSTLER / ARTISTE:

561–563 Mike Quon
565 Lionel Kalish

DESIGNER / GESTALTER / MAQUETTISTE:

561–563 Mike Quon/Bob Farber
564, 566 Jonson Pedersen Hinrichs Shakery
567 Bob Farber

ART DIRECTOR / DIRECTEUR ARTISTIQUE:

561–563, 565, 567 Bob Farber
564, 566 B. Martin Pedersen

562

561–567 Double spreads and two covers of *U&lc,* house magazine of the *International Typeface Corporation,* a typographers association. Figs. 561 and 562 refer to a feature about the Chinese signs of the zodiac; Fig. 563 shows 4681—The Year of the Boar in the Chinese calendar; Fig. 564: Cover of an issue with a special feature devoted to the history of flying (see Fig. 566); Fig. 565 is a word puzzle; Fig. 566: A feature on the Wright Brothers, inventors of the first motor-powered aeroplane and two of the most important pioneers in the history of aviation; Fig. 567 shows how type can be art as well as fun. (USA)

AGENCY / AGENTUR / AGENCE – STUDIO:

561–563 Mike Quon Design Office
564, 566 Jonson Pedersen Hinrichs Shakery

PUBLISHER / VERLEGER / EDITEUR:

561–567 International Typeface Corporation

563

564

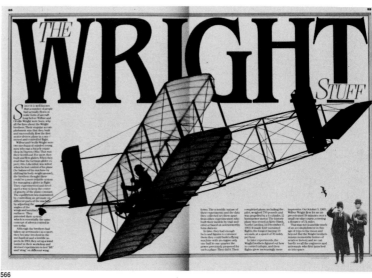

565 / **566**

561–567 Doppelseiten und zwei Umschläge von *U&lc*, Hauszeitschrift der *International Typeface Corporation*, eine internationale Typographen-Vereinigung. Abb. 561 und 562 stammen aus einem Beitrag über die chinesischen Tierkreiszeichen, Abb. 563 zeigt den Umschlag der Ausgabe, die das Jahr des Schweins im chinesischen Kalender begrüsst; Abb. 564: Umschlag einer Ausgabe mit einem Beitrag über die Geschichte des Fliegens (s. Abb. 566); Abb. 565 ist einem Wort-Puzzle gewidmet; Abb. 566: für einen Beitrag über die Gebrüder Wright; Abb. 567: «Typographie als Kunst und Spass». (USA)

561–567 Doubles pages et deux couvertures d'*U&lc*, la revue d'entreprise de l'*International Typeface Corporation*, une association internationale de typographes. Les fig. 561 et 562 illustrent un article sur le calendrier chinois, la fig. 563 représente la couverture d'un numéro annonçant l'année chinoise du Cochon; fig. 564: couverture du numéro contenant un article sur l'histoire du vol humain (cf. la fig. 566); la fig. 565 est consacrée à un rébus; fig. 566: pour un article sur les frères Wright, qui construisirent le premier avion à moteur; fig. 567: «la typographie – un art et un divertissement». (USA)

House Organs
Hauszeitschriften
Journaux d'entreprise

567

568

569

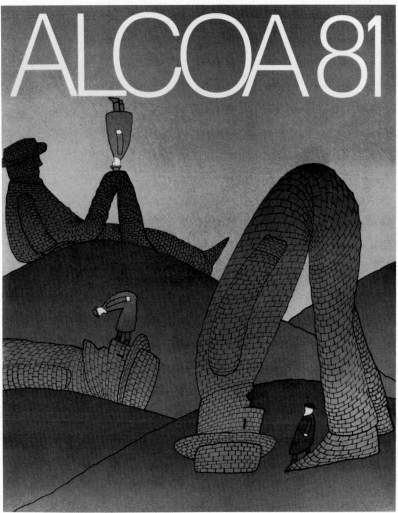

570

571

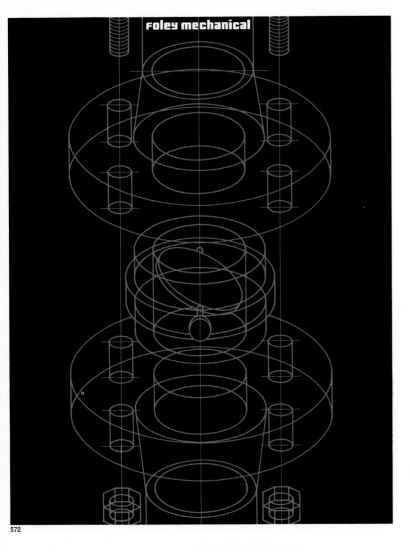

572

573

ARTIST / KÜNSTLER / ARTISTE:

568 Yoshio Okada
569 Michael Kilraine
570 Folon
571 Pierre Paul Darigo
573, 574 Jan Faust

DESIGNER / GESTALTER:

568 Mona Kesa Meyer
570 Barton Denmarsh Esteban
571 Any Dubois
572 Michael Campbell/John Wong
573, 574 Rob Hugel

ART DIRECTOR:

569 Tony Stanford/Cassandra Jardine
571 Jacques Tribondeau
572 Jim Jacobs/Michael Campbell
573, 574 Rob Hugel

AGENCY / AGENTUR / AGENCE:

568 Emphasis Inc.
570 Barton Denmarsh Esteban
572 Jim Jacobs' Studio, Inc.
573, 574 Corporate Communications
          Design & Development

PUBLISHER / VERLEGER / EDITEUR:

568 Japan Air Lines
569 Unilever PLC
570 Aluminium Company of America
571 Esso France
572 Foley Mechanical Co.
573, 574 Herman Miller, Inc.

568 Cover of *Winds*, a publication of the Japanese airline JAL. The subject of this issue is the many legends and myths emanating from Japan's economic successes. (JPN)
569 For a marketing feature in *Unilever Magazine*. (GBR)
570 Cover of *Alcoa*, house magazine of the *Aluminium Company of America*. (USA)
571 Verso of the cover of *Pétrole Progrès*, house journal of *Esso*. (FRA)
572 Cover of *Foley Mechanical*, brochure of a firm that installs plumbing, heating ventilating, etc. (USA)
573, 574 For a *Herman Miller* publication: integrating information technology into the workplace. (USA)

568 Umschlag von *Winds*, einer Publikation der japanischen Fluggesellschaft JAL. Thema der Ausgabe sind die vielen Legenden, die um den wirtschaftlichen Erfolg der Japaner ranken. (JPN)
569 Für einen Marketing-Beitrag im *Unilever Magazine*: «Freud – oder Fakten und Zahlen?» (GBR)
570 Umschlag von *Alcoa*, Hauszeitschrift der *Aluminium Company of America*. (USA)
571 Rückseite des Umschlags von *Pétrole Progrès*, Hauszeitschrift von *Esso*. (FRA)
572 Umschlag einer Firmenbroschüre von *Foley Mechanical*, Installations- und Heizungsbau. (USA)
573, 574 Für eine Publikation von *Herman Miller*: Sinnvolle Gestaltung des Arbeitsplatzes. (USA)

568 Couverture de *Winds*, une publication de la compagnie aérienne japonaise JAL. Le numéro discute les nombreuses légendes entourant le succès économique des Japonais. (JPN)
569 Pour un article de marketing: «Freud – ou des faits, des chiffres?» *Unilever Magazine*. (GBR)
570 Couverture d'*Alcoa*, revue d'entreprise de l'*Aluminium Company of America*. (USA)
571 4e page de couverture d'un numéro de *Pétrole Progrès*, revue d'entreprise d'*Esso*. (FRA)
572 Couverture d'une brochure d'entreprise de *Foley Mechanical* (sanitaires et chauffages). (USA)
573, 574 Pour une publication de *Herman Miller*: le poste de travail informatisé. (USA)

574

217

575 Cover of a paperback edition of a book by the Nobel prize-winner Pär Lagerkvist. Blue, violet, green and brown. (USA)
576 Cover of a thriller published by *Doubleday*. (USA)
577 For a novel by Ruth Rendell, published by Pantheon Books. Green shades and dark greyish-blue. (USA)
578 Cover illustration for a collection of short stories about people's characteristics and longings. (JPN)
579 Cover for a travellers' guide for London. (USA)
580 Greyish-green jacket with fiery eyes, for a collection of horror stories published by Avon Books. (USA)
581 Cover for a book of suspense stories, one of which serves as the title. (USA)
582 For a *Granada* publication. Pocket-book format. (GBR)

575 Umschlag für ein Taschenbuch des Nobel-Preisträgers Pär Lagerkvist. Blau, Violett, Grün und Braun. (USA)
576 Umschlag für einen Kriminalroman. (USA)
577 Für einen Kriminalroman mit dem Titel «Meister des Moores». Grüntöne und düsteres Graublau. (USA)
578 Umschlagillustration für eine Sammlung von Kurzgeschichten über Sehnsüchte des Menschen. (JPN)
579 Umschlag für einen Reiseführer durch London. (USA)
580 In Grau-Grün gehaltener Umschlag mit feurigen Augen, für ein Buch mit Gruselgeschichten. (USA)
581 Umschlag für ein Buch mit Kriminalgeschichten, von denen eine «Der Fieberbaum» heisst. (USA)
582 Für ein «Lexikon der Symbole», Taschenbuch. (GBR)

575 Couverture d'un livre du prix Nobel Pär Lagerkvist «Pèlerin sur la mer», paru en édition de poche. En couleurs. (USA)
576 Couverture d'un roman policier. (USA)
577 Pour un roman policier intitulé «Le Maître des marais». Divers verts, gris bleu sinistre. (USA)
578 Illustration de couverture pour un recueil de nouvelles sur les prédispositions et les nostalgies humaines. (JPN)
579 Couverture d'un guide de Londres. (USA)
580 Couverture vert gris aux yeux flamboyants pour un recueil d'histoires à donner la chair de poule. (USA)
581 Couverture d'un recueil de récits policiers, dont l'un s'intitule «L'Arbre à fièvre». (USA)
582 Pour un «Dictionnaire des symboles», en poche. (GBR)

575

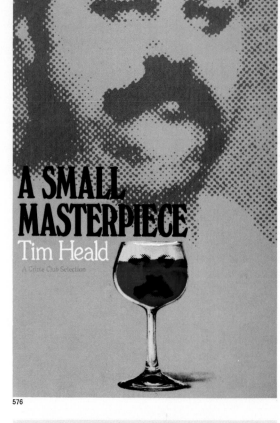

576

Over 1500 candid, opinionated, and refreshingly irreverent ratings of the restaurants, hotels, nightspots, and tourist traps of London.

579

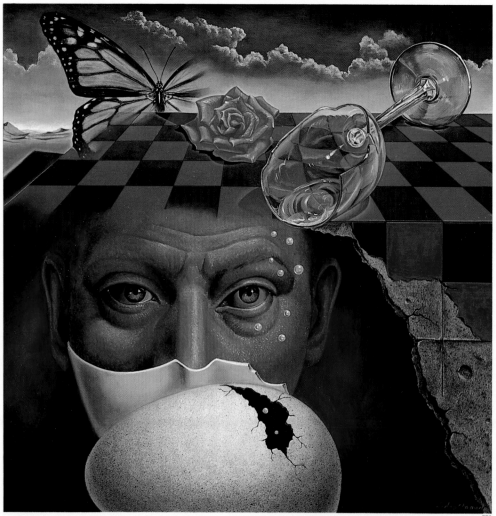

578

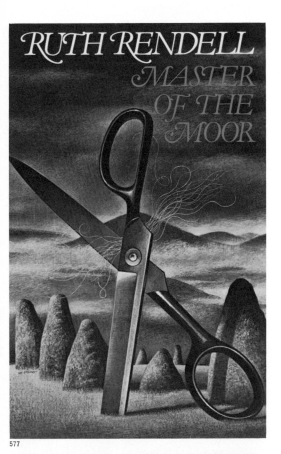

577

580

ARTIST / KÜNSTLER / ARTISTE:

575 Bascove
576 David Barnett
577, 580 Wendell G. Minor
578 Tadami Yamada
579 S. Truesdell
581 David Montiel
582 James Marsh

DESIGNER / GESTALTER / MAQUETTISTE:

575 Paul Gramarello
579 J. Bordnick / B. Olivari / J. Kouman
581 Louise Fili

ART DIRECTOR:

575 Judith Loeser
576 Peter Kruzan
577, 581 Louise Fili
578 Tadami Yamada /
    Iwao Asanuma
579 J. Bordnick
580 Stephanie Zuras /
    Nat Tepper
582 Stephen Abis

AGENCY / AGENTUR / AGENCE:

576 Barnett Design
577, 580 W. Minor Designs
579 Bordnick & Assoc.

PUBLISHER / VERLEGER:

575 Vintage Books
576 Doubleday
577, 581 Pantheon Books
578 Kojinsha Ltd.
579 Gault Millau
580 Avon Books
582 Granada Publishing

581

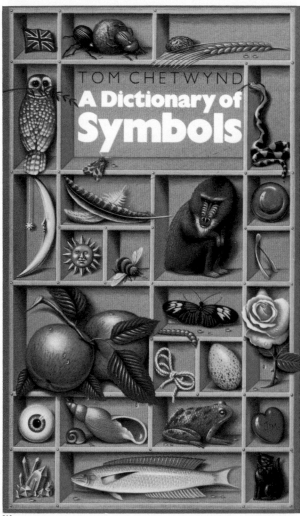

582

Book Covers
Buchumschläge
Couvertures de livres

583 Cover of a medical book on dermatology, published by Little, Brown & Co. (USA)
584 For "The peculiar dirges of the country parson Knight Michael von Jung", published by the Eulen-spiegel Verlag, Berlin. These dirges were written and composed by the parson for burial services. (GDR)
585 Cover of a factual book dealing with the current economic situation in the textile industry. (USA)
586 Cover illustration for a book published by Bert Bakker. (NLD)
587 Draft for the covers of an inexpensive twenty-volume encyclopaedia published by *Fischer*. (GER)
588 Dust jacket for a book about "Great Pianists of Our Times". In black and white. (GER)
589 Dust jacket for a book by a Jewish author, published by *Melzer*. (GER)

583 Umschlag für ein medizinisches Fachbuch über Dermatologie für dunkle Haut. (USA)
584 Für «Die sonderbaren Grablieder des Dorfpfarrers Ritter Michael von Jung». (GDR)
585 Umschlag für ein Sachbuch über die Wirtschaftslage der Textilindustrie. (USA)
586 Umschlagillustration für ein vom Verlag Bert Brakker herausgegebenes Buch. (NLD)
587 Entwurf für die Gestaltung eines zwanzigbändigen Lexikons des *Fischer*-Verlags. (GER)
588 Schutzumschlag für ein Buch über grosse zeitgenössische Pianisten. In Schwarzweiss. (GER)
589 Schutzumschlag für ein Buch eines jüdischen Autors, erschienen im *Melzer*-Verlag. (GER)

583 Couverture d'un manuel médical de dermatologie pour mélanodermes. (USA)
584 Pour «Les Bizarres Chants funèbres du pasteur de village Michael von Jung». (GDR)
585 Couverture d'un rapport sur la situation dans l'industrie du textile. (USA)
586 Illustration de couverture pour un ouvrage publié aux Editions Bert Brakker. (NLD)
587 Projet pour les couvertures d'une encyclopédie en 20 volumes des Editions *Fischer*. (GER)
588 Jaquette d'un ouvrage consacré aux «Grands Pianistes de notre temps». Noir, blanc. (GER)
589 Jaquette du livre d'un auteur juif. «Masques à Francfort» de Dahn Ben-Amotz, publié aux Editions *Melzer*. (GER)

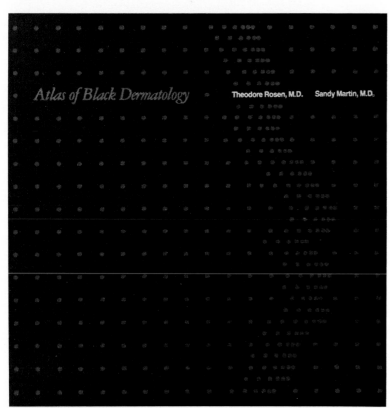

583

584

585

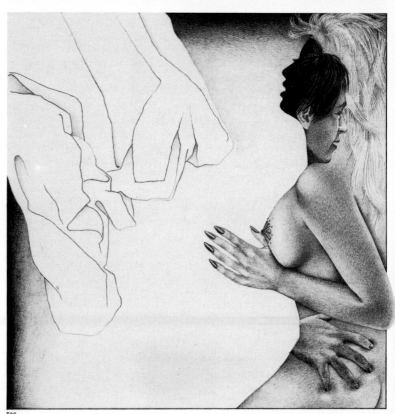

586

ARTIST / KÜNSTLER / ARTISTE:

583 Betsy Hacker
584 Jiří Salamoun
585 Gloria Marconi
586 Jelle van der Toorn Vrijthoff

DESIGNER / GESTALTER / MAQUETTISTE:

583 Betsy Hacker
585 Susan English/Jerry Hunter
586 Jelle van der Toorn Vrijthoff
587–589 Pierre Mendell

ART DIRECTOR / DIRECTEUR ARTISTIQUE:

583 Clifton Gaskill
584 Gerhard Steiner
585 Susan English
587–589 Pierre Mendell

AGENCY / AGENTUR / AGENCE – STUDIO:

585 Graham Associates, Inc.
586 Total Design
587–589 Mendell & Oberer

PUBLISHER / VERLEGER / EDITEUR:

583 Little, Brown & Co.
584 Eulenspiegel Verlag
585 Man-Made Producers Association, Inc.
586 Bert Bakker
587 S. Fischer Verlag
588 Rütten & Loening
589 Melzer Verlag

590

ARTIST / KÜNSTLER / ARTISTE:

590 James McMullan
591 Michael Hasted/Mayer-Norten Group
592 Braldt Bralds
593 Vivienne Flesher
594 Jan Niksiński
595 Sato Yamamoto

DESIGNER / GESTALTER / MAQUETTISTE:

592 Braldt Bralds
593 Louise Fili
594 Jan Niksiński

ART DIRECTOR / DIRECTEUR ARTISTIQUE:

590 Nancy Etheredge
591 Wolfgang Jeschke
592 Lidia Ferrera
593 Louise Fili
594 Jan Niksiński
595 Sato Yamamoto

AGENCY / AGENTUR / AGENCE – STUDIO:

593 Pushpin Lubalin Peckolick

PUBLISHER / VERLEGER / EDITEUR:

590 Dutton
591 Heyne Verlag
592 Alfred A. Knopf
593 Pantheon Books
594 Państwowy Instytut Wydawniczy
595 Sybex

591

590 Complete dust jacket for a romance story published by *Dutton*, New York. (USA)
591 Illustration for the cover of a book published by *Heyne*. Grey and beige. (GER)
592 Dust jacket of a book about the legend of King Arthur from a feminine point of view. (USA)
593 Dust jacket of a book by Nicolas Freeling, published by *Pantheon*. (USA)
594 Black-and-white dust jacket, with the author's name in yellow, for the book *Don Goyo*. (POL)
595 "Two Robots in Love." Full-colour cover for a *Sybex* book. (FRA)

590 Vollständiger Schutzumschlag für einen Liebesroman, erschienen bei *Dutton,* New York. (USA)
591 Illustration für den Umschlag eines im *Heyne*-Verlag erschienenen Kriminalromans. (GER)
592 Schutzumschlag für ein Buch über König Arthur, aus der Sicht von Frauen erzählt. (USA)
593 Schutzumschlag für einen von *Pantheon* herausgegebenen Kriminalroman. (USA)
594 Schwarzweisser Schutzumschlag, Name des Autors in Gelb, für das Buch *Don Goyo.* (POL)
595 «Zwei Androiden, die sich liebten.» Farbiger Umschlag für ein bei *Sybex* erschienenes Buch. (USA)

590 Jaquette complète d'un roman d'amour publié chez *Dutton* à New York. (USA)
591 Illustration de couverture d'un livre paru aux Editions *Heyne.* Gris, beige. (GER)
592 Jaquette d'un livre sur le roi Arthur à travers les femmes qui l'ont connu. (USA)
593 Jaquette d'un policier publié aux Editions *Pantheon.* (USA)
594 Jaquette noir et blanc (nom de l'auteur en jaune) du livre *Don Goyo.* (POL)
595 «Deux androïdes qui s'aimaient.» Couverture couleur d'un livre paru chez *Sybex.* (USA)

Book Covers
Buchumschläge
Couvertures de livres

592

593

594

595

596

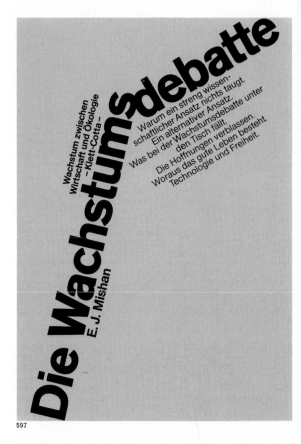

597

598

596 For "The call to another country", a novel by the painter Dahlov Ipcar. (GER)
597 For a book entitled "The Growth Debate", on the subject of economic policies. Black on yellow. (GER)
598 Cover of volume 2 of a three-volume series, "The Economy of Work—The Allocation of Work." (GER)
599 Cover of a book issued by the New York City Department of Cultural Affairs. (USA)
600 For a book of drawings of cats by Parviz Shapour. Orange and black on white. (IRA)
601 Complete cover of a book about Japanese noodles. In full colour. (JPN)
602 Illustrations for the cover of a paperback by J. M. Coetzee. (USA)

596 Für einen Roman der Malerin Dahlov Ipcar, in dem es um mythisches Brauchtum geht. (GER)
597 Für ein Buch, das für eine Gleichgewichtswirtschaft plädiert. Schwarz auf Gelb. (GER)
598 Umschlag für Band 2 einer dreibändigen Fachbuchreihe vom Klett-Cotta-Verlag. (GER)
599 Umschlag für ein vom Kultur-Dezernat der Stadt New York herausgegebenes Buch. (USA)
600 Umschlag für ein Buch mit Katzenzeichnungen von Parviz Shapour. Orange und Schwarz auf Weiss. (IRA)
601 Vollständiger Umschlag eines Buches über japanische Nudeln. In Farbe. (JPN)
602 Illustration für den Umschlag eines Taschenbuches: «In Erwartung der Barbaren.» Mehrfarbig. (USA)

596 Pour un roman de la femme peintre Dahlov Ipcar dans le registre du fantastique. (GER)
597 Pour un livre en faveur d'une économie équilibrée. Noir sur jaune. (GER)
598 Couverture du tome 2 d'un manuel scientifique en 3 volumes paru aux Editions Klett-Cotta. (GER)
599 Couverture d'un ouvrage publié par le département culturel de la ville de New York. En polychromie. (USA)
600 Pour un recueil de dessins de chats par Parviz Shapour. Orange et noir sur blanc. (IRA)
601 Couverture complète d'un livre sur les nouilles japonaises. En couleurs. (JPN)
602 Illustration de couverture pour un poche intitulé «En attendant les barbares». En couleurs. (USA)

ARTIST / KÜNSTLER / ARTISTE:

596 Heinz Edelmann
599 Seymour Chwast
600 Parviz Shapour
601 Yutaka Hasegawa
602 Bascove

DESIGNER / GESTALTER / MAQUETTISTE:

596–598 Heinz Edelmann
599 Seymour Chwast
601 Yutaka Hasegawa
602 Bascove

ART DIRECTOR / DIRECTEUR ARTISTIQUE:

596–598 Heinz Edelmann
599 Toshiaki Ide
600 Parviz Shapour
601 Tadao Koyama
602 Neil Stuart

PUBLISHER / VERLEGER / EDITEUR:

596–598 Klett-Cotta
599 New York City Dept. of Cultural Affairs
600 Morvareed Publication
601 Syufu to Seikatsu sha
602 Penguin Books

599

601

600

602

225

Book Covers
Buchumschläge
Couvertures de livres

603, 606 Covers of books from a series published by *Outlook Review*, dealing here with politics and religion. (USA)
604 Cover of a Crime Club Selection book written by Bernard St. James and published by *Doubleday*. Illustration in brown shades with black, black lettering on violet. (USA)
605 Cover for a Japanese book. Red hair, yellow skin, blue shirt with green on a light violet ground. (JPN)
607 For a Japanese guide to bakeries. In bright colours. (JPN)
608 Black-and-white dust jacket for "Passing Pairs", a book written by Botho Strauss and published by *Ex Libris*. The book deals with loneliness and lack of love in society. (SWI)
609 Dust jacket of a Japanese book. Yellow, green and magenta on structured paper. (JPN)

603, 606 Umschläge für Bücher aus einer Reihe des Verlags *Outlook Review*, hier über Auswüchse in Politik und Religion. (USA)
604 Umschlag für einen Kriminalroman mit dem Titel «Die sieben Träumer», aus einer bei *Doubleday* erschienenen Reihe. Illustration in Brauntönen mit Schwarz, Schrift schwarz auf Violett. (USA)
605 Umschlag für ein japanisches Buch. Haare rot, Haut gelb, Hemd blau und grün auf hellviolettem Grund. (JPN)
607 Für einen japanischen Konditorei-Führer. In bunten Farben. (JPN)
608 Schutzumschlag in Schwarzweiss für die bei *Ex Libris* erschienene Ausgabe eines Buches von Botho Strauss, in dem es um die Einsamkeit und Lieblosigkeit als gesellschaftliche Erscheinung geht. (SWI)
609 Schutzumschlag für ein japanisches Buch. Gelb, Grün und Magenta auf strukturiertem Papier. (JPN)

ARTIST / KÜNSTLER / ARTISTE:

603, 606 Michael David Brown
604 David Barnett
605, 609 Tadanori Yokoo
607 Kumiko Nagasaki
608 Oskar Weiss

DESIGNER / GESTALTER / MAQUETTISTE:

603, 606 Kathleen Wilmes Herring
604 David Barnett
605, 609 Tadanori Yokoo
607 Kenzo Nakagawa
608 Oskar Weiss

ART DIRECTOR / DIRECTEUR ARTISTIQUE:

603, 606 Michael David Brown
604 Peter Kruzan
605, 609 Tadanori Yokoo
607 Kenzo Nakagawa
608 Oswald Dubacher

AGENCY / AGENTUR / AGENCE – STUDIO:

603, 606 Michael David Brown, Inc.
604 Barnett Design Group
607 Bolt & Nuts Studio

PUBLISHER / VERLEGER / EDITEUR:

603, 606 Outlook Review Inc.
604 Doubleday & Co., Inc.
605 Shinchosha Publishing
607 Syufu to Seikatsu sha
608 Ex Libris Verlag
609 Shuppan Kaihatsusha Publishing

603

604

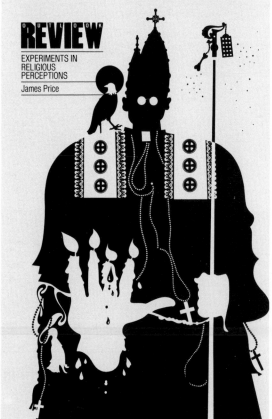

606

607

603, 606 Couvertures de deux titres d'une collection parue aux Editions *Outlook Review*, ici sur les excès en politique et en religion. (USA)
604 Couverture d'un policier intitulé «Les Sept Dormeurs», publié dans une collection *Doubleday*. Illustration en divers bruns, avec du noir, texte noir sur violet. (USA)
605 Couverture d'un livre japonais. Cheveux roux, peau jaune, chemise bleu et vert sur fond violet clair. (JPN)
607 Pour un guide des confiseries au Japon. Couleurs bigarrées. (JPN)
608 Jaquette noir et blanc de l'édition parue chez *Ex Libris* d'un livre de Botho Strauss où il est question de la solitude et du manque de chaleur qui prévalent dans la vie sociale. (SWI)
609 Jaquette d'un ouvrage japonais. Jaune, vert, rouge magenta sur papier structuré. (JPN)

605

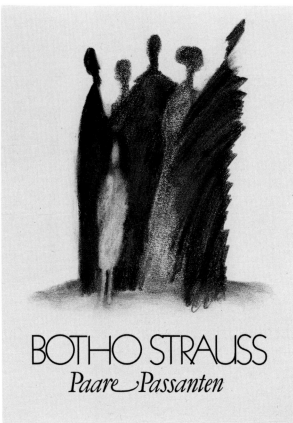

608

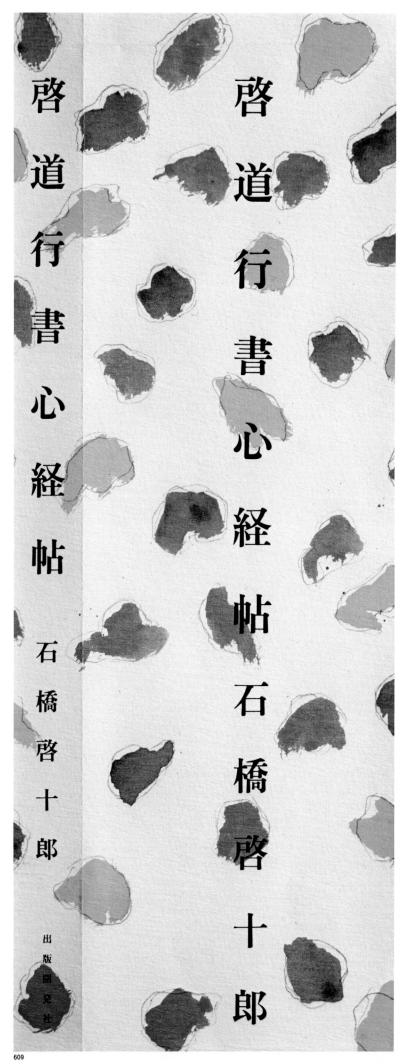

609

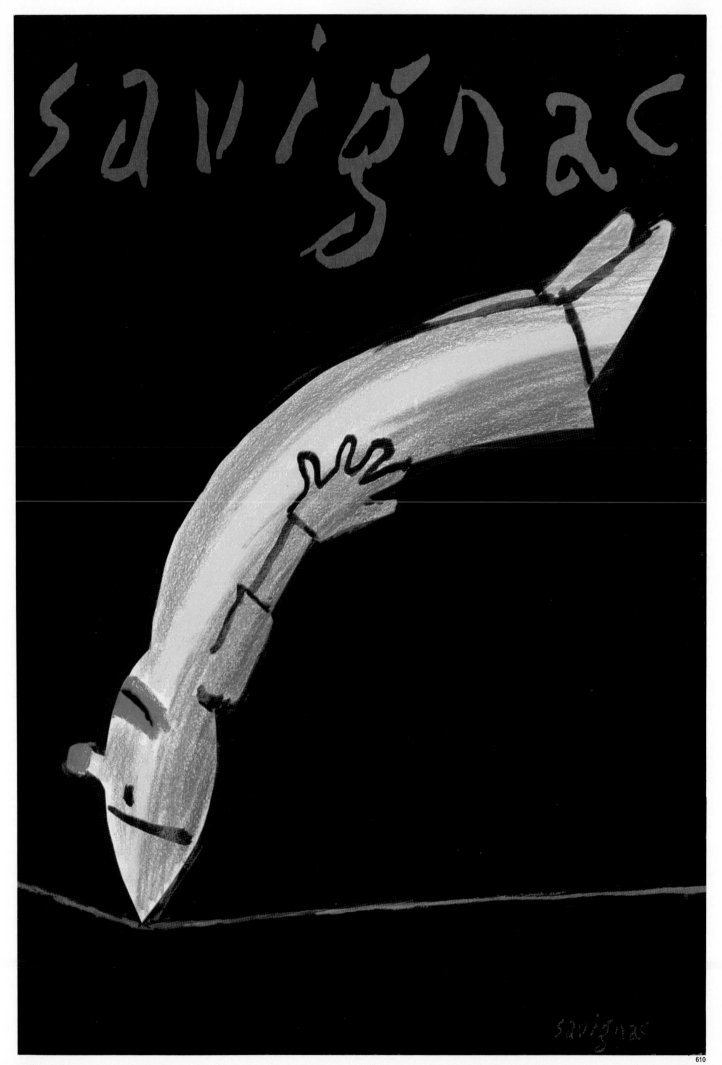

610

Book Covers
Buchumschläge
Couvertures de livres

610 Cover in actual size for a catalogue-book with works by Savignac, a French poster designer. (GER)
611 Cover of a book. Greenish-brown, bluish-pink sky. (USA)
612 For a book with illustrations referring to alcoholism, by the teachers and pupils of an art school. In full colour. (ITA)
613 Dust jacket of a thriller told solely with illustrations by Hans Hillmann. The original was written by Dashiel Hammett. (GER)

610 Umschlag in Originalgrösse für ein Katalog-Buch mit Arbeiten des französischen Plakatkünstlers Savignac. (GER)
611 Umschlag für ein Buch über das hier gezeigte Fabeltier. Grünbraun vor blau-rosa Himmel. (USA)
612 Für ein Buch mit Illustrationen zum Thema Alkoholismus, von Lehrern und Schülern einer Kunstschule. Mehrfarbig. (ITA)
613 Schutzumschlag für eine ausschliesslich mit Illustrationen von Hans Hillmann nacherzählte Kriminalgeschichte. (GER)

610 Couverture grandeur nature d'un catalogue de l'œuvre de l'affichiste français Savignac. (GER)
611 Couverture d'un «Livre des griffons». L'animal mythique y est représenté en brun vert sur fond de ciel rose bleu. (USA)
612 Pour un recueil d'illustrations sur l'alcoolisme par les professeurs et étudiants d'une école d'art. En polychromie. (ITA)
613 Jaquette d'un policier mis en illustrations par Hans Hillmann, «Papier à mouches» de D. Hammett. (GER)

ARTIST / KÜNSTLER / ARTISTE:

610 Savignac
611 Jözef Sumichrast
612 Corrado Albicocco
613 Hans Hillmann

DESIGNER / GESTALTER / MAQUETTISTE:

610 Mendell & Oberer

ART DIRECTOR / DIRECTEUR ARTISTIQUE:

610 Pierre Mendell
611 Marty Swanson
612 Antonio De Ruosi

AGENCY / AGENTUR / AGENCE – STUDIO:

610 Mendell & Oberer
611 Jözef Sumichrast Inc.

PUBLISHER / VERLEGER / EDITEUR:

610 Neue Sammlung Staatl. Museum
      für angewandte Kunst, München
611 Apple Wood Books
612 Istituto Statale d'Arte, Udine
613 Zweitausendeins

611

ALCOOLISMO
IN
FRIULI
Testi di
Domenico Pecile

Istituto
Statale
d'Arte
Udine

612

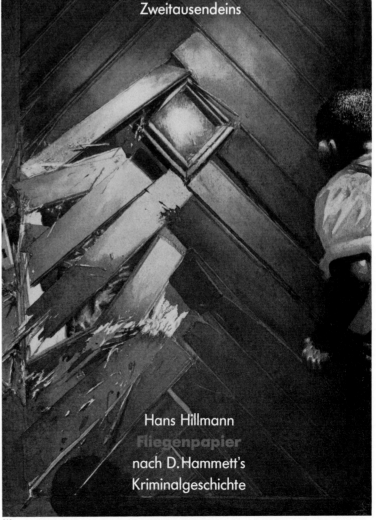

Zweitausendeins

Hans Hillmann
Fliegenpapier
nach D. Hammett's
Kriminalgeschichte

613

4

Calendars

Trademarks

Letterheads

Record Covers

Packaging

Kalender

Schutzmarken

Briefköpfe

Schallplattenhüllen

Packungen

Calendriers

Marques et emblèmes

En-têtes

Pochettes de disques

Emballages

614

Calendars / Kalender / Calendries

ARTIST / KÜNSTLER / ARTISTE:

614 Ernst Fuchs
615, 616 Walter Sägesser
617–619 Tadashi Ohashi
620, 621 U. G. Sato

DESIGNER / GESTALTER / MAQUETTISTE:

615, 616 F. de Koning
617–619 Tadashi Ohashi
620, 621 U. G. Sato
622, 623 Knut Marsen

614 "Sadness and Beauty" is the title of this drawing taken from a limited-edition calendar printed by the *Brönner* publishing company. The calendar consists of twelve full-colour large-format artwork sheets with works by Ernst Fuchs on the subject of "Eros and Myth". (GER)
615, 616 Full-colour picture puzzles from a printer's 1982 calendar: "How many knots will there be when one pulls at both ends?" and "Which pliers are meant to catch which ball?" (NLD)
617–619 Illustrations from a calendar by *Kikkoman*, makers of tinned foods and of sauces. (JPN)
620, 621 Examples of drawings by the illustrator U. G. Sato, for a calendar on the subject of birds. Fig. 620: black and white on bluish-green; Fig. 621: honey-yellow and blue shades. (JPN)
622, 623 Sheets from a calendar with children's' drawings from all over Europe—with which the *Airbus Industries* wish to demonstrate European cooperation in aeroplane development. (FRA)

614 «Betrübnis und Schönheit» ist der Titel dieser Zeichnung aus einem vom *Brönner*-Verlag in limitierter Auflage herausgegebenen Kalender. Er besteht aus zwölf mehrfarbigen, grossformatigen Kunstblättern mit Werken von Ernst Fuchs zum Thema «Eros und Mythos». (GER)
615, 116 Mehrfarbige Bilderrätsel aus dem Kalender einer Druckerei für 1982: «Wieviele Knoten ergeben sich, wenn man an den Enden zieht?» «Mit welcher Zange wird welcher Ball gefasst?» (NLD)
617–619 Illustrationen aus einem Kalender von *Kikkoman*, Hersteller von Konserven und Saucen. (JPN)
620, 621 Beispiele der Abbildungen aus einem Kalender des Illustrators U. G. Sato, dessen Thema Vögel sind. Abb. 620: Schwarzweiss auf Blau-Grün; Abb. 621: Honiggelb und Blautöne. (JPN)
622, 623 Blätter aus einem Kalender mit Kinderzeichnungen aus Europa. Die *Airbus Industries* wollen damit auf die eigene europäische Zusammenarbeit in der Flugzeug-Entwicklung hinweisen. (FRA)

614 «Affliction et beauté», voilà le titre de ce dessin qui figure dans un calendrier au tirage limité publié aux Editions *Brönner* et illustré de douze planches polychromes au grand format d'Ernst Fuchs sur le thème de «Eros et Mythos». (GER)
615, 616 Rébus polychromes illustrant le calendrier d'une imprimerie pour 1982: «Combien de nœuds obtient-on en tirant sur les bouts?» «Quelle pince saisit quelles balles?» (NLD)
617–619 Illustrations d'un calendrier de *Kikkoman*, fabricant de sauces et conserves. (JPN)
620, 621 Exemples des créations de l'illustrateur U. G. Sato pour son calendrier d'oiseaux. Fig. 620: noir et blanc sur vert bleu; fig. 621: jaune miel et divers bleus. (JPN)
622, 623 Feuillets d'un calendrier de dessins d'enfants européens pour *Airbus Industries*, qui entend ainsi souligner la coopération européenne dans la réalisation de l'Airbus. (FRA)

615

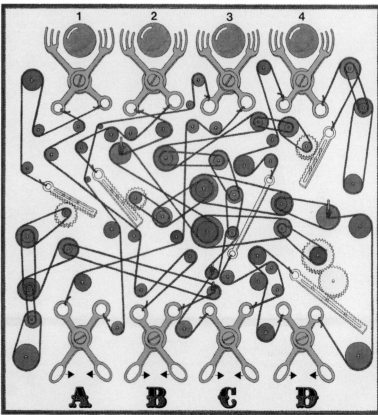
616

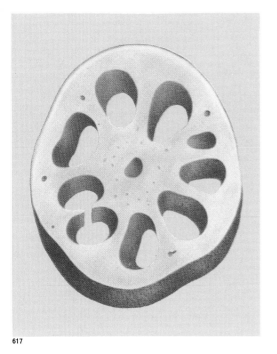

617

618

619

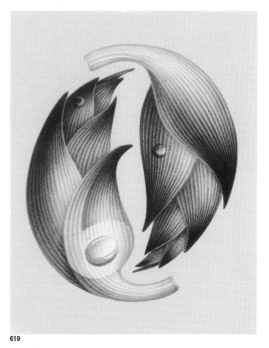

620

621

ART DIRECTOR

615, 616 K. H. Talirz
617–619 Tadashi Ohashi
622, 623 Knut Marsen

AGENCY / AGENTUR / AGENCE

615, 616 MultiCopy
          Drukwerkservice B.V.
622, 623 Airbus Industrie

622

623

624

625

ARTIST / KÜNSTLER / ARTISTE:
624–629 Haruo Miyauchi

AGENCY / AGENTUR / AGENCE – STUDIO:
624–629 Dai Nippon Printing

624–629 Drawings from a calendar for *Mitsubishi Motors*, in which reproductions of pictures by the Japanese artist Haruo Miyauchi are shown exclusively. The originals were all acryl on canvas. Figs. 624, 625: complete February sheet and the picture "Vacation", mainly in blue shades and brownish-yellow; Fig. 626: "Destination", in blue and yellow shades; Fig. 627: "Poseidia", in soft colour gradations; Fig. 628: "Strawberry Fields"; Fig. 629: "Summer Dream". (JPN)

628

626

627

624–629 Abbildungen aus einem Kalender für *Mitsubishi Motors*, in dem ausschliesslich Reproduktionen von Bildern (alle Akryl auf Leinwand) des japanischen Künstlers Haruo Miyauchi gezeigt werden. Abb. 624, 625: Vollständiges Februarblatt und das Bild «Ferien», vorwiegend in Blau- und Braun-Gelbtönen; Abb. 626: «Bestimmungsort», in Blau- und Gelbtönen; Abb. 627: «Poseidia», in sanften Farbabstufungen; Abb. 628: «Erdbeerfelder», Abb. 629: «Sommertraum». (JPN)

624–629 Illustrations d'un calendrier mural au grand format entièrement réalisé pour *Mitsubishi Motors* par l'artiste japonais Haruo Miyauchi en acryliques sur toile. Fig. 624, 625: feuillet complet de février et tableau «Vacances» dominé par les bleus et les jaune brun; fig. 626: «Destination», bleus et jaunes; fig. 627: «Poseidia», divers dégradés aux tonalités douces; fig. 628: «Champs de fraises»; fig. 629: «Rêve d'été». (JPN)

629

630

631

ARTIST / KÜNSTLER / ARTISTE:

630 Keith Laban
631, 632 Ann Sharp
633, 634 Michael Mathias Prechtl
635 Jerry Jeanmard

DESIGNER / GESTALTER / MAQUETTISTE:

630–632 Peter Celiz/Billy Mawhinney
633, 634 Michael Mathias Prechtl
635 Steven Sessions

630–632 Title spread, complete sheet and illustration from a calendar of the *Guinness* breweries. The theme throughout the calendar is that of the tucan, the company's advertising symbol. (GBR)
633, 634 Complete sheets from a hand-printed calendar with child motifs, dispatched at New Year 1983 by Reprotechnik Staudacher GmbH in a limited edition. Fig. 633: "Two Russian Girls", a pencil drawing inspired by an episode from a story by Leo Tolstoy; Fig. 634: "Pamela as a Clown", a tempera and water-colour drawing. (GER)
635 Humorous interpretations of the concept of "time". From a printer's quarterly calendar. Water-colour. (USA)

630–632 Titelblatt, vollständige Seite und Illustration aus einem Wandkalender der Bierbrauerei *Guinness*. Thema des Kalenders ist der Tukan, hier «heimkehrende Tukanvögel». (GBR)
633, 634 Vollständige Blätter aus einem handgedruckten Kalender mit Kindermotiven in limitierter Auflage, von Reprotechnik Staudacher GmbH zum Jahresbeginn 1983 verschickt. Abb. 633: «Zwei russische Mädchen», Bleistiftzeichnung zu einer Episode der Erzählung *Drei Tode* von Leo Tolstoi, Abb. 634: «Pamela als Clown», Tempera, Tusche. (GER)
635 Humorvolle Interpretationen des Begriffes «Zeit» für den vierteljährlichen Kalender einer Druckerei. Aquarell. (USA)

630–632 Page de titre, feuillet complet et illustration d'un calendrier mural de la brasserie *Guinness* consacré au toucan. Thème évoqué ici: «le retour des toucans». (GBR)
633, 634 Feuillets d'un calendrier pour 1983 imprimé à la main, en tirage limité, par Reprotechnik Staudacher GmbH et illustré de motifs d'enfants. Fig. 633: «Deux fillettes russes», crayon illustrant un épisode des *Trois Morts* de Léon Tolstoï; fig. 634: «Pamela habillée en clown», détrempe, encre de Chine. (GER)
635 Interprétations pleines d'humour de la notion de «temps» pour le calendrier trimestriel d'une imprimerie. Aquarelle. (USA)

236

632

ART DIRECTOR / DIRECTEUR ARTISTIQUE:
630–632 Peter Celiz / Billy Mawhinney
635 Steven Sessions

AGENCY / AGENTUR / AGENCE – STUDIO:
630–632 J. Walter Thompson Co. Ltd.
635 Baxter & Korge, Inc.

REPROTECHNIK **STAUDACHER** GMBH **806878**

OKTOBER	1	2	3	4	5	6	7	8	9
10	11	12	13	14	15	16	17	18	19	20	21	22	23
24	25	26	27	28	29	30	31

Montag Dienstag Mittwoch Donnerstag Freitag Samstag Sonntag Montag Dienstag Mittwoch Donnerstag Freitag Samstag Sonntag

Zwei russische Mädchen

633

REPROTECHNIK **STAUDACHER** GMBH **806878**

FEBRUAR	1	2	3	4	5	6
7	8	9	10	11	12	13	14	15	16	17	18	19	20
21	22	23	24	25	26	27	28

Montag Dienstag Mittwoch Donnerstag Freitag Samstag Sonntag Montag Dienstag Mittwoch Donnerstag Freitag Samstag Sonntag

Pamela als Clown

634

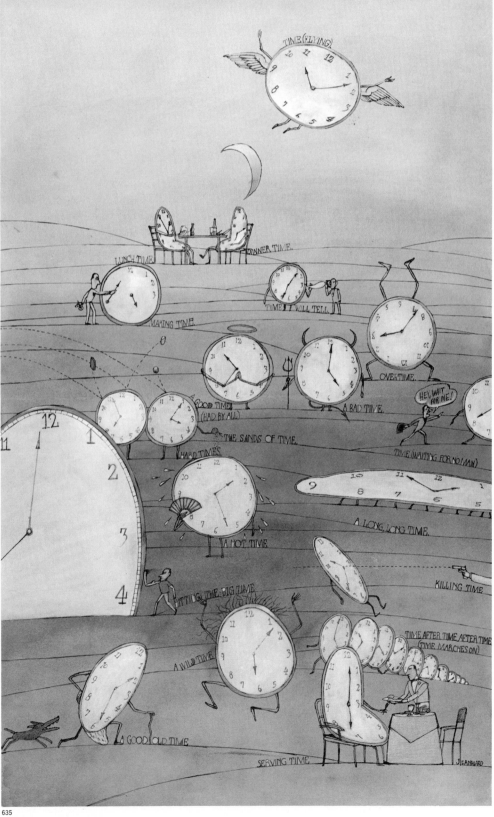

635

237

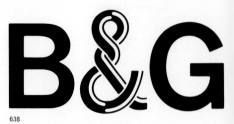

638

636, 637 Signet for the municipal council of Cartagena, Columbia, and an example for its usage as a repetitive, decorative pattern. (USA)
638 Trademark for the B & G factory, manufacturers of railings and fences. (NLD)
639 Signet for the designers' day of the German Designers Associations. (GER)
640 Symbol for *Barnett*, the British health authority. (GBR)
641 Symbol of the Spanish printers *Gala*. (SPA)
642 Symbol of *Ocean Oil*, a British oil company. (GBR)
643 Symbol for the Sorrett Publishing Pty. Ltd. (AUS)
644 Symbol of a sales location for theatre and concert tickets. (USA)
645 Motif of the initial-day imprint of the 1982 Christmas stamp. (GER)
646 Symbol of the *Middle East Bank* in Dubai. (UAE)
647 Signet of *Sylvac*, electronic precision-measuring instruments. (SWI)
648 Symbol of Color Communications, Inc. (USA)
649 Logo of *Arntz Cobra*, automobile manufacturers. (USA)
650 Company symbol of the American Savings Bank. (USA)

642

636, 637 Signet für die Stadtverwaltung von Cartagena, (Kolumbien) und Beispiel für die Verwendung als sich repetierendes, dekoratives Muster. (USA)
638 Schutzmarke für die B & G Zaunfabrik. (NDL)
639 Signet für den Designertag der deutschen Designerverbände. (GER)
640 Symbol für die britische Gesundheitsbehörde *Barnett*. (GBR)
641 Signet für die spanische Druckerei *Gala*. (SPA)
642 Symbol für die britische Ölgesellschaft *Ocean Oil*. (GBR)
643 Signet für den Verlag Sorrett Publishing Pty. Ltd. (AUS)
644 Signet für eine Verkaufsstelle von Theater- und Konzertkarten. (USA)
645 Motiv für den Ersttagsstempel der Weihnachtsmarke 1982. (GER)
646 Symbol für die *Middle East Bank* in Dubai. (UAE)
647 Signet für elektronische Präzisions-Messinstrumente der Marke *Sylvac*. (SWI)
648 Signet für die Farben-Marketinggesellschaft Color Communications, Inc. (USA)
649 Logo für den Automobilhersteller *Arntz Cobra*. (USA)
650 Firmensignet für die American Savings Bank. (USA)

636, 637 Logo pour la municipalité de Cartagena (Colombie) et exemple de son emploi répétitif comme motif décoratif. (USA)
638 Marque déposée pour la fabrique de clôtures B & G. (NDL)
639 Emblème de la Journée du design des associations allemandes de design. (GER)
640 Emblème de l'office de santé britannique *Barnett*. (GBR)
641 Emblème de l'imprimerie espagnole *Gala*. (SPA)
642 Emblème de la compagnie pétrolière britannique *Ocean Oil*. (GBR)
643 Emblème des Editions Sorrett Publishing Pty. Ltd. (AUS)
644 Emblème d'une billetterie de théâtre et de concert. (USA)
645 Symbole du timbre apposé lors de la mise en vente du timbre de Noël 1982. (GER)
646 Emblème de la *Middle East Bank* de Dubay. (UAE)
647 Emblème des instruments de mesure électroniques de précision *Sylvac*. (SWI)
648 Emblème de la société de commercialisation de couleurs Color Communications, Inc. (USA)
649 Logo pour l'usine d'automobiles *Arntz Cobra*. (USA)
650 Emblème de l'American Savings Bank. (USA)

646

636

637

650

639

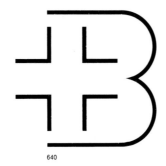

640

641

643

644

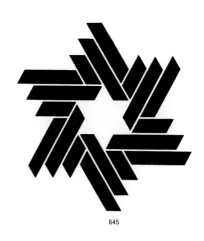

645

647

648

649

DESIGNER / GESTALTER / MAQUETTISTE:

636, 637 Stephan Geissbuhler
638 Ben Bos/Evert Snellenberg
639, 645 Bruno K. Wiese
640, 642 Marcello Minale/Brian Tattersfield
641 Nacho Soriano
643 Ken Cato
644 Michael Manwaring/Betty Barsamian/Karen Fenlon
646 Ben Bos
647 Heinrich M. Adam
648 Jim Lienhart
649 Marty Neumeier
650 Alan Peckolick

ART DIRECTOR / DIRECTEUR ARTISTIQUE:

636, 637 Stephan Geissbuhler
638, 646 Ben Bos
639, 645 Bruno K. Wiese
640, 642 Marcello Minale/Brian Tattersfield
641 Nacho Soriano
643 Ken Cato
644 Michael Manwaring
647 Heinrich M. Adam
648 Jim Lienhart
650 Alan Peckolick

AGENCY / AGENTUR / AGENCE – STUDIO:

636, 637 Chermayeff & Geismar Assoc.
638, 646 Total Design
639, 645 BK Wiese
640, 642 Minale Tattersfield & Partners
641 Nacho Soriano
643 Cato Hibberd Design
644 The Office of Michael Manwaring
648 Murrie White Drummond Lienhart & Assoc.
649 Neumeier Design Team
650 Lubalin Peckolick Assoc. Inc.

651

652

653

654

655

656

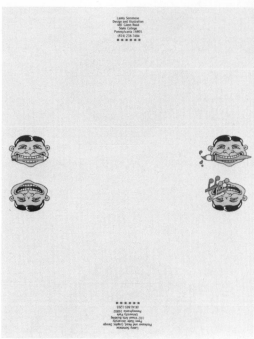

657

660

664

663

Varia

DESIGNER / GESTALTER / MAQUETTISTE:

651–656 Kyösti Varis
657 Lanny Sommese
658 Beatrix Kutschera
659 Oswaldo Miranda
660 Arthur Beckenstein
661 Garry Emery/Ken Stanley
662 Ruedi & Seraina Baur
663 Frank Nichols
664 Michael Campbell
665 Ian Mullan
666 Louisa Sugar/Harold McAnaney
667 Hanspeter Rolly

ART DIRECTOR / DIRECTEUR ARTISTIQUE:

651–656 Kyösti Varis
657 Lanny Sommese
658 Beatrix Kutschera
659 Oswaldo Miranda
660 Arthur Beckenstein
661 Garry Emery
662 Ruedi & Seraina Baur
663 Woody Pirtle
664 Jim Jacobs
665 Ian Mullan
666 Louisa Sugar/Harold McAnaney
667 Hanspeter Rolly

658

659

661

662

RS REINIGUNG

René Schmid
Gebäudereinigung
Tobelhofstrasse 326
CH-8044 Gockhausen
Telefon 01/821 18 88
PC-80-130599

Datum

Batom

AGENCY / AGENTUR / AGENCE – STUDIO:

657 Lanny Sommese Design
658 Atelier 21
659 Miran Estudio
660 Arthur Beckenstein
661 Garry Emery & Associates
662 BBV Baur, Baviera, Vetter
663 Pirtle Design
664 Jim Jacobs' Studio, Inc.
665 Ian Mullan Graphics
666 Louisa Sugar

651, 652 Symbol for a film company and for a race. (FIN)
653 Trademark of the automobile manufacturer SAAB. (FIN)
654 Symbol of a combined bakery and café-restaurant. (FIN)
655 Symbol of *Servi Systems*, a Finnish cleaning company. (FIN)
656 Symbol of one of Finland's largest magazine publishers. (FIN)
657 Notepaper for the head of the Penn State University's graphics dept. (USA)
658 Letterhead advertising a real estate company. (AUT)
659 Stationery of *Baton* (lipstick), a women's magazine. (BRA)
660 Red symbol and black address on HB Associates' letterhead. (USA)
661 Letterhead of a firm of architects. (AUS)
662 Notepaper of a cleaning company. Blue lettering. (SWI)
663 Notepaper with envelope for an advertising/marketing/PR firm. (USA)
664 Notepaper of a computer company. Woodcut, red apple. (USA)
665 Stationery for a graphic and packaging designer. Grey shades. (AUS)
666 Trademark of The Edge, a rock group. (USA)
667 Monogram of a printing firm. (SWI)

651, 652 Symbol für eine Filmgesellschaft und ein Wettlaufen. (FIN)
653 Schutzmarke für den Automobilhersteller SAAB. (FIN)
654 Symbol für eine Konditorei mit Café-Restaurant. (FIN)
655 Symbol für die Reinigungsfirma *Servi Systems* in Finnland. (FIN)
656 Symbol für einen der grössten Zeitschriften-Verlage Finnlands. (FIN)
657 Briefbogen für die Graphikabteilung der Penn State University. (USA)
658 Briefkopf als Werbung für eine Immobiliengesellschaft. (AUT)
659 Briefpapier für die Frauenzeitschrift *Baton* (Lippenstift). (BRA)
660 Rotes Signet und schwarze Adresse auf Briefkopf für HB Associates. (USA)
661 Briefkopf mit Bürogebäuden, für eine Architektur-Firma. (AUS)
662 Briefbogen einer Gebäudereinigungsfirma. Blauer Schriftzug. (SWI)
663 Für eine Werbe- und PR-Firma. Briefbogen mit Umschlag. (USA)
664 Briefbogen für eine Computerfirma. Holzschnitt, rot kolorierter Apfel. (USA)
665 Briefpapier für einen Graphik- und Verpackungsdesigner. Grautöne. (AUS)
666 Schutzmarke für die Rock-Gruppe The Edge. (USA)
667 Namenszug für eine Druckerei. (SWI)

651, 652 Emblème d'une société de cinéma et d'une course à pied. (FIN)
653 Marque déposée pour l'usine d'automobiles SAAB. (FIN)
654 Emblème d'une pâtisserie-confiserie doublée d'un café-restaurant. (FIN)
655 Emblème de l'entreprise finlandaise de nettoyage *Servi Systems*. (FIN)
656 Emblème de l'un des plus grands éditeurs de presse en Finlande. (FIN)
657 En-tête pour le chef du département Art graphique de la Penn State. (USA)
658 En-tête publicitaire d'une société immobilière. (AUT)
659 Papier à lettres du magazine féminin *Baton* (rouge à lèvres). (BRA)
660 Sigle rouge et adresse en noir d'un en-tête pour HB Associates. (USA)
661 En-tête illustré d'immeubles de bureaux, pour un architecte. (AUS)
662 En-tête d'une entreprise de nettoyage d'immeubles. Texte bleu. (SWI)
663 Pour une firme de publicité, marketing et RP. En-tête et enveloppe. (USA)
664 En-tête d'une société d'informatique. Gravure sur bois. (USA)
665 Papier à lettres pour un graphiste-emballagiste. Divers gris. (AUS)
666 Marque déposée du groupe rock The Edge. (USA)
667 Raison sociale d'une imprimerie. (SWI)

665

666

667

670

671

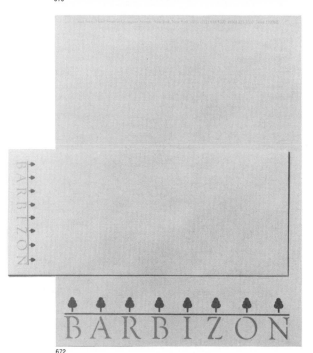

B A R B I Z O N

672

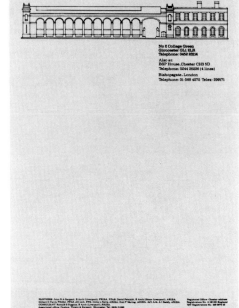

The Biggins Sargent Partnership
Chartered Architects and Consultants

No 8 College Green
Gloucester GL1 2LR
Telephone: 0452 23214

Also at:
BSP House, Chester CH3 5D
Telephone: 0244 25236 (4 lines)
Bishopsgate, London
Telephone: 01-588 4272 Telex: 299171

673

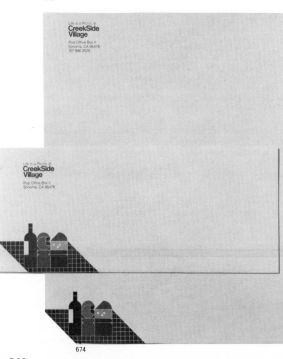

Life is a Picnic at
CreekSide
Village
Post Office Box 11
Sonoma, CA 95476
707 996 2520

674

TRAFFIC

675

670 Beige stationery of a wood craftsman. (USA)
671 Stationery of an advertising and PR company. (USA)
672 Stationery and envelope for a hotel chain. (USA)
673 For a firm of architects and consultants. (GBR)
674 Stationery with a full-colour symbol. (USA)
675 Letterhead of an agency for printed matter. (NDL)
676 Stationery of the national theatre of Lyon. (FRA)
677 Envelope and stationery of a printing firm. (USA)
678 For Bob Coonts Graphic Design Inc. Employees' heads are portrayed on the stationery. (USA)
679 Stationery and envelope of a North American association. Black symbol with light yellow initials. (USA)
680 Letterhead of Beaver Tower Inc. The sailing boat illustration is imprinted in red. (USA)
681 A restaurant's logo and envelope. Green and pink. (USA)
682 Trademark of a graphic design studio. (GBR)

670 Beiges Briefpapier für einen Holzfachmann. (USA)
671 Briefpapier einer Werbe- und PR-Firma. (USA)
672 Briefpapier und Umschlag für eine Hotelkette. (USA)
673 Für eine Architektur- und Beraterfirma. (GBR)
674 Briefbogen und Umschlag für eine Wohnsiedlung. (USA)
675 Briefkopf einer Drucksachenagentur. (NDL)
676 Briefpapier für das Nationaltheater von Lyon. (FRA)
677 Umschlag und Briefpapier für eine Druckerei. (USA)
678 Für Bob Coonts Graphic Design Inc. Die Köpfe der Mitarbeiter sind auf dem Briefpapier dargestellt. (USA)
679 Briefpapier und Umschlag für den Beleuchtungs-Ingenieurverein von Nordamerika. (USA)
680 Geprägte Segelschiffillustration in Rot. Briefkopf für Beaver Tower Inc. à New York. (USA)
681 Logo und Umschlag für ein Restaurant. (USA)
682 Schutzmarke für ein graphisches Atelier. (GBR)

670 En-tête beige pour un spécialiste du bois. (USA)
671 En-tête d'une société de publicité et de RP. (USA)
672 En-tête et enveloppe pour une chaîne d'hôtels. (USA)
673 Pour un bureau d'architecte et de conseils. (GBR)
674 En-tête et enveloppe pour un lotissement. (USA)
675 En-tête d'un bureau d'adresses. (NDL)
676 En-tête du Théâtre national de Lyon. (FRA)
677 Enveloppe et papier à lettres d'une imprimerie. (USA)
678 Pour Bob Coonts Graphic Design Inc. L'en-tête est illustré des têtes des collaborateurs. Irisation. (USA)
679 En-tête et enveloppe pour l'association nord-américaine des ingénieurs éclairagistes. Emblème noir. (USA)
680 Voiliers gaufrés en rouge sur l'en-tête de Beaver Tower Inc. à New York. (USA)
681 Logo, enveloppe de restaurant. Texte vert, rose. (USA)
682 Marque déposée pour un atelier graphique. (GBR)

676

677

678

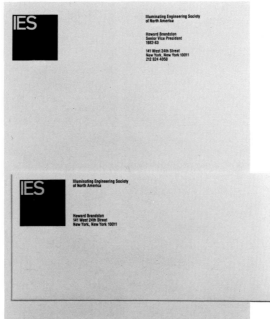

679

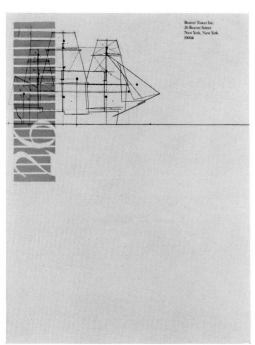

680

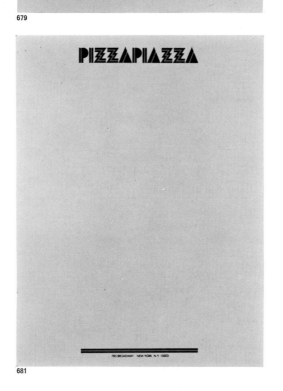

681

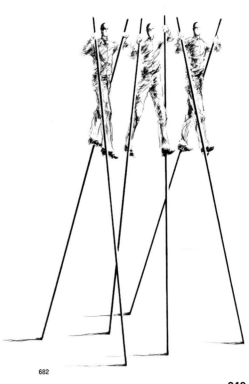

682

683

684

685

Trademarks / Schutzmarken / Marques et emblèmes

683 Symbol of the Banco de Italia in Buenos Aires. (ARG)
684 Trademark for *Wildfibers*, a clothes store specialising in textiles and natural fibre materials. (USA)
685 Symbol of the Mitsubishi Bank. (USA)
686 Trademark of the Deutsche Bank. The symbol refers to dynamics, safety and trust. (GER)
687 Symbol for the letters column in a women's magazine. (BUL)
688 Trademark for *DirectCom*. (USA)
689 Trademark of a clothes transport company. (FIN)
690 Trademark of the Berman Printing Co., specialists in lithography. (USA)
691 Symbol of a business specialising in products used for sailing. (USA)
692 Symbol for Continental Plaza, part of an urban real estate development. (USA)
693 Symbol for *Embassy Communications*, film productions. (USA)
694 Logotype of Health Services Alternative. (USA)
695 Symbol for a Houston TV station. (USA)
696 Trademark for a firm of housing administration. (FIN)

683 Signet der Banco de Italia in Buenos Aires. (ARG)
684 Schutzmarke für *Wildfibers*, ein Geschäft, das auf Textilien aus Naturfasern spezialisiert ist. (USA)
685 Signet für die Mitsubishi Bank. (USA)
686 Firmenzeichen der Deutschen Bank. Das Signet beruht auf Dynamik und Sicherheit. (GER)
687 Signet für die Rubrik Leserbriefe in einer Frauenzeitschrift. (BUL)
688 Schutzmarke für *DirectCom*. (USA)
689 Schutzmarke für eine Kleider-Transportfirma. (FIN)
690 Schutzmarke für Berman Printing Co., die auf Lithographien spezialisiert ist. (USA)
691 Signet eines Geschäftes für Segelsportbedarf. (USA)
692 Signet für Continental Plaza, eine städtische Überbauung. (USA)
693 Symbol für *Embassy Communications*, Filmproduktionen. (USA)
694 Logo für einen alternativen Gesundheitsdienst. (USA)
695 Signet für die Houston-Fernsehstation. (USA)
696 Schutzmarke für eine Hausverwaltungs-Gesellschaft. (FIN)

683 Emblème de la Banco de Italia de Buenos Aires. (ARG)
684 Marque déposée pour *Wildfibers*, un magasin de confection spécialisé dans les textiles en fibres naturelles. (USA)
685 Emblème de la Mitsubishi Bank. (USA)
686 Logo de la Deutsche Bank incarnant le dynamisme et la sécurité. (GER)
687 Emblème de la rubrique Courrier des lectrices d'un magazine féminin. (BUL)
688 Marque déposée pour *DirectCom*. (USA)
689 Marque déposée pour une entreprise de transport de vêtements. (FIN)
690 Marque déposée pour la Berman Printing Co. spécialisée dans la lithographie. (USA)
691 Emblème d'un magasin d'équipements pour la voile. (USA)
692 Emblème de Continental Plaza, un promoteur immobilier urbain. (USA)
693 Symbole pour *Embassy Communications*. (USA)
694 Logo d'un service de santé marginal. (USA)
695 Emblème de la station de télévision de Houston. (USA)
696 Marque déposée pour une société de gérance immobilière. (FIN)

689

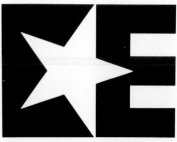

693

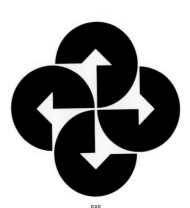

686

687

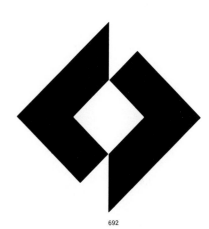

688

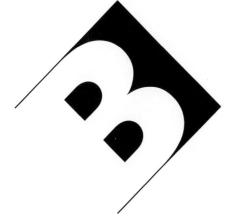

690

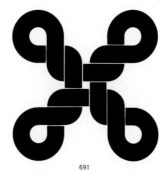

691

692

694

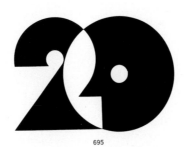

695

696

697

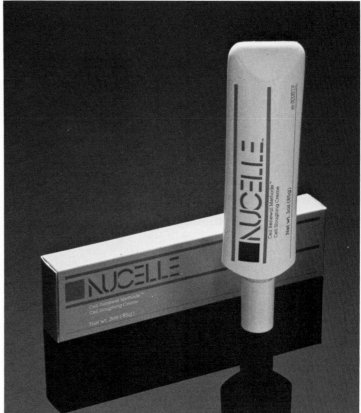

698

ARTIST / KÜNSTLER / ARTISTE:

697 Alice Brickner
699 Cheryl Craft
701 Gretchen Schields
702 Gen Naito

DESIGNER / GESTALTER / MAQUETTISTE:

697 Alice Brickner/Jeanne Greco
698 Barbara Lynk
699 Michael Gericke
700 Helmut Schmid
701 Wilson Ong
702 Gen Naito
703, 704 Ken Cato

ART DIRECTOR / DIRECTEUR ARTISTIQUE:

697 Josh Taylor
698 Kurt Meinecke
699 Henry Beer
701 Gerald Reis
702 Gen Naito
703, 704 Ken Cato

AGENCY / AGENTUR / AGENCE – STUDIO:

698 Group/Chicago
699 Communication Arts Inc.
700 Suntory Design Dept.
701 Reis & Co.
702 Gen Design Room
703, 704 Ken Cato Design Co Pty Ltd

699

Packaging
Packungen
Emballages

700

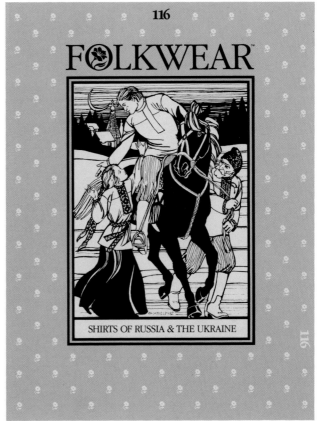

701

702

697 Boxes for cosmetic soap. Pastel colours, red, blue and green. Black lettering. (USA)
698 Packaging and tube of facial cream for sensitive skin. (USA)
699 Packaging line for *Atan* photography products. (USA)
700 Shopping bag with logotype for the *Suntory* Shopping Club. Black on white. (JPN)
701 Envelope with patterns for shirts and blouses in Russian-Ukrainian style. (USA)
702 Wrapping paper used by a Chinese restaurant. Black and red on golden yellow. (JPN)
703 Display packaging for twenty-four cigarette lighters. (AUS)
704 Display cardboard for the packaging of a dozen boxes of matches. (AUS)

697 Schachteln für Kosmetik-Seifen. Pastellfarben, rot, blau und grün. Schrift in Schwarz. (USA)
698 Verpackung und Tube mit Gesichtscrème für empfindliche Haut. (USA)
699 Packungslinie für *Atan*-Phototaschen und Zubehör. (USA)
700 Einkaufstasche mit Logo für den *Suntory*-Shopping-Club. Schwarz auf Weiss. (JPN)
701 Umschlag mit Schnittmustern für Hemden und Blusen im russisch-ukrainischen Stil. (USA)
702 Von einem chinesischen Restaurant verwendetes Einschlagpapier. Schwarz, Rot, Goldgelb. (JPN)
703 Display-Packung für vierundzwanzig Feuerzeuge. (AUS)
704 Schaukarton als Verpackung von zwölf Zündholzschachteln. (AUS)

697 Cartons de savons cosmétiques. Tons pastel rouge, bleu, vert. Texte noir. (USA)
698 Emballage et tube de crème pour le visage pour peaux sensibles. (USA)
699 Gamme d'emballages pour les sacoches et accessoires photo *Atan*. (USA)
700 Sac à commissions du *Suntory* Shopping Club, avec logo. Noir sur blanc. (JPN)
701 Emballage de patrons de blouses et chemises de style russo-ukrainien. (USA)
702 Papier d'emballage d'un restaurant chinois. Noir, rouge sur jaune or. (JPN)
703 Emballage-présentoir pour vingt-quatre briquets. (AUS)
704 Carton de vente-exposition pour douze boîtes d'allumettes. (AUS)

703

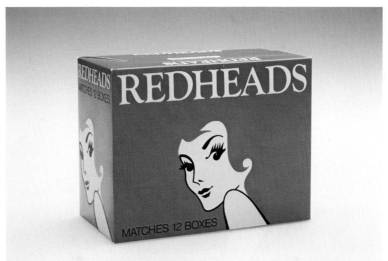

704

705

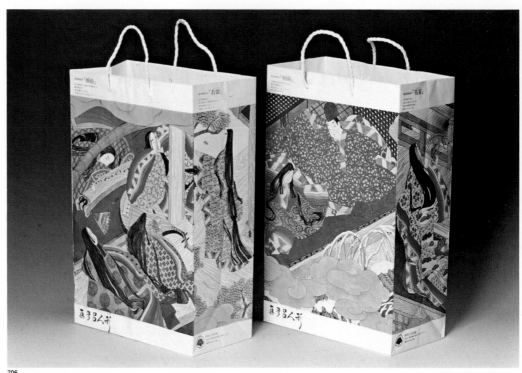

706

707

ARTIST / KÜNSTLER / ARTISTE:

706 Takeru Niwa
710, 711 Heather Cooper
712 Shozo Kakutani

708

709

705 Label and bottle design for the Italian cream liqueur *Bisleri*. (USA)
706 Paper carrier bag of a special store for the sale of *Mataro* dolls. (JPN)
707 Boxes for Japanese confectionery. Blue and white on an olive-green ground. (JPN)
708 Bottle design for *Koshu*, a Japanese white wine. (JPN)
709 Packaging for three different kinds of green tea. (JPN)
710, 711 Label design for condiment glasses with herb mixtures. (CAN)
712 Carrier bag for traditional Japanese pastries and confectionery. In white and grey. (JPN)
713 Paper carrier bag on the occasion of an exhibition about the future, organised by *Gimbels* department store in New York. (USA)

705 Etikett und Flaschengestaltung für den italienischen Crème-Likör *Bisleri*. (USA)
706 Papiertragtasche eines Spezialgeschäftes für den Verkauf von *Mataro*-Puppen. (JPN)
707 Schachteln für japanisches Konfekt. Blau und weiss auf olivgrünem Grund. (JPN)
708 Flaschengestaltung für den japanischen Weisswein *Koshu*. Goldfarbene Kapsel. (JPN)
709 Verpackungen für grünen Tee in drei verschiedenen Varianten. (JPN)
710, 711 Etikettgestaltung für Gewürzgläser mit Kräutermischungen. (CAN)
712 Tragtasche für traditionelles japanisches Gebäck und Konfekt. In Weiss und Grau. (JPN)
713 Papiertragtasche anlässlich einer Ausstellung über die Zukunft, die von dem Kaufhaus *Gimbels* organisiert wurde. (USA)

705 Etiquette et étude de bouteille pour la crème de liqueur italienne *Bisleri*. (USA)
706 Cabas en papier d'un magasin spécialisé dans la vente des poupées *Mataro*. (JPN)
707 Emballages de confiserie japonais. Bleu et blanc sur fond olive. (JPN)
708 Etude de bouteille pour le *Koshu*, vin blanc japonais. Capsule dorée. (JPN)
709 Emballages de thé vert en trois versions différentes. (JPN)
710, 711 Etiquettes de bocaux d'épices contenant des mélanges d'herbes. (CAN)
712 Sac pour le transport des gâteaux et sucreries japonais traditionnels. Blanc, gris. (JPN)
713 Sac en papier réalisé à l'occasion d'une exposition de futurologie organisée par les grands magasins *Gimbels* à New York. (USA)

DESIGNER / GESTALTER / MAQUETTISTE:

705 Joe Feigenbaum
706 Takeru Niwa
707 Kenji Maezawa
708 Nobuhiro Nakasaki/Taizen Sugano
709 Gen Naito/Ken Huang
710, 711 Heather Cooper
712 Shozo Kakutani
713 Robert P. Gersin/Pam Virgilio

ART DIRECTOR / DIRECTEUR ARTISTIQUE:

705 Joe Feigenbaum/Doug May
706 Takeru Niwa
707 Kenji Maezawa
708 Toshihiko Daimon
709 Gen Naito
710, 711 Heather Cooper
712 Shozo Kakutani
713 Robert P. Gersin

AGENCY / AGENTUR / AGENCE – STUDIO:

705 Carnase, Inc.
709 Gen Design Room
710, 711 Burns, Cooper, Hynes Ltd.
713 Robert P. Gersin Associates

710

711

712

713

714

715

716

717

718

Packaging
Packungen
Emballages

DESIGNER / GESTALTER / MAQUETTISTE:

714 John Nowland/Katy Timotheon
715, 716 Ken Cato
717 Joan Marquès
718 Takashi Kanome
719 Kenji Maezawa

ART DIRECTOR / DIRECTEUR ARTISTIQUE:

714 John Nowland
715, 716 Ken Cato
717 Enric Huguet
718 Takashi Kanome
719 Kenji Maezawa

AGENCY / AGENTUR / AGENCE – STUDIO:

714 John Nowland Graphic Design
715, 716 Ken Cato Design Co. Pty Ltd
717 Enric Huguet
718 Kanome Design Office

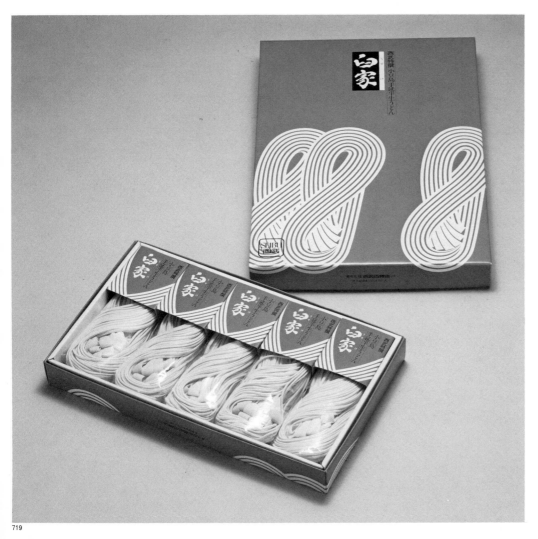

719

714 Packaging and bottle design for an Australian port wine. First shipment in 1983. (AUS)
715 Example of a label design for jam. (AUS)
716 Bottle and can for *Tarax,* a mineral water with bubbles. Trademark in green and white. (AUS)
717 Can design for vegetables and dumplings. (SPA)
718 Gift carton of the Japanese company Imaraya Co. Ltd. White on blue, turquoise and gold ribbon. (JPN)
719 Packaging for pasta sold by the *Seibu* store. (JPN)

714 Verpackung und Flaschengestaltung für den australischen «Fine Old Tawny Port». Erste Verschiffung 1983. (AUS)
715 Beispiel der Etikettgestaltung für Konfitüren. (AUS)
716 Flasche und Dose für *Tarax,* kohlensäurehaltiges Mineralwasser. Markenzeichen in Grün und Weiss. (AUS)
717 Dosengestaltung für Gemüse und Knödel. (SPA)
718 Geschenkschachtel der japanischen Firma Imaraya Co. Ltd. Weiss auf Blau. Türkis- und Goldband. (JPN)
719 Verpackung für Teigwaren des Kaufhauses *Seibu.* (JPN)

714 Carton et bouteille pour le «Fine Old Tawny Port» australien. Première cuvée 1983. (AUS)
715 Exemple d'étiquette pour confitures. (AUS)
716 Bouteille et boîte pour l'eau minérale gazeuse *Tarax.* Marque déposée en vert et en blanc. (AUS)
717 Etude de boîte pour conserves de légumes et de boulettes. (SPA)
718 Boîte-cadeau de la société japonais Imaraya Co. Ltd. Blanc sur bleu. Ruban or et turquoise. (JPN)
719 Emballage de pâtes pour les grands magasins *Seibu.* (JPN)

720

721

722

723

724

725

726

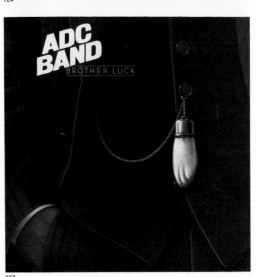

727

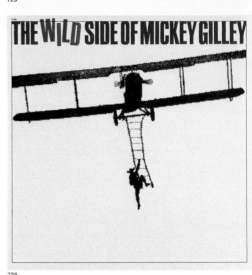

728

720 Record cover for recordings by the jazz pianist Cecil Taylor. Light green finger and white nail on black. (SWI)
721 Full-colour record cover for an album of the Japanese techno-pop group Yellow Magic Orchestra. (USA)
722 Cover of an album featuring the singer Rodney Franklin. Green shades, blue sky, white lettering. (USA)
723 Cover for an album of Belgian piano music. (BEL)
724 Record cover for a pop group's album. (USA)
725 For a record featuring Freddy Salem & The Wildcats. Fiery eyes, green tongue, violet ground. (USA)
726 Record cover for a collection called Swingtime Compilation, interpreted by two brothers. (USA)
727 Cover for an album featuring the funk band ADC. (USA)
728 Black-and-white record cover for a production of country Western and rock music by Mickey Gilley. (USA)
729, 730 Illustration and complete cover for an album of Albert King masterpieces. (USA)

720 Plattenhülle für Aufnahmen des Jazzpianisten Cecil Taylor. Hellgrüner Finger und weisser Nagel auf Schwarz. (SWI)
721 Mehrfarbige Hülle für Aufnahmen der japanischen Gruppe Yellow Magic Orchestra, die im Technopop-Stil spielt. (USA)
722 Für eine Schallplatte mit Aufnahmen des Sängers Rodney Franklin. Grüntöne, blauer Himmel, weisse Schrift. (USA)
723 Hülle für Aufnahmen mit belgischer Klaviermusik. (BEL)
724 Hülle für die Pop-Gruppe The Boomtown Rats. (USA)
725 Für eine Platte der Rock-Gruppe Freddy Salem & The Wildcats. Feurige Augen, grüne Zunge, violetter Grund. (USA)
726 Plattenhülle für eine Sammlung von Unterhaltungstiteln interpretiert von Les + Larry Elgart. (USA)
727 Hülle für Aufnahmen der Funk-Band ADC. (USA)
728 Schwarzweisse Hülle für eine Produktion mit Country-Western- und Rock-Musik von Mickey Gilley. (USA)
729, 730 Illustration und vollständige Schallplattenhülle mit populären Titeln von Albert King. (USA)

720 Pochette de disque pour des enregistrements du pianiste de jazz Cecil Taylor. Doigt vert clair, ongle blanc, sur noir. (SWI)
721 Pochette polychrome pour un disque du groupe japonais Yellow Magic Orchestra, qui a adopté le style technopop. (USA)
722 Pour un disque du chanteur Rodney Franklin. Divers verts, ciel bleu, texte blanc. (USA)
723 Pochette de disque de pianistes belges. (BEL)
724 Pochette de disque du groupe pop The Boomtown Rats. (USA)
725 Pour un disque du groupe rock Freddy Salem & The Wildcats. Yeux de braise, langue verte, fond violet. (USA)
726 Pochette réalisée pour un disque de variétés interprété par Les + Larry Elgart. (USA)
727 Pochette d'un disque pour le groupe ADC. (USA)
728 Pochette noir et blanc d'un disque de country music et de rock enregistré par Mickey Gilley. Texte brun, vert, rouge. (USA)
729, 730 Illustration et pochette entière d'un disque réunissant les meilleurs morceaux d'Albert King. (USA)

730

729

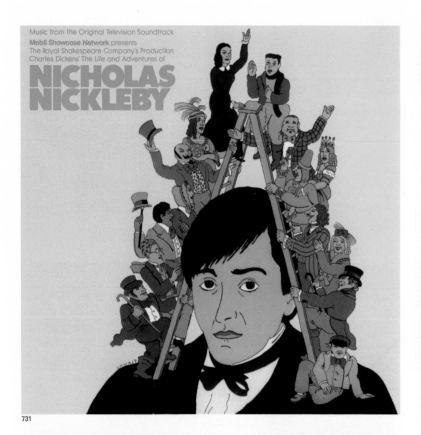

731

732

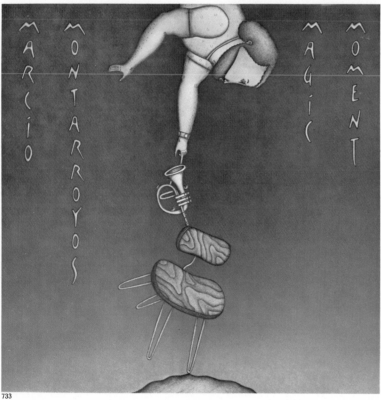

733

734

ARTIST / KÜNSTLER / ARTISTE:

731 Seymour Chwast
732, 735 Milton Glaser
733 Jerry McDonald
734 Lou & Pearl Beach
736 Robert Rodriguez
737 Lou Beach
738 Martin Springett

DESIGNER / GESTALTER

731 Seymour Chwast
732, 735 Milton Glaser
736 Robert Rodriguez
737 Lou Beach

Record Covers
Schallplattenhüllen
Pochettes de disques

731 Full-colour record cover for a recording of a production by the Royal Shakespeare Company. (USA)
732 Record cover for an album of blues tracks by the pianist Professor Longhair. (USA)
733 Cover of a CBS record starring the trumpeter Marcio Montarroyos. (USA)
734 Record cover of an album featuring rock music from America's southern states. (USA)
735 Recto of a record cassette with recordings by Ray Charles. (USA)
736 Full-colour cover of a *Capitol* album featuring dance music. (USA)
737 Cover of a CBS jazz album. In full colour. (USA)
738 Full-colour cover of a jazz album produced by *Illuminated Records*. In blue and beige. (USA)

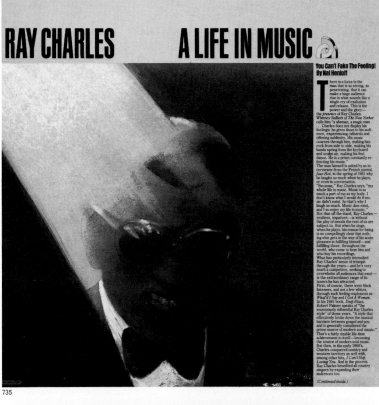

RAY CHARLES   A LIFE IN MUSIC

You Can't Fake The Feeling!
By Nat Hentoff

There is a force in the man that is so strong, so penetrating, that it can make a huge audience rise in what sounds like a single cry of exaltation and release. This is the power and the glory—the presence of Ray Charles, Whitney Balliett of *The New Yorker* calls him "a shaman, a magic man ... Charles does not display his feelings; he gives them to his audience, experiencing catharsis and offering authority. His music courses through him, making his hands spring from the keyboard and sculpt air, making his feet dance. He is a prism constantly refracting his music."

The man himself is asked by an interviewer from the French journal, *Jazz-Hot*, in the spring of 1981 why he laughs so much when he plays, or even in conversation. "Because," Ray Charles says, "my whole life is music. Music is as much a part of me as my body. I don't know what I would do if music didn't exist. So that's why I laugh so much. Music does exist, and I so enjoy my life in music." Not that, of the stand, Ray Charles—restless, impatient—is without the play of moods the rest of us are subject to. But when he sings, when he plays, his reason for being is so compelling clear that nothing else gets in the way of his acute pleasure in fulfilling himself—and fulfilling those, throughout the world, who come to hear him and who buy his recordings.

What has particularly intensified Ray Charles' sense of triumph through the years—and he's very much a competitor, seeking to overwhelm all audiences that exist—is the extraordinary range of listeners he has attracted. First, of course, there were black listeners, and not a few whites, through such feeling-explosions as *What'd I Say* and *I Got A Woman*. In his 1981 book, *Deep Blues*, Robert Palmer speaks of "the enormously influential Ray Charles style" of those years. "A style that effectively broke down the musical barriers between gospel and pop and is generally considered the prime source of modern soul music."

That is a fairly sizable life-time achievement in itself—becoming the source of modern soul music. But then, in the early 1960's, Charles conquered country and western territory as well with, among other hits, *I Can't Stop Loving You*. And in the process, Ray Charles benefited all country singers by expanding *their* audiences too.

(Continued inside.)

735

736

737

738

ART DIRECTOR / DIRECTEUR ARTISTIQUE:

731 Cyd Kilbey
732, 735 Milton Glaser
733 Tony Lane
734 Chuck Beeson
736 Peter Shea
737 Nancy Donald
738 Russ Walker

AGENCY / AGENTUR / AGENCE – STUDIO:

731 Pushpin Lubalin Peckolick
732, 735 Milton Glaser, Inc.

PUBLISHER / VERLEGER / EDITEUR:

731 DRG Records
732, 735 Atlantic Recording Corp.
733, 737 CBS Records
734 A & M Records
736 Capitol Records
738 Illuminated Records

731 Hülle für eine Produktion nach Dickens Roman *Leben und Abenteuer Nikolas Nicklebys*. (USA)
732 Schallplattenhülle für Blues-Aufnahmen des Pianisten Professor Longhair. (USA)
733 Umschlag einer Schallplatte des Jazztrompeters Marcio Montarroyos (CBS Records). (USA)
734 Plattenhülle für Aufnahmen mit amerikanischem Südstaaten-Rock. (USA)
735 Vorderseite einer Plattenkassette mit Aufnahmen von Ray Charles. (USA)
736 Mehrfarbige Hülle für eine von *Capitol* herausgegebene Platte mit Tanzmusik. (USA)
737 Hülle für eine Jazz-Platte von CBS. In Farbe. (USA)
738 Mehrfarbige Hülle einer Jazz-Platte von *Illuminated Records*: «Köpfe am Himmel». (USA)

731 Pochette polychrome pour *La Vie et les Aventures de Nicolas Nickleby*, d'après Dickens. (USA)
732 Pochette de disque pour les blues du pianiste qu'est le professeur Longhair. (USA)
733 Pochette d'un disque du trompettiste de jazz Marcio Montarroyos (CBS Records). (USA)
734 Pochette d'un disque de rock sudiste. (USA)
735 Recto d'un album de disques de Ray Charles. (USA)
736 Pochette polychrome d'un disque de musique de danse produit par *Capitol*. (USA)
737 Pochette d'un disque de jazz CBS. En couleurs. (USA)
738 Pochette polychrome d'un disque de jazz *Illuminated Records*: «Têtes au ciel». Bleu, beige. (USA)

Paper / Papier: Papierfabrik Biberist–Biber art paper, super white, glaced,
130 gm² and Biber Offset SK3, pure white, machine-finished, 140 gm² /
Biber-Kunstdruck ultra weiss, glaciert, 130 gm²
und Biber-Offset SK3, hochweiss, maschinenglatt, 140 gm²

Printed by / gedruckt von: Offset + Buchdruck AG, Zürich
(Colour pages and dust jacket / Farbseiten und Schutzumschlag),
BDV Basler Druck- und Verlagsanstalt AG, Basel (black and
white / schwarzweiss)

Typesetting / Lichtsatz: Sauerländer AG, Aarau
(Univers, MONOTYPE-Lasercomp)

Binding / Einband: Buchbinderei Schumacher AG, Bern/Schmitten

Glossy lamination / Glanzfoliierung: Durolit AG, Pfäffikon SZ